Vocational Curriculum for Individuals with Special Needs

Vocational Curriculum for Individuals with Special Needs

Transition from School to Adulthood

Edited by
Paul Wehman
Pamela Sherron Targett

pro·ed
An International Publisher

8700 Shoal Creek Boulevard
Austin, Texas 78757-6897
800/847-3202 Fax 800/397-7633
Order online at http://www.proedinc.com

© 1999 by PRO-ED, Inc.
8700 Shoal Creek Boulevard
Austin, Texas 78757-6897
800/847-3202 Fax 800/397-7633
Order online at http://www.proedinc.com

This book is designed in New Century School Book.

Production Director: Alan Grimes
Production Coordinator: Dolly Fisk Jackson
Managing Editor: Chris Olson
Art Director: Thomas Barkley
Designer: Jason Crosier
Print Buyer: Alicia Woods
Preproduction Coordinator: Chris Anne Worsham
Staff Copyeditor: Martin Wilson
Project Editor: Debra Berman
Publishing Assistant: John Means Cooper

Printed in the United States of America

1 2 3 4 5 6 7 8 9 10   03 02 01 00 99

Contents

♦ ♦ ♦ ♦ ♦ ♦ ♦ ♦ ♦ ♦ ♦ ♦ ♦ ♦ ♦ ♦ ♦ ♦

Preface ♦ *xi*

Part I: Foundation for Vocational Program Development ♦ *1*

Chapter 1

Vocational Curriculum ♦ *3*
Paul Wehman

Five Key Themes for Vocational Curriculum
Development ♦ *4*

Population Analysis: Knowing Each Student's
Strengths and Weaknesses ♦ *6*

Community Analysis: Involving the Community in
Vocational Planning ♦ *7*

Annual Goals ♦ *13*

Task Analysis and Skill Sequencing ♦ *15*

Developing Task Analyses for Teaching ♦ *19*

Chapter 2

Functional Vocational Assessment ♦ *25*
Pamela Sherron Targett and Katherine M. Wittig

Community-Based Vocational Program ♦ *26*

Outline for Writing a Vocational Situational
Assessment Report ♦ *46*

Appendix 2.A Student Profile ♦ *49*

Appendix 2.B Business Review ♦ *52*

Appendix 2.C Department Review ♦ *55*

Appendix 2.D Skills and Learning Analysis ♦ *57*

Chapter 3

Business Partnerships ◆ *63*
David Michael Mank and George P. Tilson

Evolving Roles for Employers and Support Personnel
in the Employment of People with Severe Disabilities ◆ *63*

Overlapping Trends in Supported Employment
and Business ◆ *63*

Typicality and Employment Outcomes ◆ *64*

Ideas for a New Partnership with Business ◆ *65*

Employers as Customers of Supported Employment
Professionals ◆ *68*

Obstacles to Mutual Understanding ◆ *70*

Essential Customer Service Principles for Job Placement
and Supported Employment Professionals ◆ *72*

Summary ◆ *74*

Chapter 4

Supported Employment and Vocational Program Development ◆ *77*
Paul Wehman

Overview of Supported Employment for Persons
with Severe Disabilities ◆ *77*

Work Supports and Individual Placement in
Supported Employment ◆ *78*

Implementation Configurations ◆ *82*

Outcomes of the Individual Approach ◆ *83*

Trends and Issues Associated with the
Individual Placement Approach ◆ *86*

How Well Does Supported Employment Work? ◆ *89*

A Status Report on Movement from Segregated to
Competitive Employment ◆ *90*

Conversion from Segregated Day Programs to
Competitive Employment ◆ *91*

A Rationale for a Conversion Strategy ◆ *92*

Summary ◆ *93*

Chapter 5

Vocational Training ◆ *97*
Paul Wehman

Techniques ◆ *98*

Reinforcement Procedures for Job-Site Training ◆ *105*

Fading Teacher Presence from the Immediate
Work Area ◆ *106*

Job-Site Modifications ◆ *107*

Chapter 6

Living in the Community ◆ *111*
Paula K. Davis and Ernest L. Pancsofar

Residential Options ◆ *112*

Person-Centered Planning ◆ *119*

Regular People with Real Lives ◆ *128*

Chapter 7

Job Retention and Natural Supports ◆ *131*
Michael D. West

Defining Extended Services and Need for
Ongoing Support ◆ *131*

Funding Extended Services ◆ *133*

Issues Related to Providing Extended Services ◆ *137*

Planning Services for Enhancing Job Retention
Potential ◆ *142*

Supported Employment and Natural Supports ◆ *145*

Planning and Implementing Extended Services ◆ *148*

Summary ◆ *155*

Part II: Vocational Curriculum
for Competitive Employment ◆ *159*
Pamela Sherron Targett

Building and Related Services Occupations ♦ *161*

Description of Domain ♦ *161*

Job Descriptions ♦ *161*
  1. Pool Cleaner ♦ *161*
  2. Janitor ♦ *163*
  3. Porter ♦ *165*
  4. Groundskeeper ♦ *167*
  5. General Utility ♦ *169*

Case Study ♦ *173*

Individual Transition Plan 1 ♦ *174*

Sales Occupations ♦ *181*

Description of Domain ♦ *181*

Job Descriptions ♦ *181*
  1. Customer Assistant ♦ *181*
  2. Courtesy Clerk ♦ *185*
  3. Telemarketer ♦ *186*
  4. Movie Video Clerk ♦ *187*
  5. Customer Service Representative ♦ *189*

Case Study ♦ *193*

Individual Transition Plan 2 ♦ *194*

Production and Stock Clerk Occupations ♦ *201*

Description of Domain ♦ *201*

Job Descriptions ♦ *201*
  1. Box Packer ♦ *201*
  2. Order Picker ♦ *203*
  3. Warehouse Assistant ♦ *206*
  4. Engraver ♦ *208*

Case Study ♦ *210*

Individual Transition Plan 3 ♦ *211*

Food and Beverage Preparation Occupations ♦ *217*

Description of Domain ♦ *217*

Job Descriptions ♦ *217*
  1. Linebacker ♦ *217*
  2. Dietary Aide ♦ *221*
  3. Dishwasher ♦ *222*
  4. Silverware Roller ♦ *227*
  5. Fast Food Order Taker ♦ *228*

Case Study ♦ *231*

Individual Transition Plan 4 ♦ *232*

Clerical Occupations ♦ *239*

Description of Domain ♦ *239*

Job Descriptions ♦ *239*
  1. General Office Aide ♦ *239*
  2. File Clerk ♦ *241*
  3. Mail Clerk ♦ *242*
  4. Mail Room Clerk ♦ *244*

Case Study ♦ *246*

Individual Transition Plan 5 ♦ *248*

Lodging and Related Services Occupations ♦ *255*

Description of Domain ♦ *255*

Job Descriptions ♦ *255*
  1. Houseman ♦ *255*
  2. Runner ♦ *257*
  3. Silver Polisher ♦ *258*
  4. Linen Sorter ♦ *260*
  5. Housekeeper ♦ *261*

Case Study ♦ *265*

Individual Transition Plan 6 ♦ *266*

Plant Farming Occupations ♦ *273*

Description of Domain ♦ *273*

Job Descriptions ♦ *273*
  1. Plant Installation Preparer ♦ *273*
  2. Greenhouse Assistant ♦ *276*
  3. Horticultural Worker ♦ *277*

Case Study ♦ *278*

Individual Transition Plan 7 ♦ *279*

Information and Message Distribution Occupations ♦ *285*

Description of Domain ♦ *285*

Job Descriptions ♦ *285*
  1. Telephone Secretary ♦ *285*
  2. Librarian's Assistant ♦ *287*
  3. Library Clerk ♦ *289*
  4. Receptionist ♦ *292*

Case Study ♦ *294*

Individual Transition Plan 8 ♦ *295*

Computing and Account-Recording Occupations ♦ *301*

Description of Domain ♦ *301*

Job Descriptions ♦ *301*
   1. Toll Collector ♦ *301*
   2. Bookstore Cashier ♦ *303*
   3. Accounting Clerk ♦ *306*
   4. Microfilm Clerk ♦ *309*

Case Study ♦ *314*

Individual Transition Plan 9 ♦ *315*

About the Contributors ♦ *321*

Index ♦ *323*

Preface

◆ ◆ ◆ ◆ ◆ ◆ ◆ ◆ ◆ ◆ ◆ ◆ ◆ ◆ ◆ ◆ ◆ ◆ ◆

The purpose of this text, *Vocational Curriculum for Individuals with Special Needs: Transition from School to Adulthood,* is to provide a 1990s version of a basic vocational curriculum book for teachers working with individuals who have developmental and other severe disabilities. In an earlier text (Wehman & McLaughlin, 1980), we met a need for occupational task analyses at that time; the new book, however, focuses on individualized daily sequences of work routines that occur throughout the day at a specific job, as well as the supportive task analyses. The curriculum categories encompass major *Dictionary of Occupational Titles* occupational clusters.

In the past 17 years, our vocational staff has placed over 500 people with severe disabilities into competitive employment. Most of these people have individualized daily sequences of work that incorporate clusters of task analyses. In this curriculum-oriented book, we share with teachers, vocational evaluators, counselors, and adult service personnel these specific sequences and selected supportive task analyses and objectives. Additionally, we provide chapters on implementation and assessment strategies.

The strength of this material is that it enhances the ability of the teacher to design and implement community-based work experiences, paid employment, or work–study arrangements. Whereas task analyses provided only isolated information, the individualized daily sequences take the teacher right through the type of instructional activities that might be necessary for a worker at a photocopying store.

We expect the primary audience of this text to be secondary special educators, vocational evaluators, vocational special needs teachers, and regular vocational education teachers. Adult service personnel working in the 6,000 rehabilitation facilities nationally will also be interested in this curriculum book. Occupational therapists, rehabilitation counselors, and vocational evaluators likewise may find the material of interest. Direct service personnel, such as special education teachers and work experience coordinators, are continually looking for behavioral examples of *what* and *how* to teach work skills to persons with special needs.

REFERENCES

U.S. Department of Labor, Manpower Division. (1965). *Dictionary of Occupational Titles* (3rd ed.). Washington, DC: Author.

Wehman, P., & McLaughlin, P. (1980). *Vocational curriculum for developmentally disabled persons.* Baltimore: University Park Press.

Part I

◆ ◆ ◆ ◆ ◆ ◆ ◆ ◆ ◆ ◆ ◆ ◆ ◆ ◆ ◆ ◆ ◆ ◆ ◆

Foundation for Vocational Program Development

The first seven chapters of this book present the foundation of information related to design of vocational curriculum and instruction. This curriculum is best utilized in the context of assessment, training, life in the community, employment, and long-term job retention.

In Chapter 1 the general design of a vocational curriculum is presented along with several major themes for development of the curriculum. The concepts of task analysis and skill sequence are described, as is the way to best provide analyses of student abilities and the community. Chapter 2 follows with an in-depth but practical presentation of functional vocational assessment. Chapter 3 provides lead-in to the value of business alliances and partnerships. Without employer support, no amount of vocational curriculum will be useful. Employers are key to making a vocational curriculum come alive and be truly of value. In Chapters 4 and 5 discussions of how to design supported employment programs and how to implement training techniques are presented. These two core areas of knowledge are paramount to actual implementation of the content associated with the actual curriculum (work tasks). Without this training information, only part of the employment process (preparation) can occur. Chapter 6 covers life in the community. The authors provide a rich community-oriented context for vocational competence. Chapter 7 provides the final component necessary to implementation of a vocational curriculum: job retention and natural supports. This chapter focuses on ways to help maintain individuals with disabilities in the workplace. Learning the vocational tasks is not enough; receiving key support to maintain employment is equally important.

Chapter 1

◆ ◆ ◆ ◆ ◆ ◆ ◆ ◆ ◆ ◆ ◆ ◆ ◆ ◆ ◆ ◆ ◆ ◆ ◆

Vocational Curriculum

Paul Wehman

A vocational training curriculum must reflect jobs as they exist in the community and must consider the strengths and abilities of the specific group of individuals to be served. The traditional approach to vocational education for students with special needs has been to implement traditional vocational curricula such as shop, horticulture, and home economics. Historically, these curricular topics have been used for noncollege track, high school youth with no disabilities. This approach to vocational curricula does not seem to be working, at least when measured in terms of employment, as 50% to 75% of the individuals with disabilities in the United States are unemployed (Louis Harris and Associates, 1994; U.S. Commission on Civil Rights, 1983) and thousands of young people are leaving school without jobs (Wehman, 1996).

There are some possible reasons why this traditional approach does not result in employment for individuals who have disabilities. Once a curriculum package is developed (to reflect the two or three vocational areas), a particular curriculum product tends to stay the same, not taking into account changes in the job market, automation, and so forth. When curriculum packages are updated, they frequently do not reach the service providers in time for the information to be current. Also, many schools with vocational training programs adopt these prepackaged curricula regardless of the local marketability for such skills in their respective communities. It is indeed easier to purchase a curriculum than to develop one. However, if the curriculum package includes skills inappropriate for a given community or population, the money that purchased the curriculum package is not well spent. Finally, when targeting job training for individuals with physical and other disabilities, a curriculum designed to meet the needs of the majority is unsuitable. Under these circumstances, individuals with severe disabilities are often excluded from vocational training because they are unable to perform the required tasks in a generalized vocational training curriculum.

In this curriculum guide, we present the process of curriculum development as being as important as the product. Teachers must learn how to look beyond their classroom and school into the local labor market. Visits to businesses, interviews with personnel directors at local companies, and contacts with the local Chamber of Commerce can quickly provide insight as to the value of the current vocational curricula. The process of curriculum development must start with a careful consideration of the individuals to be served, followed by a procedure for ongoing analysis of the targeted job market—that is, the local community. The first section of this chapter provides five key themes for vocational curriculum development. The next section describes two procedures for curriculum development: population analysis and community analysis. This is followed by a review of selecting relevant goals and objectives. Finally, task analysis and skill sequencing are described in detail.

FIVE KEY THEMES FOR VOCATIONAL CURRICULUM DEVELOPMENT

With the rapid and continuing change in the nation's labor force and the significant demand for well-trained workers, there is a greater need than ever for well-developed vocational curricula. The unemployment rate in the United States hovers at around a 5% level, and there is a dramatic need for labor in most industries at both skilled and unskilled levels. The United States is in the midst of a very significant labor shortage that should make opportunities for individuals with special needs such as disabilities very welcome prospects for employment. This, however, will be the case only if individuals are trained appropriately in vocational curriculum that has utility for success in business and industry. There are five major themes that are important in any vocational curriculum design. The designer of vocational curriculum, as well as the implementors such as teachers and counselors, must be sensitive to some of these points, which are described below. Table 1.1 provides a quick glimpse of these five themes.

> *With the rapid and continuing change in the nation's labor force and the significant demand for well-trained workers, there is a greater need than ever for well-developed vocational curricula.*

Business-Referenced Curricula

To establish a vocational curriculum that is going to be useful within a given community, educators and trainers must plan vocational sequences that are directly reflective of what the local market offers in the way of jobs. Too many vocational curricula have been promoted in different school systems and vocational–technical centers that have little bearing on what the evolving business needs are in a given region. This concept is critically important; it is incongru-

Table 1.1. Key Themes in Vocational Curriculum

---

1. Business-referenced curricula

2. Flexibility for cross-training

3. Rigorous detail

4. Objective and focus

5. Consistency in job descriptions and task segments

---

ous for teachers to teach agricultural skills to students who are growing up in New York City and who have little or no need for that type of training. It may not be advisable for vocational educators to teach auto mechanics to students who live in suburban communities in which there is no demand for auto mechanic positions. While at first this may seem to be very simplistic common sense, the fact remains that often vocational curriculum has not been directly tied to what business indicates is required for successful productivity.

> *To establish a vocational curriculum that is going to be useful within a given community, it is essential that educators and trainers must plan vocational sequences that are directly reflective of what the local market offers in the way of jobs.*

Cross-Training

Another important theme in the effective implementation of vocational curricula is *flexibility* in terms of teaching different skill clusters. An important concept in business, more than ever as we close out the 1990s, is that of cross-training. Cross-training refers to the capability of employees to do multiple tasks, especially on short notice if certain staff members are not available.

In the 1990s, there has been a consistent downsizing of the number of employees maintained by companies and subsequently available to work in a given department. This is because businesses have been trying to maximize productivity and reduce labor costs. Cross-training is a way of enhancing productivity through having workers who can do tasks in different parts of a department with minimal amounts of training and support. In departments in which employees are unable to be cross-trained effectively, the employees' jobs are frequently abolished, and the function is outsourced. Outsourcing, another concept that has evolved rapidly in recent years, refers to taking specialized functions within a company and contracting outside the company for their completion. Essentially, this turns over a select set of tasks to another group that specializes in the completion of these tasks in a more cost-efficient way.

> *Cross-training refers to the capability of employees to do multiple tasks, especially on short notice if certain staff members are not available.*

Rigorous Detail

A vocational curriculum must be comprehensive. In addition to reflecting what business needs are, each curriculum needs to have an extensive array of detail that describes the task sequences that are required for proficiency. In order for a fast food franchise to hire an employee who can come in quickly and immediately to provide food service skills, the vocational curriculum needs to have provided rigorous detail about the tasks, as well as detailed training that teaches specific tasks proficiently. Having a curriculum that mimics the tasks only on a surface basis may reduce the training time, but the end result is a highly ineffective mode of vocational training for the student. There needs to be sufficient rigor in the comprehensiveness of the curricula.

Objective and Focus

In an effective vocational curriculum, a well-articulated set of objectives is highly focused on what the employee needs to be able to do with proficiency. Therefore, each major segment within the curriculum area needs to have specific objectives that are behavioral in nature and can be aptly demonstrated by independent examiners. The best way to determine whether a prospective employee has learned competency in a given set of the curricula is to have him or her perform in front of an independent, objective examiner. The objectives need to be completely focused throughout the longitudinal sequence of the curriculum.

> *Each major segment within the curriculum area needs to have specific objectives that are behavioral in nature and can be aptly demonstrated by independent examiners.*

Consistency in Job Descriptions and Task Segments

The task segments within the vocational curriculum should be consistent with the different elements of job descriptions that are available in companies within the community. As noted above, identifying what jobs and career paths seem most likely in the community is an important first step. Then the vocational curriculum that will be used can be modified, redesigned, or adapted in such a way as to reflect these jobs. To do this well, educators and trainers must perform an analysis of the labor market conditions.

POPULATION ANALYSIS: KNOWING EACH STUDENT'S STRENGTHS AND WEAKNESSES

Before looking to the local community to identify potential employment alternatives, it is necessary to gather some information on the individuals to be served. The initial student assessment should be designed to identify the abilities, limitations, and supports of each individual as relevant to the long-term goal of competitive employment in the community.

Standardized assessment instruments are not recommended, for the same reason prepackaged curricula are not. The information gathered needs only to be relevant to a particular group of individuals and a particular community job market. Also, as standardized assessment instruments tend to identify and emphasize inabilities rather than abilities, many individuals with severe or multiple disabilities are thereby excluded from participation in vocational training programs based on a general or standard measure of skill requirements.

The student analysis should identify both the abilities and the limitations of each individual. However, the inabilities should not be used to exclude students from vocational training services, but rather to generate thoughts on potential supports. Knowledge of each student's abilities and support needs should be used during the community analysis phase to identify jobs and job tasks that use student abilities.

Table 1.2 illustrates the manner in which the analysis of a particular group of individuals with special needs is compared with the analysis of potential jobs in a particular community. The analysis, for example, is designed to assess a group of students whose primary disability is *motor impairment.* Therefore, much attention is given to physical abilities, self-care, independent living, communication skills, and mobility. The analysis is also designed to obtain a general idea of the cognitive abilities of the students, such as reading levels, math skills, perceptual abilities, visual acuity, and hearing. Other areas include information on social behavior, on-task behavior, parental support, and job interest. The information can be gathered using informal procedures, including (a) direct questioning of the students when possible, (b) talks with teachers and therapists, (c) direct observations, (d) talks with parents, and (e) consultation of school records.

> *As standardized assessment instruments tend to identify and empha-size inabilities rather than abilities, many individuals with severe and multiple disabilities are thereby excluded from participation in vocational training programs based on a general or standard mea-sure of skill requirements.*

Teachers also should familiarize themselves with a person-centered approach to curriculum design that provides an in-depth look at the student and his or her world (Mount, 1991; Vandercook, York, & Forest, 1989). This approach offers the most information about a student and focuses on his or her gifts, talents, and skills. The process helps all those involved focus on the best possible future for the student and establishes a set of goals and objectives that need to be accomplished in order to achieve the desired outcome. It allows students to become involved in planning for their own future, including where to work. The process can also assist with identifying a career path.

Typically, this process involves having the student invite a small group of people who know him or her well to come together to describe the person. The group should determine the student's strengths and support needs, investigate goals for the future, identify potential barriers to a desirable future, and explore strategies to achieve a desirable future. This approach is a wonderful addition to the transition planning model. When a school system moves from the traditional approach to one that is more person centered, it puts control in the hands of the student and the family.

COMMUNITY ANALYSIS: INVOLVING THE COMMUNITY IN VOCATIONAL PLANNING

Assessing the skills of students for whatever reason is a common activity for most special education or vocational education teachers. However, assessing the skill requirements of a community job market is probably not an activity in which most teachers engage as part of a program planning routine. If independent functioning in a community is the desired outcome, then the teacher must go into the community to determine the most important skills to be taught. This approach offers a refreshing break from the four walls of the classroom and adds an interesting dimension to the role of teacher.

Table 1.2. Selection of Vocational Objectives: Functional Relationship Between Student Evaluation and Job Evaluation

Student Evaluation	Job Evaluation
Physical Description	**Physical Requirements**
Hand use	Hand use
Head control	Ability to reach
Arm extension	Lifting and carrying
Mobility	Mobility
Communication Abilities	**Communication Requirements**
Oral speech	Interacting with co-workers
Alternative communication mode	Interacting with strangers
Following of multiple commands	Using telephone
	Following simple instructions
Academic Information	**Academic Requirements**
Reading skills	Approximate reading level
Math skills	Writing or typing skills
Perceptual deficits	Perceptual skills
Visual acuity	Visual acuity
Hearing	Hearing
Managing and telling time	Time management skills
Communication of phone number and address	
Endurance and Strength	**Demands of Job**
Endurance	Endurance
Physical strength	Accuracy
Manipulative capabilities	Speed
Speed of manipulation and operation of materials and equipment	Use of specific equipment
Work Behaviors and Responsibility	**Work Environment**
Promptness	Job description
Completion of work on time	Entry level
Following through and showing initiative	Job duties
Attendance	Description of social climate
Ability to work unsupervised	Dress code
Distractibility	Work hours
Transportation Needs	**Accessibility**
Type of transportation	Type of transportation available to job site
Ability to board transportation vehicle	Architectural barriers in work environment
Other	**Other**
Student work interests	Benefits
Student social skills	
Medical needs	
Self-help and independent living skills	

Conducting a community analysis basically involves the following elements. First, local businesses must be identified and contacted by the vocational training person(s). This contact can be done by telephone or by sending a letter of introduction to be followed by a phone call. Next, a visit to the business site must be arranged to allow the vocational trainer to learn more about work opportunities and, when appropriate, assess the job requirements. This initial job analysis should seek to examine the job requirements in relation to the overall abilities of the student group (see Table 1.2). If there is a potential match for one or more students, then a detailed ecological analysis of the job and work environment should be completed. Finally, a plan and schedule for updating community analysis information should be developed. Although these are the essential elements in a community analysis, reviewing and visiting other programs, as well as gathering some follow-up information on graduates of the school program, are also recommended.

> *If independent functioning in a community is the desired outcome, then the teacher must go into the community to determine the most important skills to be taught.*

Review Past Success

Before starting a community analysis, it may be useful to have some knowledge of what has been successful in other programs. What vocational training or employment efforts have shown success for individuals with the same or similar disability characteristics as those of current students? To find out, professionals can consider subscribing to a journal on state-of-the-art practices in vocational rehabilitation or maintain ongoing communications with local vocational rehabilitation counselors. Supported employment providers can also provide information regarding where individuals with severe disabilities are employed. It is also important to know what postschool adults are doing. Questions such as these are important to consider: How many postschool adults are working? How many are not working? What types of jobs do they hold? What barriers have they found while seeking employment or while competitively employed? How long have they been employed? The remainder of this section briefly describes how to conduct a community job market analysis.

Identify Labor Trends

Becoming familiar with job trends as projected by the U.S. Department of Labor's Bureau of Labor Statistics can be helpful. There will be an increasing demand for a diversified workforce in the 21st century (Kregel & Tomiyasu, 1994). Work opportunities will flourish in areas such as entry-level service occupations in the restaurant and hotel industries, the child and elderly adult care sector, the technologies, inventory management, and clerical support. These are areas in which students with disabilities, if sufficiently trained and exposed to the work environment, can make contributions to society and business while improving their own lives. A reference librarian can help locate this type of data using resources such as the *Occupational Outlook Handbook* (U.S. Department of Labor, 1998).

Identify Businesses Representative of the Local Labor Market

Use the Yellow Pages, classified ads, or other available business listings to select several local companies that are representative of the local area. Also, make use of personal acquaintances to contact businesses or for referrals.

Some examples of other resources that can be useful when developing an understanding of the future work opportunities for students are listed below:

- School placement services
- Private Industry Councils
- Public libraries
- State Vocational Rehabilitation agencies
- Associations serving the community of individuals with disabilities
- Committees on employment of people with disabilities
- Job fairs
- Independent living centers
- Professional trade and industrial associations
- Recruitment ads
- Public employment service offices
- Database services

Make Contact with Business Representatives

Once a decision is made on what businesses to approach, the next step is to make the contact. Call the personnel department and explain that you are seeking first-hand information from the local business community for the purpose of developing a vocational training curriculum for students with disabilities. This step may require talking to several individuals before reaching the one who can and will help.

Ask for an appointment to visit and explain your needs in more detail and to learn more about the job opportunities within the business. When calling a business person, be sensitive to the fact that it may not be a convenient time for a telephone conversation, and be willing to call back at another time. The business person will appreciate consideration of his or her busy schedule and will be more willing to participate at a later date.

> *Call the personnel department and explain that you are seeking first-hand information from the local business community for the purpose of developing a vocational training curriculum for students with disabilities.*

Make the Initial Business Visit

When interacting with members of the business community, it is important to conduct oneself as a competent professional. In other words, when making visits to businesses, it is important to dress neatly, be on time, offer a firm handshake, and so forth.

It is equally important to be organized and prepared to make the most of this valuable opportunity. The primary focus of this meeting is to learn more about the business visited, current and future hiring trends, and possibly the potential of developing the site for vocational assessment and training purposes. The following outline lays a foundation for the meeting:

• Explain the reason for the need to interact with the local business community. Stress the fact that you are gathering information for the purpose of developing a vocational training program.

• Give a short, general description of your students in layman's terms. If possible, give a few examples of jobs that have been successful placements for other individuals with similar abilities.

• Be able to give factual information regarding the unemployment situation among individuals with disabilities.

• Ask questions such as these to learn more about the business:
Can you tell me about your business?
What products or services do you offer?
What are the entry-level positions?
What are the qualifications for entry-level positions?
What skills or aptitudes do these workers possess?
What type of growth or downsizing do you anticipate over the next 5 years?
Do you currently employ workers with disabilities and, if so, in what areas?

• If representing students with severe cognitive or physical disabilities, briefly explain the concept of job carving and ask what positions in the company might be appropriate for job carving. Questions may include these:
Have you ever considered job carving?
How would or would this not fit into your business?

• Network and ask about other businesses with similar jobs or other jobs that might be appropriate. Get the names of other people to contact.
Who else can I contact about future employment trends and work opportunities?

• Ask to observe some of the different jobs discussed. If inconvenient, ask to schedule a follow-up visit to do your observation.

Observe Potential Work Opportunities

If the initial meeting points toward the business' becoming a good resource of future training or job opportunities for the students represented, then schedule a follow-up visit for a job analysis. During this visit, a detailed ecological analysis of the job and the work environment should be completed. This involves careful observation of the job being performed by a person who does the job on a regular basis. Frequently, with jobs involving technology, the jargon spoken by the job site personnel is difficult for the average educator to understand. For this reason, it is very important to have good observation skills; however, it is not necessary to speak the jargon to perform the task. Besides the steps involved in performing the job, the work environment needs to be examined for accessibility, maneuverability, and so forth.

After the specific job parts have been carefully analyzed, a thorough analysis of the other areas in the work environment is necessary. Besides the actual work station(s), to what other subenvironments does the student need to have access? Places such as bathrooms, breakrooms, meeting rooms, elevators, entrances and exits, and so on, need to be considered. Are bathrooms accessible for individuals in wheelchairs? Is there an entrance to the building that is wheelchair accessible? How many doors will have to be opened? Is public transportation available to this job site, and is it accessible for students with mobility impairments? If accessibility problems are identified, are there some adaptations or modifications that might alleviate the problems?

> *A detailed ecological analysis of the job and the work environment should be completed. This involves careful observation of the job being performed by a person who does the job on a regular basis.*

Besides accessibility, it is important to note the social interactions and communication skills that will be required. If the job(s) viewed is (are) a likely match for one or more of the targeted students, it may be the appropriate time to lay the groundwork for a community-based vocational training program. Details on how to do this are provided in later chapters.

Maintain Business Relationships

After each business visit, promptly send a letter to thank the business contact for his or her time and information. It is important to maintain some level of contact with the business on a long-term basis even when there is no immediate need for involvement. Sending a periodic letter to inform business contacts of how the program is progressing is one good way to keep business contacts current and involved. Maintaining business contacts also facilitates the process of updating community analysis information, which should be done on a yearly basis.

With well-maintained business contacts, a teacher can update a community analysis very efficiently. For example, during the summer months, a teacher could conceivably schedule two business visits per day for 2 weeks to update or confirm information on 20 or more jobs. If the business contacts are not maintained, more time will be required to keep a community analysis updated, as the network of contacts takes a substantial amount of time to establish.

Some individuals in the business community contribute more and show more interest than the average business contact. These people can become valuable assets to a vocational training program when formed into a business advisory committee. This contact often provides a strong and ongoing relationship between the business community and the vocational training service providers. A business advisory committee can be a valuable resource to assist with curriculum development by keeping educators abreast of business trends and labor needs, making referrals to other businesses, assisting with resolving problems, and giving feedback on marketing approaches. Of course, an active business advisory committee depends on the initiative of the vocational training teacher, because he or she most likely will be responsible for coordinating the committee. If a group meeting is impossible, the teacher can maintain contact by communicating with each member individually at his or her business.

> *A business advisory committee can be a valuable resource to assist with curriculum development by keeping educators abreast of business trends and labor needs, making referrals to other businesses, assisting with resolving problems, and giving feedback on marketing approaches.*

ANNUAL GOALS

Annual goals must be determined carefully by assessing each individual and then ordering individual needs into priorities. Because many students with special needs exhibit physical and cognitive skill deficits, the Individualized Education Plan (IEP) team must attempt to make careful decisions concerning which skills should receive the highest priority.

It is necessary to make some attempts at predicting what curriculum content will influence the child's adult functioning. This is best done by visiting numerous companies in the local community and by determining the types of vocational opportunities available as described in the previous section. As parents become more involved in the planning process, they will inquire more frequently about the relevance of the skills being taught. Educators must be prepared to defend and justify skill priorities in the vocational curriculum for each child.

Identifying Annual Goals

What are relevant vocational goals for students with special needs? More specifically, what issues should be taken into consideration when selecting skill areas for vocational instruction? At a minimum, special educators must answer the following questions in selecting appropriate curricula for students:

1. Why should the skill(s) be taught?

2. Is (are) the skill(s) necessary to prepare students to ultimately function in complex heterogeneous vocational and other community settings?

3. Could students be employable in the workforce if they did not acquire the skill(s)?

4. Are there other important skills that might be taught more quickly and efficiently?

If the selection of goals cannot be justified as appropriate, then educators may be teaching students with disabilities skills that are not critical to a long-range plan. As an illustration, consider teaching phonics skills to a secondary-level class of students with severe cerebral palsy. The purpose of these daily lessons presumably would be to expand the students' reading abilities. In all likelihood, these reading goals are not realistic, because 16- through 19-year-old students with severe physical disabilities will remain in public school only until age 21, and phonics training can be a lengthy means of attaining reading skills. An alternative, more desirable method of teaching reading involves basic sight-word recognition and comprehension skills. These skills might also facilitate employment and community living preparation.

Selecting Vocational Objectives

The selection of vocational objectives is an important program decision, which must be made in the initial stages of program development. Careful choice of what to teach is a major factor in whether the student will learn the skill, as well as in how quickly he or she will acquire the skill. Program objectives that are irrelevant, too difficult, or too easy result in needless failure and may lead to inappropriate behavior either in the classroom or at the community site.

If students with disabilities are going to reach their fullest potential, educators must be willing to tailor instruction to meet their specific goals, needs, and desires. Too often IEPs have become general education plans that essentially repeat the same objectives for all students. The IEP must be individualized.

> *Careful choice of what to teach is a major factor in whether the student will learn the skill, as well as in how quickly he or she will acquire the skill.*

It is also important that instructional objectives be logically sequenced. All students learn more quickly when material is presented in a logical progression from easy to hard. Lack of sequencing, or faulty sequencing, is unfortunately a frequent limitation of many instructional programs for students with disabilities. The inability to present objectives in a carefully developed skill sequence reduces the speed with which the objective is attained and also diminishes the effectiveness of instructional procedures.

Writing Vocational Instruction Objectives

Curriculum subject matter must be appropriate and the objectives must be functional. In order to write practical objectives, the teacher should carefully analyze the student's needs and desires, and then make a determination about whether the student will be able to use the information currently or in the future. Good common sense paired with information on student preferences can help program developers decide which skills the student needs to be learning in order to become competent at work.

Short-term objectives should be derived from the annual goals. They should reflect a specific statement of the learning conditions, the observable behavior to be attained, and performance criteria. The criteria are necessary for determining when the student has mastered the skill and is ready to move to the next skill.

A behaviorally stated vocational instructional objective involves anchoring the objective in the specific skill and the behavior desired to be learned. This involves three components: (1) a statement of given conditions under which the desired performance should occur, (2) a description of the desired performance, and (3) a listing of the criteria for adequate performance.

Specifying Performance Conditions

The performance conditions specify the testing conditions (i.e., what the student will be given or be allowed to use during the testing situation). Such statements are usually introduced by the words "Given . . ." or "Using . . ." or "Referring to . . . ," and the entire phrase generally precedes the terminal behavior.

Specifying Desired Performance

When decisions are made about the desired performance, the specific skills are selected in order to achieve the broad skill specified in the annual goals. As stated earlier, it is necessary to consult a skill sequence chart for the relevant domain and the follow-up assessment profile. Judgments should be based on what specific skills the student has mastered and what specific skills remain to be mastered before the broad skill is learned.

It is difficult to be explicit about the specific skills the pupil must learn. The key element is the verbs used. The verbs must be concrete; that is, they must refer unequivocally to behavior that is clear and observable. Usually action verbs provide the most effective descriptions.

Specifying Criterion of Adequate Performance

When the performance criterion is established, it is necessary to specify the degree to which it is part of the vocational instructional objective. This is the achievement level that a teacher considers sufficient for the student to begin work on the next highest specific skill. To specify the achievement level, it is necessary to decide about reference standards and cutting points.

Curriculum design must be adaptive and redesigned to meet the student's needs. When objectives are deemed inappropriate or new objectives are needed, the goal must be changed. When a student is continuing to have problems in learning the skills that were originally targeted, a change may be needed. However, it may take some time to reach a definitive decision about adapting an objective.

TASK ANALYSIS AND SKILL SEQUENCING

Once annual goals have been identified and instructional objectives written, then the specific skills of the instructional objectives must be sequenced and broken down into small steps for teaching.

Task analysis is the breaking down of specific skills into smaller steps that may be easier for the individual to learn. It is a process that involves a logical sequencing of material from easier to more complex. Task analysis is an important skill for teachers to have because it (a) facilitates replicability of instruction, (b) helps determine the student's specific skill level (assessment), (c) is valuable for evaluating progress in students who make gains slowly, and (d) provides a sequence for students to learn material.

Task analysis is especially valuable in determining the progress of a student with a severe disability. By assessing the number of steps in the task analysis that the individual performs independent of assistance, the teacher is able to provide a criterion-referenced means of evaluation.

A task analysis of a specific skill provides a precise description of the behaviors expected in a given instructional situation. For example, during vocational training activities, the teacher asks a question or makes a request in order to elicit specific answers about the task. The student in turn responds either correctly or incorrectly. Correct responses may be considered as target behaviors in a task analysis. See Table 1.3 for a review of how dishwashing can be task analyzed. Careful sequencing of the desired responses ensures continuity within the program, as well as facilitates learning for the student.

> *Task analysis is the breaking down of specific skills into smaller steps that may be easier for the individual to learn.*

The continual development and field testing of reliable and valid task-analyzed skill sequences that are effective with students with disabilities are important tasks facing special educators. Unquestionably, there are alternatives to the sequence provided in Table 1.3; these alternatives may be tried out and evaluated by teachers in an effort to find the most effective sequence.

What must be recognized, however, is that careful sequencing of specific skills is a critical aspect of the instructional situation between teacher and student. The most expensive materials, favorable staff ratios, and innovative teaching activities are not being used efficiently when material is not presented in a logical sequence, or worse, when no sequence is provided at all.

The arbitrary selection of isolated skills for students with disabilities is an inadequate means of providing optimal educational services. For the child's educational program to flow logically and consistently over the approximately 18 years in school, skills must be selected from relevant domains that are clearly tied to the child's longitudinal or long-range educational plan.

Task analyses must be constructed prior to student assessment and program development. A task should never be analyzed merely by sitting at a desk and mentally walking through the task components. In fact, a number of resources should be used, and the task analysis must be tested prior to using the steps in program implementation with students with disabilities. Cuvo and colleagues (Cuvo, 1978; Cuvo & Davis, 1981) suggested that validating task analyses should include the following steps:

1. Consult experts (individuals who are proficient in the task or who perform the task as part of their vocation—e.g., home economists for food preparation, tailors or seamstresses for sewing skills, janitors for cleaning skills).

2. Consult written documents (manuals that describe how to use equipment to complete a task—e.g., manuals that accompany washers and dryers or sewing machines).

3. Field test (pilot preliminary task analyses on experts).

Table 1.3. Task Analytic Assessment of Dishwashing

Intervention Instructions: Give instructions, "(*Name*), wash the dishes." Allow 3 seconds for initiation of Step 1. If correct, record (+). If incorrect or no response, proceed to verbal prompt. If correct, record (V). If incorrect or no response in 3 seconds, give model prompt. If correct, record (M). If incorrect or no response within 3 seconds, give physical prompt and record (P). Proceed through all steps in task analysis using these procedures.

Teacher: Mrs. Smith

Student(s): Joe, Bobbi

Date: November 10, 1998

Environment: Kitchen

Instructional Cue: "Wash the dishes."

Step	Response
1. Take detergent from storage location and place on sink	
2. Lift faucet to turn on water	
3. Pick up sponge	
4. Sponge out wash sink and rinse	
5. Sponge out rinse sink and rinse	
6. Put sponge down	
7. Distinguish between hot and cold water	
8. Adjust water to appropriate temperature	
9. Place stopper so that rinse sink begins to fill	
10. Fill rinse sink to half full	
11. Place stopper so that wash sink begins to fill	
12. Pick up detergent	
13. Unscrew cap	
14. Measure detergent	
15. Pour detergent from cap into wash sink	
16. Replace cap	
17. Put detergent on sink	
18. Fill wash sink half full	
19. Place utensils and plates in wash sink	
20. Pick up each piece and scrub with sponge until clean	
Knife	
Fork	
Spoon	
Plate	
21. Place each piece in rinse sink	
Knife	
Fork	
Spoon	
Plate	
22. Rinse each piece thoroughly	
Knife	
Fork	
Spoon	
Plate	

(continues)

Table 1.3. (Continued)

Step	Response
23. Place each piece in dish rack	
Knife	
Fork	
Spoon	
Plate	
24. Place glasses in wash sink	
25. Pick up each glass and scrub with sponge until clean	
26. Place each glass in rinse sink	
27. Rinse each glass thoroughly	
28. Place each glass in dish rack	
29. Place remaining dishes and pans in wash sink	
30. Pick up each piece and scrub with sponge	
Dish	
Pot	
31. Place each piece in rinse sink	
Dish	
Pot	
32. Rinse each piece thoroughly	
Dish	
Pot	
33. Place each piece in dish rack	
Dish	
Pot	
34. Manipulate stopper in wash sink so that wash sink drains	
35. Manipulate stopper in rinse sink so that rinse sink drains	
36. Rinse wash sink with sponge	
37. Rinse rinse sink with sponge	
38. Squeeze out sponge	
39. Place sponge on sink	
40. Empty debris from stopper into trash can	
41. Replace stopper in sink	
42. Place detergent in correct storage location	

4. Modify task analyses based on field tests.

5. Field test task analyses on the target population (individuals with handicaps similar to those identified to receive instruction).

6. Modify task analyses to accommodate disability.

7. Identify mandatory task steps (steps crucial to task completion vs. those extraneous to task completion—e.g., returning the salt shaker to the cabinet is not crucial to preparation of food for lunch).

DEVELOPING TASK ANALYSES FOR TEACHING

To this point, discussion has centered around the development of relevant goals and objectives and task analyses as an important instructional competency. The purpose of this section is to identify and describe how to develop vocational task analyses, such as the one relative to bedmaking provided in Table 1.4. Several specific methods of generating task analyses and locating resources that facilitate the development of instructional sequences are presented.

Look for Already Available Resources

Once relevant areas for instruction have been selected for the student, it is necessary to do a careful review of the available commercial materials. In recent years, more and more texts offer already completed and field-tested skill sequences. Through the use of these books, the teacher can save valuable curriculum development time by modifying, adapting, or replicating relevant instructional sequences.

The value of texts such as these is that replicable instructional sequences may facilitate task analytic assessment, learning in small parts, and objective evaluation. Furthermore, they usually span a large number of curricular areas across a wide range of disability categories. Clearly, the use of such commercial resources can save teacher time.

How To Adapt Curriculum Guides

Another way to select skill sequences is through careful inspection of curriculum guides that have relevant information. These may include workbooks, detailed guides for a similar population of students, or "homemade" activity books developed by other teachers.

In many ways, educational materials and resources that are already available, although not exactly suitable for a given class, are ideal for teachers to review for skill sequences. They fulfill the criterion of having been field tested by other teachers. Frequently, such materials can be located quickly and inexpensively through the public school system or possibly a nearby university.

> *Educational materials and resources that are already available, although not exactly suitable for a given class, are ideal for teachers to review for skill sequences.*

What is critical is that teachers know how to modify educational materials and curriculum guides for the purpose of implementing a logical skill sequence. A good example of the pitfalls that may result from not doing this is reflected in the extensive reliance of many teachers on commercial workbooks. Large numbers of special education classes rely solely on the content, and sequence for that content, to teach reading, arithmetic, and other subjects. This is regrettable because these workbooks may

Table 1.4. Task Analytic Assessment of Bed Making

Probe Instructions: Place chair beside bed, and start with partially made bed (sheet, blanket, and spread pulled down, wrinkled) and bed pushed into wall, pajamas under pillow. Give instructions: "*(Name)*, make the bed." Allow 5 seconds for response. If correct response, record (+). If incorrect response or no response, record (–) and complete the step for student. Proceed to the next step. Do not prompt or reinforce.

Teacher: <u>Mr. King</u>
Student(s): <u>Jane, Ray</u>
Date: <u>May 15, 1998</u>
Environment: <u>Home/School Bedroom</u>
Instructional Cue: <u>"Make the bed."</u>

Step	Response														
1. Pull bed from wall enough to walk around															
2. Place pillow and pajamas on chair, other bed, or dresser															
3. Pull top sheet with both hands to head of bed so it is straight															
4. Smooth															
5. Pull blanket with both hands to head of bed so it is straight															
6. Smooth															
7. Pull spread with both hands to head of bed so it is straight															
8. Smooth to extra spread															
9. Grasp edge, spread both hands, and fold down from head to make a 10" to 17" space															
10. Smooth spread on other side															
11. Get pajamas, fold in half, and place in pillow space															
12. Get pillow, place in space, with lower edge on spread fold															
13. Smooth pillow															
14. Grasp spread edge with both hands and pull up over pillow															
15. Tuck up under pillow with edge of hand															
16. Smooth spread top and side on near side of bed															
17. Go to other side, smooth top and side															
18. Push bed back against wall															

1. Be inadequate in terms of relevant content

2. Be culturally biased and, therefore, unfair to inner-city African American children or other minority groups

3. Fail to provide necessary breakdown of material that is being presented

4. Fail to provide a logical sequence of material

If curriculum guides and vocational workbooks are used as modifiable resources that provide only the initial curriculum content outline for instruction, then they become an invaluable means of developing individualized skill sequences relevant to each student's educational needs. Before curriculum guides can be employed effectively, however, an education plan must be established, in terms of what skills will be taught.

Second, the teacher should have the basic skill of knowing how to generate a task-analyzed skill sequence without the use of any other materials. This competency facilitates developing instructional sequences through each of the previous three methods discussed above. It is this competency of breaking down skills and logically sequencing objectives that is now discussed.

Task analyses can be obtained from curriculum guides and commercial resources. Task-analyzed skill sequences also can be derived from developmental norms and child development texts. In many cases, however, teachers must be able to generate task analyses without this assistance. This requires a logical breakdown of the skill and continual field testing of effectiveness of the analysis with students. When a series of task analyses have been cumulatively established, this may lead to the development of a curriculum. The most effective curricula are those that have come through a rigorous field-testing process.

Dividing Skills into Small Steps

In developing vocational skill sequences for youth with significant disabilities, there are seven steps that must be followed:

1. Write the instructional objective for the specific skill.

2. Review relevant instructional resources for the task analysis breakdown of the specific skills.

3. Derive the basic steps of the objective.

4. Sequence the basic steps.

5. Modify or alter selected steps based on the individual's handicap.

6. Eliminate unnecessary steps.

7. Eliminate redundant steps.

Because writing an instructional objective was discussed earlier in this chapter, it is not repeated here. It should be apparent, however, that the instructional objective is the destination that the teacher is trying to help the student reach. Following the skill sequence should move the student closer to that objective.

As noted above, it is most efficient to review any possible resources that might be considered relevant to the task of generating a sequence. However, if this search proves fruitless, as it well may, particularly for students with more severe disabilities, then the basic steps of the task analysis may be derived through several processes. Initially, it may be of value to list all the steps of a given skill that have been identified, although not sequenced in other resources, such as curriculum guides and developmental scales. These steps can then be arranged in an order that the teacher feels is a logical progression from easy to hard.

Field Testing

At this point, it may be advantageous to review the sequence and determine whether there are any steps that are unnecessary or repetitious. Furthermore, it is necessary to trial-run the sequence before fully implementing it with a whole class of students. It may turn out that what seemed logical in the analysis is very clumsy for actual instructional purposes. This is true with youth with physical disabilities who require highly individualized and modified task analysis sequences. Only through repeated field testing will the "right" task analysis become apparent.

Developing Curricula from Skill Sequences

In some skill areas there has been limited curriculum development or inadequate and limited curricula. When this is a problem, it may be advantageous to consider building a curriculum from skill sequences that have been previously acquired or developed. In this way, there will be a steady accrual of sequenced content within a given cluster of skills.

An example of one area that requires greater attention by teachers of youth with disabilities is community skills training. There is little doubt that if students with disabilities are to be included in the flow of society, then community adjustment skills must be a priority. What is required is a gradual accumulation of the skill sequences that have been generated. These sequences can then be placed together logically in a horizontal as well as vertical fashion. An illustration of this process is the functional use of money. Making change is a necessary skill required for (a) supermarket shopping, (b) going to the post office, (c) riding a public bus, and (d) going to the movie theater. Of course, the list of skills is endless and depends on the type of community setting (i.e., rural, urban) in which the student lives. Young adults with significant disabilities have all too often had their community integration severely restricted because of transportation problems, family protectiveness, or communication deficiencies. Vocational and career education must include regular training in community settings.

> *There is little doubt that if students with disabilities are to be included in the flow of society, then community adjustment skills must be a priority.*

REFERENCES

Bureau of Labor Statistics. (1998). Work at home in 1997. *United States Department of Labor, USDL 98-93.*

Cuvo, A. (1978). Validating task analysis of community living skills. *Vocational Evaluation and Work Adjustment Bulletin, 11,* 13–21.

Cuvo, A., & Davis, P. (1981). Home living for developmentally disabled persons: Instructional design and evaluation. *Exceptional Education Quarterly, 2,* 87–98.

Kregel, J., & Tomiyasu, Y. (1994). Employer attitudes toward workers with disabilities: The effect of the ADA. *Journal of Vocational Rehabilitation, 4*(3), 165–173.

Louis Harris and Associates. (1994). *The ICD survey II: Employing disabled Americans.* Washington, DC: National Organization on Disability.

Mount, B. (1991). *Person-centered planning: A source book of values, ideals, and methods to encourage person-centered development.* New York: Graphic Features.

U.S. Commission on Civil Rights. (1983). *Accommodating the spectrum of individual abilities.* Washington, DC: Author.

U.S. Department of Labor. (1998). *Occupational outlook handbook.* Washington, DC: Author.

Vandercook, T., York, J., & Forest, M. (1989). The Gill Action Planning System (NISSA): Strategies for building division. *Journal of The Association for Persons with Severe Handicaps, 14,* 205–215.

Wehman, P. (1996). *Life beyond the classroom: Transition strategies for young adults with disabilities* (2nd ed.). Baltimore: Brookes.

Chapter 2

◆ ◆ ◆ ◆ ◆ ◆ ◆ ◆ ◆ ◆ ◆ ◆ ◆ ◆ ◆ ◆ ◆ ◆ ◆

Functional Vocational Assessment

Pamela Sherron Targett and Katherine M. Wittig

A major component of transition planning for students with special needs is assessment. Secondary teachers begin this task with present level of performance assessment tools such as grades, observations, and formal assessments used by child study teams. For a student as young as age 12, it may be beneficial to conduct an informal assessment of the student's strengths, interests, and attitudes in order to create an ongoing map for transition planning and future assessment needs. As school systems nationally raise standards for academic achievement, the need for more formal vocational assessments may rise. Some students with Individualized Education Plans (IEPs) may not pass, for example, a grade-level competency test for algebra. Without that credit, the student may not receive a standard high school diploma. As those students enter high school and their corresponding vocational certificate programs, it is time to provide assessments in community and employment settings.

According to the Individuals with Disabilities Education Act Amendments of 1997 (Public Law 105-17), the following are needed for each student covered by the act:

> beginning at age 14, and updated annually, a statement of the transition service needs of child under the applicable components of the child's IEP that focuses on the child's course of study (such as vocational program); (II) beginning at age 16 (or younger if determined appropriate by the IEP team), a statement of needed transition services for the child, including, when appropriate a statement of the interagency responsibilities or any needed linkages. (*NICHCY News Digest,* 1997, p. 21)

Successful movement from school to work requires an educational foundation to prepare the student for various adult roles and the provision of postschool supports that were identified in the planning process (Wehman, Kregel, & Barcus, 1985). Individualized curriculum that promotes the development of work-related skills and commensurate appropriate support services is determined by functional vocational assessment.

This chapter advocates a functional or ecological approach to assessment that measures performance in the context in which the performance is expected (Moon, Inge, Wehman, Brooke, & Barcus, 1990). Thus, independent living skills such as using the public transportation system or shopping for goods would be evaluated in genuine community settings such as on the local bus route or in a grocery store. A student's potential work skills and traits should be analyzed within the realm of a community-based work environment. The underlying assumption of this approach is that the most accurate test of vocational skill is the one that closely approximates real work.

> *A student's potential work skills and traits should be analyzed within the realm of a community-based work environment.*

According to Wehman and Kregel (1997), *functional vocational assessment* provides a specific appraisal focusing on the needs, skills, and interests of the student within the context of future work environments. According to Kellogg (1995), the student's skills and capabilities, as well as how they are used across work settings, is determined by a functional evaluation. This practical approach to vocational evaluation, sometimes referred to as a *vocational situational assessment,* can provide valuable career development information to all members of the transition team. Situational assessments are also used to evaluate a student's skills in community and residential settings.

Some school districts and state rehabilitation agencies provide a separate setting with simulated work tasks and call it functional vocational assessment, when in fact this is far removed from what it should be. Vocational situational assessments are conducted in a variety of actual work settings and provide students with disabilities, particularly those with the most significant disabilities, with the opportunity to perform real job tasks (Moon et al., 1990). This is not to be confused with simulated work samples in a nonwork setting, in which individuals are evaluated while performing tasks that are similar to those in a real employment setting. These artificial conditions do not allow for observations of responses to stimuli in real work environments. The key component to vocational situational assessment is that the activities are conducted in the context of real community-based employment settings.

COMMUNITY-BASED VOCATIONAL PROGRAM

Community-based vocational programs are organized school activities intended to prepare students with more severe disabilities for paid employment while enrolled in school. Career explorations, functional vocational assessment, and job skills training are integral parts of a student's community-based vocational program.

Although community-based vocational programs do not have to follow any prescribed order, functional vocational or situational assessments are usually conducted prior to the student's participation in or at the conclusion of a variety of community-based training experiences. Assessments conducted prior to community training experiences can help transition team members to make decisions about what should be the focus of the student's vocational training program, whereas assessments conducted closer to the time of the student's graduation provide evidence of skills learned in addition to interest and support needs. This assessment is particularly useful to the student and others invested in helping him or her to obtain future employment. Also, it is essential for establishing eligibility for rehabilitation services during the student's final year in school (Inge & Wehman, 1993).

Not long ago standardized testing and other forms of evaluation were used to determine feasibility and readiness for vocational services by focusing on identification of skills the individual with a disability needed to improve or acquire prior to seeking employment. These efforts were used successfully to deny individuals with significant disabilities their right to work. Fortunately, due to changes in legislation and advances in the fields of special education and vocational rehabilitation, disability can no longer be equated with an inability to work (Inge & Brooke, 1993). For example, to be eligible for vocational rehabilitation services today, a student must have a disability and require assistance from vocational rehabilitation in order to achieve employment.

Final assessment results not only help direct the student's job search but also, when interpreted in relation to an actual work setting, can provide details on the pros and cons of a particular work opportunity, as well as its suitability for the student. Such details are advantageous to the student and those involved in making decisions about accepting a work opportunity. According to the U.S. Department of Labor (DOL), vocational exploration will not exceed 5 hours per job experienced and vocational assessment will not exceed 90 hours per job experienced. Please note that this is per job experienced.

> *Final assessment results not only help direct the student's job search but also, when interpreted in relation to an actual work setting, can provide details on the pros and cons of a particular work opportunity, as well as its suitability for the student.*

A community-based vocational training program helps prepare students with severe disabilities who have paid jobs by the time of graduation. During the senior year, the majority of the school day should be spent working in the community (Inge & Wehman, 1993; Moon & Inge, 1993). The DOL states that vocational training will not exceed 120 hours per job experienced.

Purpose of Vocational Assessment

A vocational assessment can provide a vast array of information that is useful for student career and curriculum development. Students get an opportunity to explore future career paths by receiving information on which to base their future work preferences; their participation can promote more active involvement in their future career decisions. Teachers learn more about the student's current abilities and potential support needs and receive direction on the most important skills to teach for a successful vocational future. The results are also a key measure of student progress. Family members gain valuable insight into how their son or daughter can have a meaningful employment outcome in their future.

As students near graduation, the vocational rehabilitation counselor can use the assessment results to determine what accommodations and support options may be needed to assist the student. Also, if potential supports do not exist, the vocational rehabilitation counselor can begin to think about creative alternatives to support provision. For instance, if assessment reveals that the student would benefit from receiving assistance from supported employment but there is no provider in the immediate area, the counselor could begin to consider other options, such as hiring a private job coach to serve the student.

Assessment results can also prove to be a valuable resource during the development of supported employment services. In fact, it is not unusual for state vocational rehabilitation agencies to request situational assessments as part of the supported employment process.

Some examples of the types of information that can be obtained from a vocational assessment are stated in Table 2.1.

Assessment Implementation

When a team works together to develop and implement a community-based vocational assessment program, it must achieve a high degree of efficiency and creativity. A guide that describes what should be done and suggests the sequence to be followed can be very valuable. Such a guide is provided in the remainder of this chapter. The reader is cautioned to keep in mind that no set of guidelines can be regarded as definitive and that discrepancy usually exists between text and the real world of practice.

Also, due to the fact that many of the activities related to development and implementation of assessment sites mirror the procedures for establishing community-based training sites, it is very important to take the time to plan the most effective way to develop a community-based vocational program. This ensures the most efficient use of everyone's time and avoids annoying potential business participants with repeated contacts. For the purposes of writing, we have approached the topic as if a vocational assessment program were the primary focus. However, in reality school systems may find it most constructive to represent the entire program, because some business sites are willing to and serve well as both a vocational assessment and job training site.

The steps in developing community-based assessment sites include (a) analyzing the local labor market, (b) analyzing student abilities and desires, (c) contacting local business representatives to locate assessment sites, (d) analyzing jobs to determine tasks for assessment, (e) designing assessment tools, (f) scheduling the assessment, and (g) conducting the assessment.

Step 1: Analyze The Labor Market

The purpose of a job market analysis is to help the transition team gain insight into potential career opportunities for students with disabilities. Assessment sites must reflect a variety of viable work options or else assessment becomes a meaningless activity. The analysis should answer the following questions:

- What types of employers are commonly found in the area?
- What businesses are anticipating future growth?
- What companies have hired people with disabilities?
- What new employers have surfaced in the area?

There are a number of ways to learn about employment options in the local community. If the job market analysis is being conducted for a large city, con-

Table 2.1. Purpose of Vocational Assessment

Topic	Questions To Consider
Interests and Preferences	• What types of job tasks does the student like and dislike? • What type of work setting does the student prefer?
Skills and Abilities	• What types of tasks does the student do well and not do well? • What are the student's responses to others in the work setting? • What work-related values has the student acquired?
On-the-Job Supports	• What training strategies promote new learning? • What are the optimal environmental conditions for promoting vocational success? • What are the student's anticipated support needs? • What types of accommodations can enhance vocational success? • Who can provide supports to enhance the student's vocational success? • What is the anticipated level of intervention needed to promote success? • Would the student benefit from supported employment services?
Ideas for Future Work	• What are some of the existing jobs in the community that the student can learn to do? • What are some of the work tasks that could be created for the student to do in the community? • What area businesses may have a need for a service that the student could provide? • What are the names of businesses where the student would like to work? • What transportation options are available to the student?
Student Evaluation and Curriculum Development	• Where is the student in terms of vocational awareness, and is additional career exploration needed? • What work skills can be taught in order to improve functioning and promote a successful vocational future? • What workplace values can be taught in order to improve functioning and promote a successful vocational future?

tacting the local Chamber of Commerce or Economic Development Office is a good place to start to learn about local businesses. Also, the state vocational rehabilitation agency should have information on area employers. The telephone directory, local employment advertisements, and riding around in the car to find out what businesses are within the realm of the student's future transportation system are ways to shed light on potential employers of students with disabilities.

> *If the job market analysis is being conducted for a large city, contacting the local Chamber of Commerce or Economic Development Office is a good place to start to learn about local businesses.*

Another way to clarify specific needs of future employers is to hold a focus group or survey local businesses by mail or telephone. Transition team members should also review their own personal networks of family, friends, and those with whom they do business, such as health care providers and retailers, to learn more about jobs. It is extremely important to keep an open mind when conducting a labor market analysis and to avoid considering only limited work options—for example, only food service industry positions such as dishwasher or potscrubber. The reality is that job options for people with disabilities reach well beyond the food service industry. Teachers must be willing to think "outside of the box" and consider nontraditional places of employment and job tasks for the future workers. Teachers also should become familiar with the concepts of job creation, such as job carving and employment proposals, because some students may not be able to compete for existing jobs.

Job carving involves showing an employer how the individual with a disability could increase business efficiency with the use of his or her unique skills and talents. One approach to job carving involves analyzing different positions within an organization and having the workers prioritize the importance of their tasks. Tasks rated as low priority are targeted as potential duties for a new job. Consider the following example: In one company, multiple job analyses revealed that many staff members spent up to 10% of their time filing documents. When presented with this information, the company manager was quick to agree that it made good business sense to relieve highly paid professionals from this task, and a part-time office aide position was created.

> *Job carving involves showing an employer how the individual with a disability could increase business efficiency with the use of his or her unique skills and talents.*

Employment proposals involve recommending services that the job seeker can offer to a business that are not presently being performed—for example, cleaning the parking lot or calling customers to evaluate business services. Familiarity with the concept of job creation, paired with knowledge of adaptive equipment, helps promote the creativity that is needed when establishing vocational goals and a direction for job search activities for students with the most significant disabilities.

A school system may desire to identify a task force of teachers or transition team members to conduct a labor market analysis. The job market analysis could also be conducted during career exploration activities for students. Regardless of who performs the analysis, a planned approach should be used to avoid overlap among those involved in this activity. This information should be updated on at least an annual basis.

Step 2: Analyze Student Abilities and Desires

After conducting a labor market analysis, but prior to contacting employers about participating in the school's vocational assessment program, it is necessary to gather some information on the students to be served. Vocational assessment sites must reflect the desires of students and represent future work opportunities in the local community. Therefore, team members need to become familiar with the expectations of the student and family members, as well as the different types of industries and potential work opportunities in the local area. Input from students and parents on career dreams and goals is needed. Surveying the student, family members, and anyone else with whom the student spends time is one way to begin to get this valuable information.

Teachers must consider creative approaches for receiving input from those who do not use symbolic communication. For students who use nonsymbolic communication, consultation with family members and the speech therapist can be helpful. An informal or formal assessment to identify the repertoire of communicative forms used by the student can be conducted. Identifying the student's forms of communication is essential for his or her participation.

Interviewing parents is also an effective method for learning about activities the student likes and dislikes, as well as their preferences for their child's future vocational outcomes. Because scheduling conflicts and other obstacles may make it difficult to meet with family members in person, an indirect approach, like the use of a questionnaire, may be used to gain initial insight into their feelings. Family members may complete written surveys at home or can be interviewed over the telephone. Optimally, however, this information would be solicited from family members during an IEP meeting.

If a parent attends the IEP meeting, it may be helpful to send information home on the topics to be covered prior to the meeting date. This gives family members plenty of time to think about comments and decreases the chances of being taken off guard or being void of an opinion at the meeting. Also, it provides an opportunity for family members who cannot be present to voice their opinions.

An assessment survey should be geared toward acquiring knowledge of a student's strengths, interests, and overall expectations of work. Consider the inquiries in Table 2.2. Whether conducted over the telephone, in writing, or in person, surveys should always be clear, concise, and easy to complete.

For parents who are feeling very uncertain or pessimistic about their son's or daughter's vocational future, teachers must be prepared to assist them in generating responses to questions concerning their child's ability. Allowing parents to talk about their child's abilities within the context of the home and community environments can help facilitate the discussion. Questions and checklists of activities associated with these familiar domains may be helpful. Consider the following type of inquiry:

> Describe a typical weekday for (student's name) from the time he or she gets up until he or she goes to bed.

As the parent explains, the teacher should probe for details of the child's performance in the home environment. Consideration must be given to the fact that some parents may provide much more support to the child in the home environment than what is given in school, which could lead to an inaccurate perception of the student's true abilities. Thus, the teacher should point out any discrepancies between parental reports and what has been observed in the school setting.

For parents who are feeling very uncertain or pessimistic about their son's or daughter's vocational future, teachers must be prepared to assist them in generating responses to questions concerning their child's ability.

Table 2.2. Questions to Generate Student Profile Data

Topic	Questions To Consider
Interests and Preferences	• What are (student's name) 's favorite things to do at home? • What does (student's name) dislike doing at home? • Describe your dream job for (student's name).
Skills and Abilities	• What type of chores does (student's name) perform? • When (state home activity) how long does (student's name) stay on task before needing a break? • How long is the break? • How quickly does (student's name) do it; would you say at a slow pace, average pace? • What are (student's name) 's skills and abilities? • How do you see (student's name) 's talents being used in a work setting? • What equipment or tools does (student's name) use at home? • Related to learning something new, what are (student's name) 's greatest accomplishments? • How long did it take (student's name) to learn it? • How was he or she taught?
On-the-Job Supports	• What accommodation(s) does (student's name) use at home?
Ideas for Future Work (These questions may be most suitable for students in their last year of school.)	• Name businesses at which you would like to see (student's name) employed, and do you have a connection at any of these businesses? • What days of week and times of day is (student's name) available to work? • What type of transportation options are available to assist (student's name) with getting to and from work?
Student Evaluation and Curriculum Development	• Does the student have insight into what type of work he or she would like to perform? • What skills can be taught or practiced to promote a successful vocational future?

Parents of a child with a severe disability may need persuasion to envision their son or daughter at work. An explanation of supported employment as a possible service option, when paired with case examples of other students with significant disability who went on to work successfully in the community, may provide parents the encouragement they need to become more actively involved in vocational planning.

Another approach involves holding a PATH (Personal Alternatives for Tomorrow with Hope). The PATH process can be used to identify each customer's dreams and goals for employment, specify accomplishments that will occur in a 1-year time period, and establish intermediate 3-month, 1-month, and 1-week objectives and activities toward meeting the customer's career goal. A PATH is led by a group facilitator and a graphic recorder. These two individuals are preferably "neutral" and not members of the customer's support team. They guide a brainstorming meeting by recording the discussion pictorially (Brooke, Inge, Armstrong, & Wehman, 1997).

Another way to gain student and parental input is to share a list of potential assessment sites categorized by business or job tasks using data from the job market analysis. As discussed in Chapter 1, a job market analysis involves identifying major employers in the community and learning more about the types of opportunities commonly available to which students will likely have access. This information can be prioritized in order of student preferences and provide direction on the businesses to contact.

Student information can also be gathered using other procedures, such as (a) direct observation, (b) talking with teachers and therapists, and (c) consulting current school records, including the results of previous vocational assessments.

All of the information obtained about the student can be organized into a student career profile. A sample is included in Appendix 2.A at the end of this chapter. Later the student profile data can be compared to information on the assessment sites to help with site selection and the establishment of objectives for the evaluation. Armed with knowledge of the student's expectations and the local labor trends, the team should begin to contact businesses.

Step 3: Contact Local Business Representatives

There is virtually no way to predict in advance which employers will be receptive to the teacher's request to provide a site for vocational assessments. However, the odds of being well received are enhanced by using a professional and well-prepared approach.

Approaching business people requires excellent communication skills, patience, confidence, perseverance, and, above all, a positive attitude. Most business contacts are made by telephone or through letters of introduction to the company's human resources office or upper members of management. The method for communicating with companies depends upon the teacher's abilities, time constraints, and comfort level, and the nature of the business. No matter which strategy is used, the teacher should know why the business is being called and the desired outcome of the contact.

> *Approaching business people requires excellent communication skills, patience, confidence, perseverance, and, above all, a positive attitude.*

Making Contact. Business contacts by telephone can be very effective if the teacher can get beyond the receptionist, who is there to decide if the call is valuable enough to forward. Foreknowledge of the proper business representative with whom to speak and confidently requesting to be connected to that person is often effective (e.g., "Good afternoon. This is Pam Wittig with Johnson County Schools. Would you please connect me with Kathy Targett?"). If the desired contact is repeatedly unavailable or not returning messages, the teacher should attempt to identify the best time of day to reach that person or an alternative contact.

Once contact is made, the teacher should be ready to ask the business representative for a personal meeting. The following outline may be used to script the approach:

- Greet the person
- Identify who you are
- Identify whom you represent
- Briefly state the nature of your request
- Briefly state how the service offered may benefit the community
- Request time to meet to explain the program in more detail

If telephone contact fails or if the nature of the business requires it, written correspondence should be considered. The letter should briefly state the reason for your request, the benefits to the community, acknowledgment of the value of the person's time, and a time for future telephone contact to schedule a personal meeting.

A drop-in visit has the obvious advantage of getting a "foot in the door"; however, sensitivity must be given to the time constraints placed on an employer who has not set aside time for the visit. This method may be most suitable for the food service industry during "slower" times of day, which are usually after the lunch rush and before dinner. Often, an appointment to meet with the employer at a later date will need to be scheduled. However, if the employer is interested and has time, a presentation should be made on the spot.

BUSINESS MEETING GUIDELINES. The content of the presentation will vary depending on the employer's demeanor. Some may want a brief, well-organized presentation, whereas a detailed description may appeal to others. Regardless of the approach used, the teacher must know what is desired and what is required of the business prior to the meeting.

The following text lays a foundation for the business presentation.

▶ *Set the Stage.* At the onset of the meeting, the teacher should thank the employer and begin to set the stage for the meeting by reiterating the reason for the contact, as in the following example:

> Thank you for agreeing to meet with me today. As I mentioned (over the telephone or in my letter), your county schools are attempting to locate community business leaders who would be willing to participate in the school's vocational assessment program.
>
> In the past, we have provided instruction for children with special challenges in the classroom environment. What we found was that after graduation many of these young adults lacked a number of skills that could assist them with entering into the world of work. Unfortunately, many of these individuals could expect only to sit at home and do nothing or go to work for a business that paid less than minimum wage. With advances in the field of special education and with the advent of new technologies, we have found that students, including those with the most significant disabilities, are employable and can provide a valuable service to the business community.
>
> We have also discovered that the best way to prepare these students for future functioning in the workplace is to assess and teach them skills in a real work setting. The classroom is an artificial setting, and it has numerous drawbacks. For instance, it is difficult to teach a student to do x task (related to the employer's business, e.g., stuffing chicken wings into bags)

using something in the classroom (poker chips and paper bags). Also, the students I teach often have difficulty transferring skills taught in the classroom to the world of work. In addition to these reasons, one of the greatest advantages students receive from participating in community-based programs is that students learn more about future career paths and educators are able to see what skills the student has and figure out ways to adjust their teachings to build on existing talents. This will increase their opportunities for future vocational success. Business participation is critical to brightening the futures of these young people.

▶ *Cover the Basics.* Next, the teacher should provide an overview of the vocational assessment process with emphasis on the responsibilities of the business, school, and student.

> Today I would like to provide you with an overview of the program and answer any questions you may have so you can decide if you will be able to participate. Establishing a vocational assessment site would involve learning more about the different types of work performed at your business. Usually, this requires a brief meeting with department heads or a tour of the company with someone who is knowledgeable about most facets of the business. Based on my observations, I would then be able to recommend the types of tasks that we would like to assess the students performing. I would present this information to you in a proposal. If you approve, I would then give you a formal agreement that will clearly spell out the roles and responsibilities of the involved parties. Here is an example of such an agreement.

> Afterwards, we would begin to schedule the assessments. A teacher accompanies each student to the worksite and makes observations on the student's skills and whether or not he or she likes the type of work. (If you are already familiar with the type of business, give some examples of the types of tasks that may be appropriate here.) This information is essential for making decisions about future instruction. The assessment is simply a time-limited, unpaid experience for the purposes of vocational exploration and evaluation only.

> At any time, if you decide to participate no longer, all you will need to do is contact me for an immediate termination of our agreement. I think, however, you will find that this can be a rewarding experience for both you and your employees.

> **Note.** The teacher must be prepared to discuss DOL regulations.

It is important to develop an agreement among all parties involved that specifically states the purpose of the situational assessment, including the DOL guidelines. The teacher must be sure that all the criteria in the federal and state DOL guidelines are met in order to prove that an employment relationship does not exist. For further discussion on this topic, the reader is referred to *Life Beyond the Classroom: Transition Strategies for Young People with Disabilities* (Wehman, 1996).

▶ *Address Concerns.* Next, the teacher would be wise to address possible concerns, particularly those related to insurance, liability, and safety, in a straight-forward and logical way.

> You may have some concerns about liability. I want you to know that I (the teacher) would be covered through my employer's worker's compensation policy, and the school has taken out a school-sponsored policy to cover any injuries to the students. As far as safety is concerned, we would not want to observe a student performing a potentially dangerous task. Also, I will be here during the assessment.

(For additional ideas on how to approach these subjects, the reader is referred to the employer concerns presented in the following section.)

▶ *Answer Questions.* Prior to concluding the meeting, the business repre-sentative should be invited to ask questions. Community business leaders are much more open to listening and considering the nature of the request to develop assessment sites if the teacher is well prepared and can respond to questions and concerns without hesitation. Therefore, prior to meeting with a business, the astute teacher will have anticipated answers to some typical employer questions or objections that may include overcoming incorrect perceptions related to working with individuals who happen to have disabilities.

> *Community business leaders are much more open to listening and considering the nature of the request to develop assessment sites if the teacher is well prepared and can respond to questions and concerns without hesitation.*

Consider the following employer concerns.

CONCERN: How do these services benefit this organization?

POSSIBLE SOLUTIONS: To answer this question, the school will need to be creative. Consider the following possibilities:

- arrange for a public relations recognition certifi-cate from the local Vocational Advisory Council
- offer to mention the company in an annual newsletter
- offer to provide information on the Americans with Disabilities Act of 1990 to the company

QUESTION: Do I have to pay the student workers?

POSSIBLE ANSWER: No, there is no cost to you. We are looking for opportunities to assess the skills and abilities of students. This will help them with making deci-sions about future jobs. We do not want to place the student into a paid or volunteer position.

CONCERN:

What about insurance? What if someone is injured during this assessment? This also may cause my rates to go up?

POSSIBLE ANSWER:

The students are covered by school insurance, and I am covered through my employer's worker's compensation program. I can provide written verification of this for you. However, injury to anyone due to negligence by the employer would be the responsibility of the business' insurance.

Note: The teacher must check with the school. Students may be covered by an existing policy, if community-based assessment is included as a goal in the IEP (Inge & Wehman, 1993). One program had the school's attorney review the existing policy to be sure the students were covered if an accident occurred on the business' premises. Another program required parents to take out a school-sponsored policy at a nominal charge that would cover medical expenses in case of emergency (Inge & Wehman, 1993). School personnel are usually covered under worker's compensation insurance that is provided by the employer, as long as community-based services are written into the individual's job description.

OBJECTION:

It sounds as though this would be too disruptive to our workplace.

POSSIBLE ANSWER:

I would be here working with and supervising the student the entire time. It is noteworthy to mention that employers who hire workers with disabilities report that workers with disabilities are no more difficult to supervise than workers without disabilities (Louis Harris and Associates, 1994). Also, I can supply references from other community businesses that have participated.

OBJECTION:

This is a dangerous workplace; I do not think it is a good idea to have a bunch of kids hanging around here.

POSSIBLE REBUTTAL:

I will be right by the student throughout the entire process. Also, I would do a job analysis in advance and naturally we would steer away from observing students performing any task that has the potential to be dangerous. We are very concerned about safety too. By the way, a survey among employers who actually hired workers with disabilities states that most employers agreed that workers with disabilities have fewer accidents on the job than workers without disabilities (Louis Harris and Associates, 1994).

QUESTION: What will my employee do while the student is doing his or her work?

POSSIBLE ANSWER: This process will not displace your employee. As a matter of fact, that would be against the DOL regulations. Instead, the student could work side by side with your employee. This will not interfere with your organization's daily activities. I will design the assessment approach so that we are not in the way during your busiest periods, or we can move to another space if things become hectic.

QUESTION: We really do not have any positions here that could be performed by a student with a disability.

POSSIBLE ANSWER: That may be true, but you do have certain tasks or parts of a job that a student could do. This is why I would perform a job analysis. This would help discover the tasks in which students may participate. Many students will need to have a job created for them after graduation. This involves performing select tasks for a business. (Follow up with examples of what students have done in the past at other sites or suggest what they may be able to do there.)

QUESTION: I tried this program once before, and it did not work out. It was a big waste of my time.

POSSIBLE ANSWER: I have worked with several of your colleagues from the (Rotary, Kiwanis, etc.), and I am sure that any one of them will provide a good reference for my program. If you are willing, can we discuss the issues you had before? (As the employer describes the problem, be sure to offer a rebuttal that explains why and how your program is different or better.)

The teacher should keep in mind that the best way to circumvent these types of employers' questions and concerns is to incorporate this information into the initial dialogue.

▶ *Wrap Up.* At the end of the meeting, the teacher should reassure the employer that he or she will personally respond to any concerns immediately and that the business may halt participation at any time without advance notice. Then the teacher should solicit a timeline for a decision. If the business is responsive, the teacher should ask permission to set up a time to learn more about the job tasks; if the business is not interested, the teacher should thank the person for his or her time and leave. All contacts, regardless of the outcome, should be followed with a thank you letter. A database or written record of all contacts should be kept for future reference. A tool such as the Business Review provided at the end of the chapter (see Appendix 2.B) can be used for these purposes.

Step 4: Analyze Jobs To Determine Tasks for Assessment

Once the business has agreed to move forward, the teacher needs to identify which job tasks are available for assessment purposes by meeting with department heads or supervisors to learn more about the different positions and specific job duties. If it is a big business, then the teacher may want to send a letter of introduction to the identified personnel and follow up with a telephone call to schedule a meeting. Another approach is to arrange to present the program at a staff meeting prior to the individual meetings. This approach allows the supervisors more time to think about the request and identify potential job tasks. Eventually, the teacher will need to meet with the members of management individually to discuss and initially identify tasks suitable for assessment. Usually this entails observations and informal interviews with the staff members who are performing the different types of work. Teachers must be mindful not to take up too much of the supervisor's time. Using a tool such as the Department Review located at the end of this chapter (see Appendix 2.C) can help the teacher collect pertinent information in a timely manner.

Conducting a Department Review involves gathering information on the general work area characteristics, job functions, sequence of job duties, the employer's openness to accommodation, and potential times for scheduling the assessment. This information can be used to help the teacher with writing the assessment proposal. An additional analysis related to the specific elements that could be measured during an assessment will be gathered once a final decision is rendered on whether or not particular job tasks can be included as part of the assessment protocol.

After observing a variety of jobs and completing the Department Review, the teacher should discuss the findings with the appropriate business representative in order to gauge his or her receptivity to using the sites selected and make the final negotiations to proceed.

Step 5: Design Assessment Tools

Once the particular tasks have been agreed upon, the teacher should begin to set up the assessment site. This includes designing data collection tools for evaluating student interests, abilities, and support needs. For each job task, the teacher should complete an analysis of the skills and learning. These detailed data on the specific job tasks are used to develop the data collection tools and can also be compared to the student's profile to help determine what sites may be most appropriate for achieving the objectives of the evaluation.

During the analysis, the types of factors that can be evaluated during the assessment process are identified. The categories include interests, physical factors, communication requirements, perceptual skills, reading, handwriting, typing and calculation, equipment and tool use, interpersonal skills and social interactions, endurance, and production. A sample tool, the Skills and Learning Analysis, is located at the end of the chapter (see Appendix 2.D).

During the assessment the teacher must use a variety of instruments to collect data. For example, insight into the student's ability to perform a task independently, as well as what instructional techniques can be used to promote learning, can be measured by collecting and analyzing performance data. All measurement techniques should be designed for the specific situation in which they will be used; being aware of the fundamental guidelines for constructing or adapting these tools is useful.

> *Insight into the student's ability to perform a task independently, as well as what instructional techniques can be used to promote learning, can be measured by collecting and analyzing performance data.*

The majority of the data collected during an assessment is based on observations and interview. Observations involve watching the student and recording specific behaviors. Some of the most common data collection tools, such as surveys, task analysis, checklists, and production recording are described next.

Surveys. Interviews are face-to-face individual question-and-answer sessions. They may be preplanned and structured or open ended and flexible. They are most appropriate for obtaining information that cannot be easily quantifiable such as feelings, attitudes, and reactions. During assessment, the interview can be used to probe student interests and preferences. Again, the teacher must have preplanned how to measure interest of students who do not use symbolic communication. Often, the student's reaction can provide an indication of his or her likes and dislikes; using pictures that show the student performing the task is one method that may help to generate feedback. The photos can also be used later when the student is trying to make a comparison between preferences for certain job settings or tasks.

Task Analysis. Students must either be taught to attend to naturally occurring cues or be taught a task in a way that eliminates the need to attend to the cue. A task analysis should be developed that teaches attendance to naturally occurring cues. During the assessment, if a student is not able to learn the task, then the teacher can modify the task analysis to eliminate the need for the student to attend to the cue. The task analysis is also used to measure performance, as the teacher scores the student's ability to perform the task.

Writing a task analysis involves breaking down a job into its components for the purpose of instruction. It can be used to individualize instruction, and to monitor and evaluate the student's knowledge. Examples of task analysis are provided in Part II of the book.

The following rules should be kept in mind when writing a task analysis:

- Always use an active form of the verb.

- If a step has the word *and* in it, you may want to consider breaking it down into two steps.

- Write the steps in the task analysis in the forms of a verbal cue in case it is needed to verbally instruct the student on that step.

- Build quality into task analysis; specify exactly where something should go (e.g., "Place the cap on the right top corner of the table").

If significant physical disability is a characteristic of the students being served, then after writing the task analysis, the teacher should consider examples of adaptations and modifications that correspond to the activity to be performed. Potential accommodations for cognitive disability can be included too. Consider the following example:

Task Analysis	Accommodations
1. Turn on computer	1. Connect a larger flat wall switch
2. Press control and reset simultaneously	2. If the student cannot hold down two switches at once: a. toggle key b. key guard with a toggle key
3. Type A–B–C	3. If the student cannot use his or her hands to type: a. use a head pointer b. use a mouth stick
4. Pick up paper	4. Finger rubber, fingertip moistener, dycem

Once the assessment begins, the teacher should revise the task analysis to reflect the student's abilities. This may require breaking the steps down further and in a way that details the specific movements the student should make or, for the less challenged student, broadening the steps into a sequence of tasks to be completed.

Checklists. The teacher may design checklists or rating scales to record observations of specific behaviors or skills. For example, a checklist on interpersonal and social skills that can be used across assessment sites may include the following items:

- Maintains social etiquette
- Maintains personal space
- Does not use foul language
- Does not physically display anger
- Recognizes and responds to social cues of others

Production Data Recording. Another measure of performance is based on the interpretation of production data. The teacher needs to set the criteria for the average rate of production of a new learner by timing him or her performing the task. The teacher can also collect data on the employee. However, if used, it is important to note how long the worker has been doing the job, because experienced employees are likely to be much faster than new learners. Production standards may be determined by the length of time it takes to perform a task or by counting the number of units completed during a given time period. Instructions on data collection are in the next section.

It takes time to develop the assessment site up front, but once everything is in place, additional evaluations can be conducted on a regular basis with usually just a telephone call to the employer to schedule the assessment. Also, using a systematic approach will help cut down on the time involved.

Step 6: Schedule the Community-Based Assessment

The next step is to identify the students to receive vocational assessment and schedule the assessments. If not previously done, an IEP or ITP (Individualized Transition Plan) meeting should be held in order to discuss the purposes of the assessment with the transition team members. At this time, the goals and objectives should be written into the student's IEP and the community-based assessment agreements should be signed by the student, parents, and teacher. The employer also needs to sign this agreement prior to performing the assessment. If insurance coverage is required for liability, this should be addressed with the parents. Also, this is when the sites are selected and a schedule for transportation is developed.

One of the greatest challenges teachers face is transportation. The school must try to be creative in its efforts to overcome this barrier. Possible transportation solutions include using parents or volunteers with mileage reimbursement, public transportation, or school vehicles. One school system arranged for the assessment sites to be on the school bus's route back to the garage. This allowed the driver to pick up the students at the school and drop them off at the assessment sites.

> *Possible transportation solutions include using parents or volunteers with mileage reimbursement, public transportation, or school vehicles.*

Another challenge is staffing. How can the teacher be everywhere at one time? The possibility of even establishing a community-based assessment site may seem overwhelming to the teacher with limited resources. Again, creativity and a willingness to persevere can go a long way. Staffing problems may be resolved using volunteers, graduate students, student teachers, or paraprofessionals.

During the assessment, the teacher collects data on the student's likes and dislikes, responses to different types of instructional strategies, skills and abilities, personality characteristics, response to environmental conditions, and interpersonal relations. To make the upcoming assessment a valuable activity for all students, including those with severe disabilities, the teacher should review the considerations listed in Table 2.3.

Students with significant disabilities most likely will need some type of accommodations in order to increase functioning during the assessment. When considering accommodations, teachers are cautioned to adapt only when necessary. This requires considering the needs of the students when recommending the use of accommodations. Adaptations should also be considered as temporary measures, and whenever possible, the teacher and the student should work toward unadapted performance (Wehman, Wood, Everson, Goodwyn, & Conley, 1988).

The teacher should also become familiar with positioning considerations. The student's posture greatly affects his or her ability. Thus, it is essential to consider the importance of posture and support to motor control and assess the student's seating prior to implementing assistive technology. The proper placement of equipment and work supplies is another consideration. If the student has difficulty using one hand, the work should be positioned near the dominant side.

Table 2.3. Vocational Assessment Considerations

Does the student have the physical abilities to perform the tasks? If not, what modifications are needed to enable the student to participate in performing the tasks, or is the purpose to learn more about supports? If needed, are the modifications readily available, and if not, how long will it take to get them?

Does the student have the sensory abilities to perform the tasks? If not, what modifications are needed to enable the student to participate in performing the tasks, or is the purpose to learn more about supports? If needed, are the modifications readily available, and if not, how long will it take to get them?

Does the student have a medical condition, physical limitation, or environmental restriction that would preclude his or her participation in the assessment?

Is the student on any medication? What are the side effects and how will administration be handled during assessment activities?

How should instruction be delivered, or is the purpose to learn more about effective instructional techniques? Is the use of picture cues, lists, or other such items needed? If so, are these already in place or will they need to be developed during the course of the assessment?

If the student has unusual or maladaptive behavior, will the environment allow for corrective actions?

How does the site relate to current interests or is it being selected to learn more about interests?

How will the student get to the assessment?

Have all agreements been signed? Have all insurance and liability issues been addressed?

Has this activity been documented in the student's Individualized Education Plan or Individualized Transition Plan?

Have all parties received a copy of the student's schedule?

Have parents received notification of issues related to appearance and dress?

Choosing specific accommodations for the student's movements requires an understanding of his or her abilities. The interaction of the student and the task must be analyzed in order to devise a plan for equipment and modification. For students with significant disabilities, determining the need for technology is a primary goal of assessment. Afterward, teachers are advised to plan ahead for the future assessments or training so that the needed equipment or modifications can be fabricated or purchased in advance.

When choosing an assessment site, a major consideration is whether the task requires a physical ability that the student does not or will not have. If so, accommodation will be needed. If accommodation is not possible due to the student's disability and the student will not be able to perform the task, another work task should be chosen.

Step 7: Conduct the Assessment

During the situational assessment, the teacher will observe the student performing work tasks in a variety of employment settings and collect information on interests and preferences, skills and abilities, and support needs.

Interests and Preferences. The student can use this opportunity to help pinpoint his or her likes and dislikes related to the specific job tasks performed as well as environmental characteristics. The teacher should probe and keep a record of the student's thoughts and reactions to these factors. Teachers also need to be creative in their approach for assessing the preferences of students who cannot communicate using symbolic communication. A structured approach such as eliciting responses to a preestablished set of questions or an unstructured approach such as keeping an anecdotal record of the student's responses can be used.

> *Teachers need to be creative in their approach for assessing the preferences of students who cannot communicate using symbolic communication.*

Skills and Abilities. The student and teacher will also begin to identify current skills, abilities, and potential on and off the job support needs. Data related to the student's ability to do the job as well as the types of strategies needed to teach him or her the task are collected using a task analysis or checklist. Detailed instructions on systematic instruction and data collection techniques are provided in the next chapter. It is recommended that the teacher try to take probe data at least once a day on all tasks observed. If possible, prompt data should be taken at the start, middle, and end of the task cycle in order to get an overall representation of specific task performance. Latency for instructional prompt delivery should be varied according to the student's cognitive and motor skills.

Any time a student is unable to perform a task independently or fast enough, the teacher should give consideration to potential on and off the job supports that may enhance outcomes. If an accommodation is put in place during assessment, the teacher should be sure to incorporate its use into the steps of the task analysis.

The teacher should make observations of the student's social and interpersonal skills. A checklist can be used to indicate the student's abilities. If the student demonstrates an unusual or socially unacceptable behavior, the incident should be recorded. The teacher can use the ABC recording technique: Antecedent = event(s) that occurred prior to the behavior; Behavior = the behavior itself; and Consequence = event(s) that occurred after the behavior. If behaviors occur often, the teacher can begin event recording by making a list of the behaviors, and recording the time each behavior starts and finishes. This may shed light on ideas for behavioral program design.

The teacher may also gain insight into the student's endurance and productivity. One measure of endurance is to record when and how often the student requires a break. This information may help with decisions related to full- or part-time employment and best times of day for work. If a student seems to fatigue easily, the teacher may want to consider the nature of the task, the influence of shorter breaks held more often during the assessment period, and sleep patterns. Also, choosing to extend incrementally the length of time the student is on a site may help with making a determination regarding whether fatigue is related to the need to build personal stamina.

Students also should be timed as they complete tasks to record level of productivity. The teacher can follow the instructions below for determining productivity by either length of time or the number of units completed (Barcus et al., 1987).[1]

A. Determining Production Rate Defined by Length of Time

1. Note the time the employee begins the job duty.

2. Observe the employee performing the task.

3. Note the time the employee completes the task.

4. Subtract the beginning time from the ending time to determine the amount of time it takes to complete the task.

5. Divide the company standard by the time it takes to complete the task.

6. Record on data sheet.

B. Determining Production Rate Defined by the Number Completed

1. Identify two short time periods during the day to sample and record the employee's production rate.

2. Count and record the number of units completed (i.e., number of pots scrubbed) during the identified sample time period (i.e., 10 minutes).

3. Divide the number of units the employee completes by the company standard number to determine the production rate (percentage of standard).

4. Record rate on data sheet.

5. Collect and record rate at least two times during the day for 2 consecutive days.

The data should be reported as the percentage of the employer's standard completed, as well as by rate, which can be calculated using one of the strategies just presented.

Support Needs. During the assessment, the teacher should document any difficulties the student experienced. Choosing specific accommodations involves analyzing the student's movements and problems in completing the task. When observing the student attempting the task, the teacher should consider the following questions if the student has a physical disability:

- Does the student's positioning allow him or her to perform the task?

- Is the work arranged to promote maximum efficiency and in a way that uses the student's strengths?

- Can the steps in the task be changed to bypass the problematic step while still allowing the student to achieve the required outcome in the same amount of time?

---

[1]From *An Instructional Guide for Training on a Job Site: A Supported Employment Resource,* by J. M. Barcus et al., 1987, Richmond: Virginia Commonwealth University, Rehabilitation Research and Training Center. Reprinted with permission.

- What adaptive devices or modifications could be made? Will the equipment simplify the task, and does the student have the skill to use or learn to use the equipment?

- What are the visual demands of the task? Can the student see adequately? Are there any ways to reduce the visual demands of the task?

- What are the perceptual or processing components of the task? What physical demands might prevent the student from doing the task? Can the perceptual demands of the task be changed?

Teachers must use existing resources, such as input from the student, family members, occupational therapist, physical therapist, vocational rehabilitation counselor, and rehabilitation engineers, to help brainstorm solutions to the problems that are not easily remedied. The good news is that many solutions can be forged by using common sense and ingenuity. The Job Accommodation Network is also a good resource for ideas on accommodations, and the local vocational rehabilitation agency should also be able to provide resources on supports. The data collected during assessment can be used when generating accommodations with the team members.

One way to generate solutions is to follow the steps below:

- State the problem; define specifically.

- Generate options.

- Evaluate the negative prospects.

- Determine the advantages.

- Weigh the evidence and select a solution.

- Evaluate the solution to determine whether it solved the problem. If not, repeat the above.

Another important consideration is to identify effective instructional strategies to determine what level of intervention was needed. Reviewing the student's performance data should provide an indication of how much and what type of support was necessary. The teacher should also keep in mind the effect that environmental characteristics (i.e., lighting, noise, temperature, sleeping habits, and medication side effects) might have had on outcomes.

All of the results from the assessment need to be analyzed and written into a final report. An outline for reporting writing is provided in the next section.

OUTLINE FOR WRITING A VOCATIONAL SITUATIONAL ASSESSMENT REPORT

Section I of the Vocational Situational Assessment Report should provide some general student information and a description of the assessment site and activities. (Pull data from the Business Review and Department Review. If a database is designed, general information on the assessment site and activities can easily be retrieved and inserted into the report.)

- Provide the student's name, current status in school, and date of report. State the reason for the assessment, such as exploring interests and preferences, and identifying skills, abilities, on-the-job support needs, ideas for future work, and/or curriculum development.

- Give a brief description of the assessment site, such as company name, mission, overview of department and environmental characteristics, and brief rationale for site selection.

- Provide a general description of the assessment activities, including what the task involves, when the assessment took place, dates, time, and so on.

Section II should report the results from the assessment. The information included should relate back to the objectives or reasons for the assessment. It may include information on one or all of the categories listed below.

1. *Interests and Preferences.* If an objective of the assessment was to help the student with identification of career interests and preferences, the teacher may want to summarize responses to the following questions: What job task(s) did the student like? What task(s) did the student dislike? This should include a reference to how the conclusion was drawn, such as informal observations of the student's reactions (give specific examples), structured interview, and so forth.

Did the student seem to prefer any particular characteristics of the work setting? The teacher could relate information on the work area characteristics from the department review and indicate how the student responded to these specific items. If a standard checklist or survey was used, it could be attached for additional details.

2. *Skills and Abilities.* If the objective of the assessment was to look at the student's current skills and abilities, the teacher may want to comment on the following for each task using the format that follows:

Initiation and Independent Work Rate: Include data from task analysis on percent of steps completed correctly (probe data) and level of independence (prompts data); provide information on reinforcement, interfering behaviors, and compensatory strategies implemented when applicable.

Performance of Tasks: Summarize what tasks were done well and what tasks were not done well. For each, indicate supports that may enhance performance.

Response to Instruction and Performance Feedback: Indicate how the student responded to the teacher's instruction and feedback on performance.

Endurance and Breaks: Include information on when and for how long the duty was performed (length of time) by the student, when breaks were given, and how breaks were initiated.

Production: Report the employer's standard and the student's performance; indicate prompting procedures or accommodations used to increase productivity when applicable.

Response to Others in the Workplace: Provide a description of how well the student related to others. Cite specific examples.

3. *Future Supports.* Make recommendations for future training strategies, optimal environmental considerations, accommodations, level of intervention at work.

4. *Ideas for Future Work.* Comment on ideas for future work, types of jobs, and business (if known). If there is a strong indication that a job creation may be needed, list any ideas.

Section III should summarize recommendations for curriculum development. Comment on the following: Is additional career exploration needed? If *yes,* give possible areas. What vocational skills or work-related skills should be focused on to improve future vocational functioning? Give ideas on how and where these activities can and should occur.

The final report should be disseminated to all members of the transition team. The information will help guide future planning. It can also be used to update the student profile.

APPENDIX 2.A
STUDENT PROFILE

I. Interests and Preferences: Document the student's, parents', and teacher's views for each question.

    A. What are the student's interests?

    B. What are the person's good student/worker traits?

II. Skills and Abilities: For the following, note the student's strengths and state any limitations using functional terms. For any limitation noted, indicate accommodations being used or ideas for future accommodation.

    A. Physical Abilities

        Mobility

        Hand Use

        Reaching

        Lifting and Carrying

        Other

    B. Communication Skills

        Expressive

        Receptive

        Nonverbal

    C. Perceptual Abilities

        Visual

        Visual Motor

        Auditory

    D. Reading, Writing, Typing, and Mathematics

        Reading

        Handwriting

        Typing

        Calculation

E. Equipment or Tools: What does or has the student use(d)?

F. Endurance: How often does the student break? What is the student's physical strength?

G. Production: Describe a situation that demonstrates how quickly the student can accomplish certain activities.

H. Interpersonal Skills and Social Interactions: What are the student's skills, and are there any unusual behaviors? If unusual behaviors exist, how can these be addressed on the job site?

III. On and Off the Job Supports

A. Describe the student's learning style and what is reinforcing to the student at home and in school.

B. Give examples of the student's learning achievement at home and in school. Indicate how instruction was delivered and how long it took the student to learn the task.

C. Does the student have any accessibility needs?

D. Will the student require job creation? If *yes,* list ideas.

E. How will future transportation to and from work be provided? (Final-year students only)

F. Other

V. Assessment Objectives and Curriculum Development: What is the purpose of assessment? Explore interests and preferences, examine skills, abilities, on-the-job supports, ideas for future work, curriculum development, and so on.

VI. Attending: _____

_____
Date

APPENDIX 2.B
BUSINESS REVIEW

Company _____   Phone_____
Address _____   Contact_____

Location: Provide directions and approximate travel time to the site by auto-mobile using the school as the base.

Availability of Transportation: How do employees get to work? Include information on use of public transportation (if on bus line, attach schedule information), including street crossing, ride sharing with other employees, accessibility to specialized transportation, and so on.

Company's Mission: Provide a brief overview of the business. Include information on mission, type of company, how long it has been around, size, and other details.

Employment Opportunities: List departments and existing entry-level jobs and ideas for job creation.

Career Opportunities: What is the company's philosophy regarding growth and new employee development?

Receptivity: How diverse (disability related) is the workforce and how receptive is the business?

Future Contact: Will you pursue site development? If *no,* why?

Accessibility: Indicate if the following areas are accessible in the work environment. Be sure to consider in terms of access for persons with sensory as well as physical disabilities.

	No	Yes	Comments
1. Parking	☐	☐	_____
2. Route to building	☐	☐	_____
3. Entrance	☐	☐	_____
4. Elevators	☐	☐	_____
5. Work areas	☐	☐	_____
6. Break area	☐	☐	_____
7. Water fountain	☐	☐	_____
8. Public telephone	☐	☐	_____
9. Vending machines	☐	☐	_____
10. Restroom	☐	☐	_____
11. Other: _____	☐	☐	_____

Environmental Exposure and Safety: Indicate whether the work environment allows exposure to the items listed.

	No	Yes	Comments
1. Noxious odors	☐	☐	_____
2. Fumes and gases	☐	☐	_____
3. Dust	☐	☐	_____
4. Mold or mildew	☐	☐	_____
5. Pollen	☐	☐	_____
6. Extreme vibrations	☐	☐	_____

7. Electrical currents	☐	☐	_____
8. Heights	☐	☐	_____
9. Moving mechanical	☐	☐	_____
10. Moving machinery	☐	☐	_____
11. Moving vehicles	☐	☐	_____
12. Extreme temperatures	☐	☐	_____
13. Uneven terrain	☐	☐	_____
14. Steps	☐	☐	_____
15. Inadequate lighting	☐	☐	_____
16. Noise	☐	☐	_____
17. Long shifts	☐	☐	_____
18. Very fast pace	☐	☐	_____
19. Heavy lifting and carrying	☐	☐	_____
20. Using chemicals	☐	☐	_____

What type of emergencies and hazards must the employee be able to recognize, report, and respond to?

_____

_____

_____

_____

_____

_____

Describe the employee emergency evacuation procedures and note accessibility.

_____

_____

_____   _____
Signature   Date

APPENDIX 2.C
DEPARTMENT REVIEW

Job Description and Task Requirements (Complete one for all positions reviewed)

Position _____   Department _____

Contact _____   Phone _____

Description (attach employer's description if available):

Work Area Characteristics

Describe the following environmental characteristics.

1. Atmosphere:

2. Setting:

3. Co-worker and Customer Interactions:

4. Dress Required:

5. Accessibility:

Job-Related Tasks

Describe what is required of the worker in the following tasks.

1. Checking in and out of work:

2. Going to work station:

3. Taking breaks:

4. Responding to emergencies:

5. Responding to hazards:

6. Communicating with worksite personnel:

Essential Job Functions

Tasks	Days of Week	Time of Day	Comments
1.			
2.			
3.			
4.			
5.			
6.			

Marginal Job Functions

Tasks	Days of Week	Time of Day	Comments
1.			
2.			
3.			
4.			
5.			
6.			

Proposed Tasks for Assessment

Tasks	Days of Week	Time of Day	Comments
1.			
2.			
3.			
4.			
5.			
6.			

_____   _____

Signature   Date

APPENDIX 2.D
SKILLS AND LEARNING ANALYSIS

Department_____ Position_____ Job Duty_____

Interests and Preferences: This type of work and environment may appeal to students who like:

Recommendations for Site Use:

Skills and Abilities: Based on your observations, employer interview, and job description, briefly describe in functional terms what is being done that requires the use of the element listed below. Then indicate the importance (*unimportant, somewhat important,* or *critically important*) of using that particular skill for task completion. For all items rated as somewhat or critically important, indicate what types of accommodations could be made.

A. Physical Factors: In addition to the above, indicate how frequently the physical skill is used as well as the duration of time it is used. Also, describe objects that are manipulated.

1. Mobility:

2. Hand Use:

3. Reach:

4. Lifting and Carrying:

5. Other Physical Factors:

B. Communication Requirements

1. Expressive: Ability to be quickly and easily understood (generation).

2. Receptive: Ability to process language of varying complexity (comprehension) or respond to questions.

3. Nonverbal: Task completion dependent upon being able to use nonverbal skills when expressing self (gestures, expression, eye contact) or interpreting nonverbal skills of others.

C. Perceptual Skills

1. Visual: The ability to process visual stimuli into meaningful patterns, sequences, or forms.

2. Visual Motor: The ability to coordinate visual input (vision) with motor output (movement).

3. Auditory: The ability to process auditory sensory input into meaningful patterns.

D. Reading, Writing, Typing, and Mathematics

1. Reading:

2. Handwriting (letters, words, numbers, or symbols):

3. Typing:

4. Calculation:

E. Equipment and Tool Use: Describe the type of equipment or tools used during task performance. List any safety or emergency shutoff features as appropriate:

F. Endurance: How often do employees break? When are the best times for the student to break?

G. Production Standard: Include standard for new learner (the teacher) and worker.

H. Interpersonal Skills and Social Interactions: Describe the organization's social norms and limits including how tolerant the environment is of unusual behaviors. What and how often can social interactions be observed?

I. Learning: Which of the following represents the highest level of learning required?

_____ *Stimulus Response:* Worker must remember the correct reaction to a particular stimulation.

_____ *Sequence Learning:* Worker required to react in a series of steps.

_____ *Perception:* Worker must learn to react to situation involving a variety of input, must organize stimulus and select appropriate response.

_____ *Concept Learning:* Worker must screen and filter an assortment of information and miscellaneous data in order to select what is relevant and to eliminate from consideration what is not.

J. Instructions for Site Use

Contact Name _____ Position _____ Phone _____

Notice Needed _____

_____

Appearance and Dress Required_____

_____

Checking In and Out_____

_____

Attach data collection tools (i.e., interest survey, task analysis, social observation checklist, production data worksheet, and so forth)

REFERENCES

Americans with Disabilities Act of 1990, 42 U.S.C. §12101 *et seq.*

Barcus, J. M., Brooke, V., Inge, K. J., Moon, M. S., Goodall, P., & Wehman, P. (1987). *An instructional guide for training on a job site: A supported employment resource.* Richmond: Virginia Commonwealth University, Rehabilitation Research and Training Center on Supported Employment.

Brooke, V., Inge, K. J., Armstrong, A., & Wehman, P. (1997). *Supported employment handbook: A customer-driven approach for persons with significant disabilities.* Richmond: Virginia Commonwealth University, Rehabilitation Research and Training Center on Supported Employment.

Individuals with Disabilities Education Act Amendments of 1997, 20 U.S.C. § 1400 *et seq.*

Inge, K. J., & Brooke, V. (Eds.). (1993, Winter). *Rehabilitation Act Amendments of 1992 Newsletter.* Richmond: Virginia Commonwealth University, Rehabilitation Research and Training Center on Supported Employment.

Inge, K. J., & Wehman, P. (1993). *Vocational options project: Designing community-based vocational programs for students with severe disabilities.* Richmond: Virginia Commonwealth University, Rehabilitation Research and Training Center on Supported Employment.

Kellogg, A. (1995). *Guidelines for conducting functional vocational assessments.* Madison: University of Wisconsin, Department of Public Instruction.

Louis Harris and Associates. (1994). *The ICD survey II: Employing disabled Americans* (pp. 6–8). Washington, DC: National Organization on Disability.

Moon, M. S., & Inge, K. J. (1993). Vocational training, transition planning, and employment for students with severe disabilities. In M. Snell (Ed.), *Systematic instruction of persons with severe disabilities* (4th ed.). Columbus, OH: Merrill.

Moon, M. S., Inge, K. J., Wehman, P., Brooke, V., & Barcus, J. M. (1990). *Helping persons with severe mental retardation get and keep employment: Supported employment issues and strategies.* Baltimore: Brookes.

NINCHCY News Digest. (August, 1997). National Information Center for Children and Youth with Disabilities, p. 21.

Wehman, P. (1996). *Life beyond the classroom: Transition strategies for young people with disabilities* (2nd ed.). Baltimore: Brookes.

Wehman, P., & Kregel, J. (1997). *Functional curriculum for elementary, middle, and secondary age students with special needs.* Austin, TX: PRO-ED.

Wehman, P., Kregel, J., & Barcus, J. M. (1985). From school to work: A vocational transition model for handicapped students. *Exceptional Children, 52*(1), 25–37.

Wehman, P., Wood, W., Everson, J. M., Goodwyn, R., & Conley, S. (1988). *Vocational education for multihandicapped youth with cerebral palsy.* Baltimore: Brookes.

Chapter 3

◆ ◆ ◆ ◆ ◆ ◆ ◆ ◆ ◆ ◆ ◆ ◆ ◆ ◆ ◆ ◆ ◆ ◆ ◆

Business Partnerships

David Michael Mank and George P. Tilson

EVOLVING ROLES FOR EMPLOYERS AND SUPPORT PERSONNEL IN THE EMPLOYMENT OF PEOPLE WITH SEVERE DISABILITIES

Employment opportunities for people with severe disabilities have improved in important ways in the last decade. Integrated employment opportunities have emerged from small demonstration programs to become accepted and expected options for people with significant disabilities (e.g., Mank, 1994; Nisbet, 1992; Rehabilitation Act Amendments of 1992). The right to jobs in the community is repeatedly affirmed, as the abilities of people with significant disabilities to contribute in the workplace has been repeatedly demonstrated. Changes in the business community are resulting in attention to improved quality as well as an increasingly diverse workforce (e.g., Harper, 1993; Juran, 1989). The initiatives for improved employment for people with significant disabilities are occurring at the same time as business interests expand in workforce diversity and implementation of the Americans with Disabilities Act of 1990 (Callahan, 1992; Mank, Oorthuys, Rhodes, Sandow, & Weyer, 1992; Kiernan, Butterworth, Schalock, & Sailor, 1993; Sailor, Pumpian, & Zivolich, 1991).

OVERLAPPING TRENDS IN SUPPORTED EMPLOYMENT AND BUSINESS

People with disabilities and others see the convergence of disability employment initiatives and the interests of the business community as an important opportunity for full inclusion in the workforce (Hagner, Cotton, Goodall, & Nisbet, 1992; Nisbet, 1992; Ramsing, Rhodes, Sandow, & Mank, 1993; Sandow, Olson, & Yan, 1992). Several trends are evident in the recent past that relate to how employment opportunities are created; these trends also relate to the relationships among people with disabilities, those who seek to support their employment, and the business community.

TYPICALITY AND EMPLOYMENT OUTCOMES

The supported employment initiative began by offering an alternative to segregated workshops for people with mental retardation (Bellamy, Rhodes, Mank, & Albin, 1988; Wehman, 1988; Will, 1984). Supported employment initially was defined through four primary models of employment (Mank, Rhodes, & Bellamy, 1986): small business enterprises, work crews, enclaves within industry, and individualized job placements. These models represented an improvement on the segregation of sheltered workshops and activity centers. Over time, small business enterprises, enclaves, and mobile work crews were shown to continue to represent segregation of workers with disabilities from others in the workforce (e.g., Rhodes, Sandow, Mank, Buckley, & Albin, 1991; Rusch, Johnson, & Hughes, 1990). In the last few years, ideas have been developed that change the role of job coaches from primarily supporting the employee with disabilities to supporting co-workers and the larger context of an individual's employment (Hagner, 1989; Hagner & Dileo, 1993; Yan, Mank, Sandow, Rhodes, & Olson, 1993). In this progression, it is clear that each improvement in employment options represents a step toward employment conditions that are typical of other workers in the workforce. Employment for people with disabilities has become less specialized, less segregated, and less different from the employment of other members of the workforce. Each step has resulted in increased integration and more typical employment status.

> *In the last few years, ideas have been developed that change the role of job coaches from primarily supporting the employee with disabilities to supporting co-workers and the larger context of an individual's employment.*

Increasingly Diverse Workforce

The country's workforce is changing. In the late 1970s and early 1980s, the workforce was largely white, male, and young. By the year 2000, the workforce will include far more women, persons from varied ethnic backgrounds, people for whom English is a second language, people across the age spectrum, and people with disabilities (Johnson & Packer, 1987; Smith, 1989; Swaboda, 1990). Accommodating this diversity is in the best interests of business and industry (Goldschmidt, 1992; Jacob, 1991; Ong, 1988; Thomas, 1990). An increasing number of businesses now offer a host of support services to employees, including employee assistance programs, flexible benefit packages, flexible work schedules, job sharing, paid course work at community colleges and universities, child care, elder care, and personal and family counseling. In a growing number of businesses, the notion of a diverse workforce includes people with disabilities (Bloom, 1993; Fabian, Luecking, & Tilson, 1994; Harper, 1993; Sandow, 1993). These changes in the interests and capacity of the business community are happening at the same time as the expectations of people with mental retardation are changing. In addition, the business community is attempting to implement the employment provisions of the Americans with Disabilities Act of 1990 (ADA).

> *An increasing number of businesses now offer a host of support services to employees, including employee assistance programs, flexible benefit packages, flexible work schedules, job sharing, paid coursework at community colleges and universities, child care, elder care, and personal and family counseling.*

"Natural Supports": An Emerging Strategy To Improve Employment Outcomes

The phrase *natural supports* has emerged as a representation of the inclusion of employees with disabilities in the same employment training and support structures that benefit other employees in the workforce (Fabian et al., 1994; Hagner & Dileo, 1993; Nisbet, 1992; Rhodes et al., 1991). Appearing in the literature only a few years ago, the term natural supports has moved extremely rapidly from concept to inclusion in federal regulation (Rehabilitation Act Amendments of 1992). This inclusion in regulation creates an opportunity to incorporate improvements into supported employment. However, it also creates a responsibility to better define the term and gather data about its effects (Wehman, 1993). Some concern has been expressed that natural supports represent an unnecessary dichotomy with supported employment and job coaching (Kregel, 1994). Supported employment developers also must develop strategies to align natural supports with the workforce diversity and transition initiatives discussed previously.

IDEAS FOR A NEW PARTNERSHIP WITH BUSINESS

This context of business interests and the continued need for good jobs for people with severe disabilities create the opportunity to redefine the relationship between supported employment developers and the business community. In the sections that follow are several illustrations of how this relationship can be fostered.

Supported Employment Fits Well with the Investment in Workforce Diversity

Employers and business groups are indicating to supported employment developers that employment of people with disabilities can fit well within the concept of workforce diversity. As the workplace becomes more diverse, companies are expanding training programs as well as employee assistance programs. Disability issues are becoming, at least in some instances, a natural part of the discussion about diversity. As the workforce begins to include an aging population, some of their needs align closely with people with disabilities.

Business Culture Should Be Explored and Better Understood

Supported employment has had some measure of success in developing jobs for people with severe disabilities on a person-by-person basis. Developers of supported employment are now seeing the intersection of the interests of the business community and the interests of people with severe disabilities in working. From a broader perspective, this creates the need to better understand business culture in order to more effectively support the workforce needs of business. Conventional wisdom in supported employment has focused on the need to understand tasks and job duties. Now, in addition to these aspects, the culture of individual workplaces and different industries should be understood. Supported employment personnel understand aspects of disability and the supports that individuals may need for success. Within businesses, supervisors, managers, and co-workers understand how work is accomplished, how people interact with one another, and the culture unique to the workplace. Supported employment for people with severe disabilities is improved if the culture of the workplace is better understood and the relationship between business and supported employment is strengthened.

Expand Relationships with Business Organizations

Similar to the notion of developing jobs for people "one person at a time," supported employment has tended to focus on developing relationships "one employer at a time." While this has been successful, supported employment also benefits from relationships with the structures and the organizations of the business community itself. Trade associations, Chambers of Commerce, and other business networks are the places where ideas and concerns about business, employment, and the future take place. This suggests that employment for people with disabilities will benefit from being aligned with the broader sweep of workforce change rather than simply being an "add-on" disability focus for individual employers. By participating in the broader workforce and exploring employment issues, supported employment developers become ongoing contributors in the community.

Supported Employment Personnel Have Skills that Are Valuable to Business

Many supported employment professionals have experienced situations wherein the job design created for an employee with disabilities becomes the preferred job design for a much larger number of employees in the workplace. Instructional strategies, self-management, job analysis, job design, and creative supervision strategies are skills that benefit employees and businesses well beyond the specific needs of employees with severe disabilities. In the past, these skills have been viewed as so disability specific that they were of little interest to supervisors and managers. Experiences in the United States and other countries have emerged that demonstrate that supported employment developers' skills are useful in a broader employment context. While supported employment may introduce these skills in the interest of an employee with disabilities, it is also important to consider that these skills might be applied in workplaces in ways that benefit all employees.

Invest in Training Opportunities Sponsored by Business Networks

The notions of teamwork, job analysis, creative job design, and individualized supports for employees are issues that many companies must address independent of disability issues in the workplace. Examples are emerging where supported employment developers are working with trade associations or other business groups to design training opportunities that focus on the broader issues of workforce development, making disability issues a part of the focus rather than the exclusive focus. This provides a new context for introducing disability issues as well as contributing to the broader concerns of the business community. This idea aligns with expanding our relationships with business and the importance of understanding business culture.

> *The notions of teamwork, job analysis, creative job design, and individualized supports for employees are issues that many companies must address independent of disability issues in the workplace.*

Develop Materials that Support Business Training Programs

Training tools should be designed that assist employers to educate their own managers and employees about disabilities. Videos, training modules, and articles in business publications are being developed that highlight issues about disability, demonstrate how people with disabilities are already contributing in the workforce, and align with the overall goals of business. Such materials, if professionally prepared, can support business interests, help expand the concept of workforce diversity, and serve the interests of people with disabilities.

Cultivate a Consultant Role with Business

In the past, the role of a job coach was viewed largely as a supporter of the employee with severe disabilities. The job coach's purpose was defined, either by design or default, as building the independence of the employee. As the concept of natural supports has evolved, job coaches have become facilitators of working environments, with efforts extended to include roles for co-workers without disabilities as they support the employee with disabilities. As a result, the job coach's role has become one of supporting the environment and supporting co-workers rather than simply supporting the employee with disabilities. As this evolves, job coaches become consultants to business in designing jobs and in problem solving.

> *As the concept of natural supports has evolved, job coaches have become facilitators of working environments, with efforts extended to include roles for co-workers without disabilities as they support the employee with disabilities.*

Invest in Enhancing the Typical Human Resource Practices in Companies

As supported employment developers become more attuned to the culture of workplaces and discover how supported employment techniques can benefit all employees, it also becomes important to understand the typical human resource processes that a company uses to bring new employees into their workforce. While supported employment personnel bring knowledge and skills about disability, it is the human resource managers who deal daily in the business of recruiting, interviewing, hiring, orienting, and training new employees. Rather that supplanting the typical human resource process, supported employment developers have begun to invest in learning the typical personnel processes and working with human resource professionals to enhance and adjust this process of working with employees with disabilities. For example, the interview process might be adjusted to allow a person with a disability to gain a better understanding of the job expected. Adding to the interview process a tour of a worksite and the opportunity to observe another employee doing the job expected of a new employee can benefit the applicant with disabilities and enhance the process already used in the business. Supporting and enhancing the typical process rather than replacing it can help ensure that the employee with disabilities is less different. This assurance is important in the employee–employer relationship.

Contribution in the Workplace Is More than Productivity

The experience of implementing supported employment has included a lesson about how contribution in the workplace is viewed by the business community. One of the early assumptions in supported employment appears to have been that contribution in the workplace is largely defined by productivity. Although productivity is clearly important, supported employment programs have discovered that many companies have a much broader definition of a meaningful contribution to the workplace. That is, contribution often also includes regular attendance, flexibility, attitude, social skills, and quality, as much as it includes sheer volume of work performed. Supported employment developers should invest in understanding how each employer defines contribution.

EMPLOYERS AS CUSTOMERS OF SUPPORTED EMPLOYMENT PROFESSIONALS

The most obvious customers for job placement professionals are job seekers with disabilities who are more commonly called "clients, recipients, consumers, [and] special education students" (Fabian et al., 1994). However, the nature of the work demands that supported employment professionals begin to view employers as equally important customers. These customers have unique and varied expectations, abilities, preferences, temperaments, desires, and needs for accommodation. Taking a customer service approach with employers is a powerful mechanism for opening doors that typically have had to be pried open. This notion is particularly exciting in its simplicity: Everything you can relate to when you yourself are a customer, applies to the services you would give to targeted employers and to clients with disabilities.

Friendliness, responsiveness, honesty, willingness to listen, creativity, ability to encourage and address complaints, follow-through, "product delivery," and so forth, are all examples of the kinds of things customers want. These characteristics are certainly apropos of interactions with employers to whom supported employment professionals represent applicants and workers with disabilities.

Tom Peters (1993), a business guru, wrote that successful enterprises do not merely satisfy their customers, they dazzle them. Are supported employment professionals up for dazzling their employer customers as well as their job-seeking customers? Adopting a customer service attitude is more than a pleasant notion; it is essential to one's long-range success in marketing expertise, developing job opportunities, achieving placements, and ensuring employment retention and satisfaction.

Customer service encompasses considerable terrain. The bedrock of this landscape is the concept of *mutual benefit.* Prospective partners—whether business associates or people in one's personal life—base their interactions on the degree to which they perceive a benefit from the association. Everyone has a bottom line. Businesspeople are in business to achieve product and service goals that will subsequently make money for their companies. Friends want moral support and companions with whom they can share ideas and activities. In either example, if one party fails to perceive a benefit, the partnership does not take hold, or dwindles.

> *Businesspeople are in business to achieve product and service goals*
> *that will subsequently make money for their companies.*

Too often, job placement and supported employment professionals have expected that employers should "just do their part" and hire their clients with disabilities, without giving much thought to the employer's questions, "Why should I hire someone?" and "Why should I work with you and your agency?" These are good questions and competent professionals can provide the answers.

There are numerous ways for competent service professionals to help employers who associate with them. Job placement and supported employment professionals are good workplace problem solvers (who know how to accommodate people with diverse special needs). By knowing the job seekers and employees they represent, they offer applicants who have been prescreened and matched to companies' expectations. They help local employers identify talent that might otherwise be overlooked or underused. Job placement professionals are experts in the area of diversity management, in identifying and facilitating effective accommodation strategies. They offer excellent opportunities for productive and meaningful activities for those companies actively committed to being "good corporate neighbors" through outreach to the wider community. Yet, how well does the supported employment professional get these ideas across to business contacts? To what extent have these professionals successfully marketed themselves to this constituency group? Have they moved beyond, "Do you have any job openings?" to "May I come in and learn more about your business and find out what your needs are?"

In their book, *A Working Relationship: The Job Development Specialist's Guide to Successful Partnerships with Business,* Fabian et al. (1994) defined marketing in a very basic way. They described this activity as any strategy whereby a target group or individual is informed that a certain product or service (1) exists and (2) is worthwhile or has value. Obviously, Step 1 is a matter of advertising or publicizing what one does and has to offer. For supported employment and job placement organizations, this might mean using public service ads, making marketing presentations, or hosting a special event. For individual professionals, it means good, old-fashioned networking, and lots of handshaking, business card exchanges, and follow-up correspondence. Step 2, demonstrating that one's services are worthwhile, can be accomplished only by delivering the kinds of services that make people sit up and take notice, the kinds of services that have people singing one's praises (and that of one's organization) to other employers.

What about the other side of the partnership equation? What do job placement and supported employment professionals gain through close association with businesspeople? Certainly, the service professionals learn about the specific industries that exist within their communities. They discover the unique expectations and idiosyncrasies of different workplaces. As Yogi Berra, baseball icon extraordinaire, said, "You can learn a lot just by watching!" Service professionals need to become avid students of the business sector, to appreciate why a business is in business to begin with—namely, to turn a profit. This attention to "bottom line" should be a critical notion adopted by the profession. Think of the efficiency, creativity, organization, flexibility, and other characteristics that top-performing companies must exhibit in order to maintain their bottom line, and the effort that must go into their enterprises if their goal is to flourish and even surpass their competition.

At TransCen, Inc., a nonprofit rehabilitation organization, every staff person is expected to have a firm grasp on the business sector, and to be known by numerous business contacts throughout the community. What are they doing? What are their concerns? What do they do really well? Who are their chief competitors? What distinguishes them from those competitors? Who are their customers, suppliers, and vendors? What is the overall "feel" or culture of a particular company site? Too often supported employment professionals have focused solely on job and task analyses—overlooking the forest for the trees.

OBSTACLES TO MUTUAL UNDERSTANDING

One obstacle to partnerships between service providers and employers is that their circles rarely cross *except* when a service provider is helping a job seeker look for a position. And the two rarely speak the same language. Typical business jargon includes these terms: outsourcing, contingency labor, right-sizing, telecommuting, self-directed teams, performance objectives. Likewise, service providers use unique terms: job coaching, natural supports, antecedent behaviors, fading, primary reinforcers, situational assessment, individualized rehabilitation plan. The two have to find out where common ground lies, and how to speak a mutually understood lingo.

Other factors confound partnerships between businesses and service professionals. The two have different perspectives on the same issues. For example, TransCen conducted two focus groups, one comprising business representatives and the other comprising rehabilitation and job placement professionals (Tilson, 1996). Both groups were asked to respond to the question, "What characterizes agencies, businesses, and professionals as good partners?" Table 3.1 lists the top 10 responses from job placement and supported employment professionals indicating what they look for in businesspeople. Table 3.2 lists the responses from businesspeople regarding what they look for in job placement and supported employment professionals.

Clearly, these very different responses to the same issue suggest that these two groups hold substantially different perceptions. The service professionals cite personal characteristics of employers as major factors. Words such as flexibility, openness, and willingness suggest that the service professionals are looking for caring and understanding on the part of businesspeople. Employers, on the other hand, identified customer service indicators such as follow-up, responsiveness, and knowledge as critical factors; they sought out attributes of competency and skill on the part of supported employment professionals.

Table 3.1. What Job Placement Professionals Are Looking for in Businesspeople

1. Flexibility
2. Creativity
3. Willingness to accommodate
4. A company culture that encourages diversity
5. Openness to communication
6. Frankness about expressing their reservations
7. Willingness to take risks
8. Willingness to ask questions
9. Receptivity to challenges
10. Previous success with employees with disabilities

Table 3.2. What Businesspeople Are Looking for in Job Placement and Supported Employment Professionals

1. Provide follow-up
2. Understand needs of supervisors
3. Understand job requirements
4. Are concerned with making good job matches
5. Know applicant's abilities
6. Show up quickly when concerns are presented
7. Are knowledgeable about business needs
8. Have ability to match skills with job needs
9. Learn everything about jobs in which applicants are placed
10. Can identify applicants for many positions

ESSENTIAL CUSTOMER SERVICE PRINCIPLES FOR JOB PLACEMENT AND SUPPORTED EMPLOYMENT PROFESSIONALS

Armed with this information, the staff at TransCen renewed their commitment to deliver the kinds of customer service desired by the business community. The outcomes have been impressive. The following are a few tricks of the trade that we have found to be invaluable techniques in our work with employers of all sizes and descriptions.

Solicit Customer Feedback

Sometimes the easiest way to find out what customers want is to ask. This can be done at any time in the job placement process. For example, we often ask employers after a placement is made to fill out a simple, quick form that asks what they did and did not like about working with us. Even more frequently, we ask *before* the placement what we can do to make life easier for them.

Quicken Response Time

When the employer calls, we respond as quickly as possible. When possible, we drop everything and attend to the employer's need. Even when there is no immediate need to respond, successful service professionals often adopt a policy of returning all phone calls within 24 hours—a simple, but frequently overlooked customer service technique that is easy for any job placement agency to adopt.

Customize Service

Because every workplace is different and every job seeker is different, service must be adapted for each customer. The more agencies and employment specialists can avoid either the appearance or the reality of a rigid "model" of service, the better they will be at satisfying employer customers. By and large, employers are not interested in whether agencies provide "supported employment," facilitate "natural supports," or subscribe to any other service or placement model. They are interested in whether or not agencies can meet their needs, just as any customer would.

Provide Value-Added Service

A question that an employment specialist might ask is "What else can I offer employers besides a job applicant?" ADA training? Diversity training? Consultation on job descriptions? Help in designing the training of new employees? One employment specialist we know once arranged an accommodation for an employee that he later helped the employer adopt for all of the employees in that worksite. Value-added service is really no more complicated or difficult than doing a little something extra.

Beg for Complaints

Why would anyone beg for complaints? This may seem absurd, yet the idea is a simple one: Successful businesses have learned that the customer who complains is a valuable customer. By making our customers know and believe that we care about quality and want to hear of any dissatisfactions, three important things happen: (1) the customer is likely to give us another chance if things happen to go wrong; (2) we are able to focus on improving our services; and (3) the customer is very likely to give us positive publicity. The next time an employer, or anyone else for that matter, complains, use it as an opportunity to improve your service.

Offer "Silk Ties" When Mistakes Occur

Tom Peters, the noted management guru and author of numerous management and customer service books, tells the story of the business executive who bought a suit at Nordstrom's department store because of the store's reputation for customer service. The suit needed alterations and he was promised the suit the next day before he left on a business trip. He was disappointed to learn that the alterations were not complete when he returned the next day. He left on his trip with a less than favorable impression of Nordstrom's fabled customer service. However, the next day an express package was delivered to his hotel with not only his suit, but also two matching silk ties, free of charge. He was converted from a disgruntled customer to a loyal one. In job placement, "silk ties" may be useful in many situations, such as when a placement does not work out or when a promised employee decides not to take the job. The possibilities are virtually limitless. Silk ties may include taking the employer to lunch, offering complementary information on the ADA, offering a free accessibility audit, and so forth. The key is to offer to compensate the employer in some way, however small, when for some reason the employer or customer is not pleased. Chances are that the relationship will continue to flourish. Use caution, however: Only offer a silk tie *after* a sincere and prompt apology has been made. Sometimes a genuine apology actually serves as a silk tie.

Convert Competence to Outstanding Performance

To paraphrase an often-expressed belief of Tom Peters, "good is nice, but only terrific will keep you in business." Many services that assist job seekers and employees with disabilities are good. Yet as funding becomes scarcer (and agencies begin competing even more for existing dollars to operate) and as rehabilitation consumers begin to really exercise their freedom to choose the services they want and like, agencies that are merely good will lose out to those that are recognized as excellent. Excellence is what every agency and every professional should be striving for at all times.

Make the Whole Agency a "Customer Service Department"

From the people who answer the phones to the agency director, everyone should be part of the effort to "delight the customer." Training in customer service is useful for *all* staff. Also, implementing procedures that are user friendly, such as promptly returning phone calls, gives the strong impression that the service professional is there to help.

To encourage excellent staff customer service, one organization instituted a "wall of fame," an easy and inexpensive way to promote good customer service behavior and create a positive organizational image. Letters received by the agency praising particular staff members for their work were framed and mounted in a prominent place on the wall in the agency's reception area. Every month, new letters were added to replace older ones, which were then put in the employees' personnel files.

Progressive agencies and effective employment specialists are well on their way to taking advantage of the new climate for job development. In fact, they are learning to view every element of their operation through the customer's eyes. The importance of customer perceptions cannot be overemphasized. Little things mean a great deal to customers. Customer responsiveness will surely be the trademark of those agencies and employment specialists who develop the most enduring partnerships with employers and, as a result, they will be most successful in assisting job seekers with disabilities.

SUMMARY

The relationship between the business community and supported employment developers has evolved in significant ways in the 10 years of implementation of supported employment. The overlap of needs of people with severe disabilities for good jobs and the interests of the business community to employ a more diverse workforce converge to create the potential for a new partnership with business. This new partnership takes the form of new relationships with individual employers as jobs for people with disabilities are developed and in new partnerships between the supported employment community and business networks as interests overlap.

REFERENCES

Americans with Disabilities Act of 1990, 42 U.S.C. §1400 *et seq.*

Bellamy, G. T., Rhodes, L. E., Mank, D. M., & Albin, J. M. (1988). Strategies for change in facility-based programs. In G. T. Bellamy & R. Horner (Eds.), *Supported employment: A community implementation guide* (pp. 139–159). Baltimore: Brookes.

Bloom, K. (1993). The creation of disability. *Journal of Vocational Rehabilitation, 3*(4), 26–29.

Callahan, M. J. (1992). Job site training and natural supports. In J. Nisbet (Ed.), *Natural supports in school, at work, and in the community for people with severe disabilities* (pp. 257–276). Baltimore: Brookes.

Fabian, E. S., Luecking, R. G., & Tilson, G. P., Jr. (1994). *A working relationship: The job development specialist's guide to successful partnerships with business.* Baltimore: Brookes.

Goldschmidt, N. (1992, February). Solving a human crisis. *Oregon Business,* p. 59.

Hagner, D. C. (1989). *The social integration of supported employees: A qualitative study.* Syracuse, NY: Syracuse University, Center on Human Policy.

Hagner, D. C., Cotton, P., Goodall, S., & Nisbet, J. (1992). The perspectives of supportive co-workers: Nothing special. In J. Nisbet (Ed.), *Natural supports in school, at work, and in the community for people with severe disabilities* (pp. 241–256). Baltimore: Brookes.

Hagner, D., & Dileo, D. (1993). *Workplace culture, supported employment, and people with disabilities.* Cambridge, MA: Brookline.

Harper, J. (1993). Securing a role for people with disabilities in the workforce. *Journal of Vocational Rehabilitation, 3*(4), 70–73.

Jacob, J. E. (1991). Developing productive people. *Vital Speeches of the Day, 153*(2), 623–626.

Johnson, W. B., & Packer, A. H. (1987). *Workforce 2000.* Indianapolis, IN: Hudson Institute.

Juran, J. M. (1989). *Juran on leadership for quality: An executive handbook.* New York: The Free Press, Macmillan.

Kiernan, W. E., Butterworth, J., Schalock, R. L., & Sailor, W. (1993). *Enhancing the use of natural supports for people with severe disabilities.* Boston: The Training and Research Institute for People with Disabilities.

Kregel, J. (1994). *Natural supports and the job coach: An unnecessary dichotomy.* Richmond: Virginia Commonwealth University, Rehabilitation Research and Training Center.

Mank, D. (1994). The underachievement of supported employment: A call for reinvestment. *Journal of Disability Policy Studies, 5*(2), 1–24.

Mank, D., Oorthuys, J., Rhodes, L., Sandow, D., & Weyer, T. (1992). Accommodating workers with mental disabilities. *Training and Development Journal, 46*(1), 49–52.

Mank, D., Rhodes, L., & Bellamy, G. T. (1986). Four supported employment alternatives. In W. Kiernan & J. Stark (Eds.), *Pathways to employment for developmentally disabled adults* (pp. 139–153). Baltimore: Brookes.

Nisbet, J. (1992). *Natural supports in school, at work, and in the community for people with severe disabilities.* Baltimore: Brookes.

Ong, J. D. (1988). Workplace 2000—Managing change: National Alliance of Business Conference. *Vital Speeches of the Day, 61,* 471–473.

Peters, T. (1987). *Thriving on chaos.* New York: Harper Perennial.

Peters, T. (Speaker). (1993). *The new manager and the new organization* (Cassette recording). Boulder, CO: CareerTrack Publications.

Ramsing, K. R., Rhodes, L., Sandow, D., & Mank, D. (1993). A paradigm shift: Quality responsibilities for vocational rehabilitation professionals. *Journal of Vocational Rehabilitation, 3*(4), 5–16.

Rehabilitation Act Amendments of 1992, 29 U.S.C. §706 *et seq.*

Rhodes, L., Sandow, D., Mank, D., Buckley, J., & Albin, J. M. (1991). Expanding the role of employers in supported employment. *Journal of The Association for Persons with Severe Handicaps, 16*(4), 213–217.

Rusch, F. R., Johnson, J. R., & Hughes, C. (1990). Analysis of co-worker involvement in relation to level of disability versus placement approach among supported employees. *Journal of The Association for Persons with Severe Handicaps, 15*(1), 32–39.

Sailor, W., Pumpian, I., & Zivolich, S. (1991). *California's natural support project: Innovative service delivery options—Transitioning students from school to adult life* (Proposal submitted to Department of Health and Human Services). San Francisco: Author.

Sandow, D. (1993). *Developing employers' capacity to support employees with severe disabilities: From analysis to synthesis.* Eugene: University of Oregon, Specialized Training Program.

Sandow, D., Olson, D., & Yan, X. (1992). *The evolution of support in the workplace.* Eugene: University of Oregon, Specialized Training Program.

Smith, G. M. (1989). Coping with the upcoming labor shortage. *Vital Speeches of the Day, 60*(21), 669–671.

Swaboda, F. (1990, July 20). The future has arrived. *Washington Post,* pp. F1, F4.

Thomas, R. R. (1990). From affirming action to affirming diversity. *Harvard Business Review, 2,* 212–215.

Tilson, G. (1996). *Focus groups of employers and their responses.* Rockville, MD: TransCen, Inc.

Wehman, P. (1988). Supported employment: Toward zero exclusion of persons with severe disabilities. In P. Wehman & M. S. Moon (Eds.), *Vocational rehabilitation and supported employment* (pp. 3–14). Baltimore: Brookes.

Wehman, P. (1993). From the editor. *Journal of Vocational Rehabilitation, 3*(3), 1–3.

Will, M. (1984). *Supported employment for adults with severe disabilities: An OSERS program initiative.* Washington, DC: Office of Special Education and Rehabilitative Services.

Yan, X., Mank, D., Sandow, D., Rhodes, L., & Olson, D. (1993). Co-workers' perceptions of an employee with severe disabilities: An analysis of social interactions in a work setting. *Journal of The Association for Persons with Severe Handicaps, 18*(4), 282–291.

Chapter 4

◆ ◆

Supported Employment and Vocational Program Development

Paul Wehman

To this point in this book, the design of vocational curriculum, indirect assessment, and establishing alliances with business have been discussed. However, the vocational curriculum cannot be successfully implemented without vocational training and work supports. Designing appropriate work supports is critical in helping many clients make their curriculum objectives become reality. The use of an employment specialist is one way to help administer work supports, usually through an individual model of supported employment. This chapter presents information on how supported employment can be used to implement the vocational curriculum.

OVERVIEW OF SUPPORTED EMPLOYMENT FOR PERSONS WITH SEVERE DISABILITIES

Competitive employment historically has been viewed as beyond the reach of millions of Americans with disabilities. Congress and the Social Security Administration have supported this belief by providing long-term payments to persons with disabilities for *not* working (Stapleton, 1996). However, these policies ignore recent advances made in employment services, such as job coaches, natural supports, and assistive technologies, as well as legislative mandates such as the Americans with Disabilities Act of 1990 (P.L. 101-336). Sadly, what has resulted is long-term placement of many persons with significant disabilities in nursing homes (Braddock, Hemp, Bachelder, & Fujiura, 1995), in segregated employment or day programs such as adult activity centers and sheltered workshops (Murphy & Rogan, 1995), or on waiting lists (Hayden & Abery, 1994).

Individuals in segregated work options are the primary focus of this chapter. Segregated options go by such names as sheltered workshops, work activity centers, day treatment centers, or day support centers. In these types of facilities, contracted work is brought in for participants to perform. Most facilities are certified by the U.S. Department of Labor to pay salaries below the national minimum wage if the productivity of participants is determined to be substantially less than that of workers without disabilities performing similar work. Many such centers lack steady contract work, and many focus primarily on teaching prevocational or social skills rather than providing remunerative employment (Schuster, 1990).

An alternative vocational approach that has been developed specifically for individuals with severe disabilities is supported employment. This employment option combines time-limited training and adjustment services provided at the place of employment, with ongoing follow-along services to the consumer and/or employer to promote job maintenance (Wehman & Kregel, 1985). According to current Vocational Rehabilitation regulations (*Federal Register,* June 24, 1992), the target population consists of those with "the most severe disabilities" who traditionally have not had access to competitive employment, that is, those who have been served in segregated options or have been unable to access vocational services altogether. The supported employment program has grown from fewer than 10,000 participants in 1986 to over 140,000 in 1995 (Wehman & Revell, 1996).

WORK SUPPORTS AND INDIVIDUAL PLACEMENT IN SUPPORTED EMPLOYMENT

The individual approach to supported employment, sometimes referred to as the supported work model of competitive employment, is founded on the general premise that one employment specialist will support only one consumer at a job site. The employment specialist's time on-site initially matches the consumer's work hours, but gradually tapers off until only periodic contact with the consumer, on or off the job site, occurs. These two fundamental characteristics contrast with the basic attributes of group models, which advocate training of more than one person at a job site and the ongoing presence of a trainer or supervisor during most of the workday and throughout the life of the job.

> *The individual approach to supported employment, sometimes referred to as the supported work model of competitive employment, is founded on the general premise that one employment specialist will support only one consumer at a job site.*

The placement and training technologies used to provide the support to consumers in the individual approach are job development, consumer assessment, job placement, job-site training, and ongoing assessment and follow-along. Figure 4.1 illustrates how these technologies, discussed briefly in the following text, relate to each other.

Job Development

The process of identifying vacancies within the local labor market is referred to as job development. The initial step in job development is screening the community job market. The purpose of this screening process is to acquaint the employment specialist with the local labor market and general requirements for the various employment sectors found in the labor market. After this initial screening is complete, the employment specialist makes contact with employers who

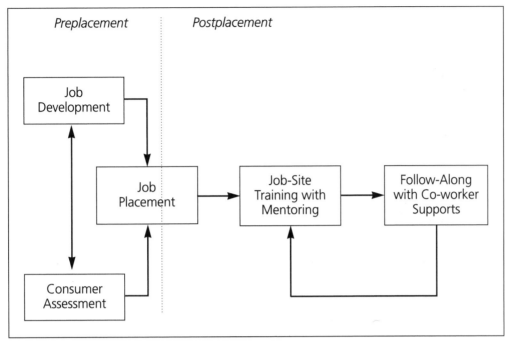

Figure 4.1. Supported employment technologies.

may have positions suited for the consumers with whom the employment specialist works. As appropriate job vacancies are located and employers demonstrate a willingness to work with supported employment, specific job requirements and duties are identified. The result of the job development process is a pool of potential jobs that can be filled by the consumers in the employment specialist's caseload.

Consumer Assessment

The purpose of consumer assessment is to identify consumer attributes and interests that will potentially facilitate or inhibit employment. Consumer assessment generally occurs concurrently with job development. The processes used to conduct consumer assessment include interviewing the consumer and significant others; observing the consumer in a variety of settings; gleaning salient information from formal educational, psychological, vocational, and medical evaluations; and sometimes conducting a situational assessment, during which the consumer can be observed performing tasks in a worklike situation for short periods of time. Consumer assessment results in a robust appraisal of consumer characteristics that will ultimately be used to determine which available job vacancy will be filled by the consumer. Unlike many assessment processes, consumer assessment in supported employment does not typically yield standardized or normative data. Likewise, the information obtained through consumer assessment is not used to "qualify" someone for supported employment.

> *Consumer assessment results in a robust appraisal of consumer characteristics that will ultimately be used to determine which available job vacancy will be filled by the consumer.*

Job Placement

Job placement refers to the process of matching a particular consumer with a particular job vacancy and securing of employment in that vacancy. At this point in the supported employment process, many resources have been allocated to carefully scrutinizing a variety of jobs and painstakingly assessing the consumers to be served. Based on the specific job and consumer attributes, a "match" between job and consumer is made. Once a pairing of job and consumer has occurred, the employer is approached and job interviews occur. The result of job placement is the acquisition of a job for a consumer.

Job-Site Training

Individuals with disabilities, like all people, come to new jobs needing training in certain areas. The job-site training phase of supported employment assures that consumer training needs are addressed systematically and efficiently. Most often this training is facilitated by the employment specialist, who obtains assistance from the employer, direct supervisor if different from the employer, and coworkers. Specific techniques, such as applied behavior analysis, counseling, and cognitive strategies, may be used to facilitate job-skill acquisition. The strategies selected depend entirely upon the consumer attributes and the job setting and are therefore necessarily individualized. Strategies typically used with various disability groups are discussed later in this chapter. The outcome of effective job-site training is a consumer who possesses all of the job duty–specific and social skills needed to maintain the job.

Ongoing Assessment and Follow-Along

A characteristic that distinguishes supported employment from other vocational rehabilitation services is its never-ending nature. During the follow-along phase of supported employment, the employment specialist makes recurrent contact with the employer and consumer to ensure that both are satisfied with the job placement. Should problems arise, as they often do, the employment specialist initiates the necessary corrective actions to remediate the problems. Corrective action may involve job restructuring, additional job-site training, and/or referral to other services.

As part of follow-along, natural supports (e.g., Test & Wood, 1996) play an important role. The literature on natural supports has described and, to a far lesser extent, investigated the way features of the workplace, interpersonal relations, and public, personal, and familial resources singly or in combination help sustain and enhance a worker's performance. Natural supports are usually discussed in terms of either strategies (i.e., strategies to overcome barriers to performance) or support systems (i.e., the interplay of various aids to performance). Natural supports are defined as formal (dedicated) and informal (voluntary) resources, such as policies, practices, and instrumental aid that serve as mechanisms for sustaining the employment viability of all workers, including disabled workers, to varying degrees.

> *Natural supports are usually discussed in terms of either strategies (i.e., strategies to overcome barriers to performance) or support systems (i.e., the interplay of various aids to performance).*

Natural Support Strategies

Strategies are often articulated in terms of one of three approaches, distinguished by their emphasis on how to effect natural supports for the benefit of employee work performance, pay, and tenure:

- Customer consultation
    Employer as first customer
    Consumer as first customer
- Networking the environment
- Employee integration

Some authors who have emphasized the central role of the job coach as "consultant" and "facilitator" of the process of realizing natural supports may be said to adopt a *customer consultation strategy.* Others have emphasized the activation and/or creation of networked supports emanating to and from the workplace. This approach can be summarized under the general heading of *networking the environment.* Finally, a third distinct perspective is articulated by authors who emphasize the integration of workers into existing workplace relations, practices, and routines. This can be termed the *employee integration strategy.*

Natural Support Systems

In discussing the support systems in terms of natural supports, there has been discussion about what are the components of natural employment supports. The support systems undergirding workplace performance do not strictly speaking "end" at or emanate from the actual job site. An entire battery of resources—financial, interpersonal, transportational, and so on—"follow" the employee to and from work. Without these often "invisible" interlocking systems of support, workplace performance might be compromised or rendered altogether impossible.

Because the nature of the support system (and who or what is contained therein) often changes very substantially with the "location" of the support system, it makes sense to differentiate support systems according to whether they are located at the worksite (worksite), at home (home-based), or bridging the two (ancillary):

- Worksite
    Co-worker and supervisor
    Employer
    Policies and procedures
    Work routines
- Home-based
    Family and friends
- Ancillary
    Transportation

IMPLEMENTATION CONFIGURATIONS

The processes portrayed in Figure 4.1 and described previously are fundamental to all individual (and most group) approaches to supported employment. However, the individual placement model has been implemented through more than one configuration. Included under the general heading of individual placement approach are three configurations: basic, multiple, and cluster placements. Figure 4.2 illustrates the different configurations graphically, and each is described in the following sections.

Basic Placement

The basic placement configuration is the way most early individual placements were made. In this configuration, only one supported employee works within a job site. As with all of the individual approaches, after a job match is made and placement occurs, the employment specialist proceeds through a period of initial training (during which the employment specialist facilitates the acquisition of all work-related skills), stabilizing (during which the employment specialist facilitates maintenance and behavioral generalization of acquired skills across materials and supervisors), and fading (during which the employment specialist systematically and gradually withdraws from the job site). The initial consumer placed at the job site is the only consumer who works at that site at one time.

Multiple Placement

The multiple placement configuration can be conceptualized as a consecutive series of more than one basic placement within the same business. Typically, the first consumer is placed at a job site as described above. After fading is complete,

Basic	Multiple	Cluster
One placement per site	Several placements in a business, dispersed by shift or workspace	Discrete placements in different businesses which are co-located
Advantages		
Represents more opportunity for integration	Facilitates job development and analysis	Facilitates follow-along
Disadvantages		
Potentially the most time consuming for both job development and follow-along	May be stigmatizing May cause "halo" effects	

Figure 4.2. Individual supported employment approach configurations.

another consumer is placed at the same job site either during a different shift or in a location that is physically distinct from the initial placement. There are several advantages to this configuration. First, during the first placement, rapport between the employment specialist and the employer is often strengthened, making job development for a second position easier. Second, job analysis procedures can be implemented during the fading phase of the first placement, thus efficiently utilizing the employment specialist's time at the job site. Finally, during the follow-along phase, fewer resources are needed because of the proximity of the consumers to one another.

There are also disadvantages to this configuration. The first disadvantage, and perhaps the one that contraindicates use of the multiple configuration in many cases, relates to the often negative stigmatization that occurs when disproportionate numbers of disabled persons work in one location (e.g., sheltered workshops or segregated educational settings). Suspect are those multiple placement configurations in which the proportion of workers with disabilities to workers without disabilities exceeds the proportion of individuals with disabilities in the general population. Second, problems that arise on the job site with one worker with disabilities may influence the perceptions of the co-workers and supervisors about the other worker(s) with disabilities. This may lead to a multiple job loss.

Cluster Placement

In the cluster placement configuration, multiple supported employees are placed in different businesses that are in the same geographic proximity. This works particularly well when the placements are within a shopping mall or other location in which businesses are congregated. This configuration makes use of the follow-along and, to some extent, job development advantages of the multiple placement configuration, but generally alleviates the disadvantages. The criteria of natural proportion should, however, be considered in this placement configuration.

OUTCOMES OF THE INDIVIDUAL APPROACH

Supported employment is said to be an outcome-oriented vocational option. The outcomes (i.e., benefits that accrue for consumers in supported employment and the rehabilitation service system) that result from the individual approach can be categorized into four interrelated areas: wages, integration, ongoing support, and economic benefit–costs. The magnitude of each of the outcomes is best described in terms of its relation to group supported employment approaches and traditional vocational rehabilitation programs.

An important value of supported employment is that individuals, regardless of disability, earn fair wages for real work. One may assume, though errantly, that access to at least minimum wage is available to all Americans. Many persons with disabilities, and in particular, persons with severe disabilities, have not been afforded this opportunity through more traditional vocational rehabilitation services, such as work or day activity and sheltered employment. For example, wages earned within day activity centers range from nothing (some states disallow paid work) to $2.00 per day. Kiernan, McGaughey, and Schalock (1988) reported that the average sheltered employment wages for persons with developmental disabilities was $1.47 per hour for full-time workers and $1.24 per hour for part-time workers. More than 50% of the workers earned less than $1.09 per hour. Persons in sheltered workshops typically earn one third of the prevailing minimum wage. The wage data favor the individual approach, in a large part, because individuals served in sheltered workshops and group supported employment options are frequently paid under a subminimum wage certificate issued by the U.S. Department of Labor. Under this special certificate, workers with disabilities can be paid wages commensurate with their productivity. Although on the face this seems fair, critical access to appropriate training and support is often unavailable; therefore, individuals paid these commensurate wages may not have an opportunity to reach their maximum productivity. Consumers with disabilities who are placed using the individual approach most often work for employers who do not possess a subminimum wage certificate and are therefore bound to pay at least minimum wage to all workers. It can be argued that no individual should be paid less than the prevailing minimum wage. To do so with persons who have disabilities is establishing a "class" distinction based on disability and can be argued as discriminatory. Unfortunately, this argument is not supported by statute or practice at this time.

Inclusion

Historically, persons with severe disabilities have been both physically and socially segregated in vocational, educational, and residential settings from persons without disabilities. Ready examples include sheltered workshops, special public schools that serve only persons with disabilities, intermediate care facilities for the mentally retarded (ICF-MR), and the Special Olympics. In each of these cases, access to social and cultural aspects of life have been limited due to the service delivery systems created by federal, state, local, and private entities.

The social and cultural attributes of a job setting are considered important as each individual decides whether or not to accept or retain a given position. The concept of vocational inclusion or integration professes that workers with disabilities have as much access to these important social and cultural job characteristics as do workers without disabilities. Mank and Buckley (1988) described vocational integration as "adherence to regular and ordinary patterns of minute-to-minute and day-to-day working life" (p. 320). They went on to describe four levels of integration, including physical integration, social integration, relationships, and social networks.

> *The concept of vocational inclusion or integration professes that workers with disabilities have as much access to important social and cultural job characteristics as do workers without disabilities.*

Data empirically documenting the total vocational inclusion of persons using the individual placement approach are somewhat limited. In one study, the physical and social inclusion of 1,608 supported employees was measured on a 5-point Likert scale. Individuals in the individual placement model had a higher mean level of integration than any of the group models. There was a statistically significantly lower level of integration for supported employees in work crews and enclaves.

Intuitively, the individual approach offers more physical integration because the supported employees are co-located with nondisabled individuals. This contrasts with the usual implementation of the group models in which supported employees are located next to other persons with disabilities. Placement is a critical consideration with group models, in general, and enclaves, in particular.

The degree to which social integration (e.g., elective personal interactions) is occurring within job sites using the individual approach is unclear. In the most pertinent study to date, Parent, Kregel, Wehman, and Metzler (1991) found similar frequencies of interactions for workers with mental retardation and nondisabled workers. However, the nondisabled employees interacted more during break time and participated in more work-related interactions than did workers with disabilities. Again, by structure, it would appear that more opportunity for social integration exists for persons served in the individual approach than in traditional sheltered work facilities or other group approaches to supported employment.

The development of relationships and social network building of supported employees have also not been adequately researched to date. One tool that measures all aspects of inclusion is *The Vocational Integration Index* (Parent, Kregel, & Wehman, 1992); it measures company, work area, employee, and benefits indicators that lead to enhanced vocational integration.

Ongoing Support

Prior to supported employment, persons placed in competitive job sites often did not (and still do not) enjoy ongoing support. Supported employees, by statute, must receive ongoing support. At least two monthly on-site visits are required to meet the federal definition of supported employment.

A basic assumption of all group models is the nearly continuous presence of a supervisor allocated specifically to the group of supported employees. Persons served in the individual placement model "lose" the continual presence of their job coach during the fading and follow-along phases. Thus, supported employees in the individual approach receive the least amount of ongoing support from service providers when compared to consumers in group models.

In an effectively operating individual approach program, frequent information gathering and retraining as needed are always provided. The fewer actual on-site hours afforded by the individual model is not a negative aspect of the approach. In fact, continual ongoing support, as provided in the group models, tends to stigmatize the workers and increase the likelihood of prompt and artificial reinforcement dependency. Indeed, the use of natural supports (utilizing existing job-site personnel and material resources) may be enhanced with the individual placement approach out of necessity of job-coach fading.

> *In an effectively operating individual approach program, frequent information gathering and retraining as needed are always provided. The fewer actual on-site hours afforded by the individual model is not a negative aspect of the approach.*

Benefit–Cost

A program evaluation that examines economic outcomes is typically called benefit–cost analysis. Writing about the individual approach to supported employment, Hill stated, "It is indeed rare for consumers and taxpayers alike to prosper financially through the implementation of a social program." The positive benefits relative to costs of the individual approach to supported employment have been empirically demonstrated (for persons with mental retardation). For example, using Virginia consumers served by a university project as a database, Hill found that each consumer gained (after loss of government benefits) an average of $3,894 per year. State taxpayers saved over $4,063 annually through the implementation of the individual approach.

Similar in-depth benefit–cost data are not available for the other approaches of supported employment. However, fiscal year 1988 cost data (no benefit data) comparing the four approaches to one another have been aggregated. The data indicate near equivalency of the four models, with the average annual cost of the individual approach being $5,244, enclaves $5,154, work crews $5,008, and, based on an extremely small sample, entrepreneurial $6,072. The data reported were not standardized for the severity level of disabilities of consumers served.

No supported employment approach is inherently better than another. By its very nature, the provision of supported employment services is individualized, and a particular approach should be used only after careful consideration by service providers, rehabilitation professionals, the consumer, and significant others in the consumer's life. The quality of life of the consumer and his or her preferences and functional abilities should form the basis of all employment decisions. It is also very important to recognize that, in most cases, the individual approach should be the first choice of approach because of generally better wages, a higher probability of integration with nondisabled individuals, and its relative cost-effectiveness.

> *The quality of life of the consumer and his or her preferences and functional abilities should form the basis of all employment decisions.*

TRENDS AND ISSUES ASSOCIATED WITH THE INDIVIDUAL PLACEMENT APPROACH

Supported employment services and use of the individual placement approach, specifically, increased dramatically during the 1980s. Growing from a few demonstration projects to a major, national vocational rehabilitation initiative, the implementation of the individual approach is now occurring in every one of the United States. With this growth, several trends seem to be emerging, and several issues have yet to be resolved. A most notable trend has been the use of the individual approach with persons who have disabilities other than mental retardation. Critical issues that have evolved include, among others, continued funding for supported employment, the utilization of employers to implement supported employment, and, perhaps most important, the way in which services to individuals with severe disabilities are delivered. Each trend and issue is discussed in the following sections.

Application Across Populations

Supported employment was first used primarily for persons with mental retardation. Recently, efforts have been made to expand supported employment overall and in particular to the individual placement approach and to consumers who have disabilities other than mental retardation. For example, this approach has been used with persons with sensory impairments, criminal offenders, and individuals with traumatic brain injuries, psychiatric disorders, and physical disabilities. A brief description of the current status of supported employment with three of the most prevalent populations follows.

Traumatic Brain Injuries

Individuals with traumatic brain injuries have received a head injury usually resulting in posttraumatic amnesia, unconsciousness, or both. This group differs quite dramatically in terms of demographics and functional characteristics. For example, most of these consumers held a job prior to their injury. Cognitive deficits, especially problems with memory, and a high incidence of alcohol or substance abuse are frequently associated with this population.

Supported employment does work for this population. Wehman, Parent, Wood, Kregel, and Inge (1989) found in a study of 20 consumers that the mean hourly wages for supported employees with traumatic brain injuries before injury, after injury but before supported employment, and with supported employment were $5.11, $3.45, and $4.52, respectively. Thus, although supported employees in this group did not return to preinjury wages, there was a significant change after supported employment.

There is also a growing literature base that indicates that the individual approach is effective with consumers who have sustained brain injuries (Wehman, West, Kregel, Sherron, & Kreutzer, 1995). The direct service technologies needed to effect job acquisition and retention for this group have yet to be fully articulated and empirically demonstrated. The reader is referred to Kreutzer and Wehman (1990) for a more detailed discussion of the individual approach to supported employment with this population.

Long-Term Mental Illness

Persons with chronic and persistent mental illness are also beneficiaries of the individual approach to supported employment (Bond, 1998; Marrone, Balzell, & Gold, 1995). Long served by transitional employment programs, these individuals do not typically need the intensive on-site job training traditionally provided by the individual approach. Therefore, the emphasis with this population is more on appropriate job selection that matches the personality and job-ability strengths of the consumer with the job. A second and equally important aspect is the significant amount of ongoing support needed to assist the consumer with coping with the job-site environment (Gervey, Parrish, & Bond, 1995).

The Center for Psychiatric Rehabilitation has developed an innovative "Choose–Get–Keep" approach that uses many of the basic tenets of supported employment to provide ongoing vocational services to persons with long-term mental illness. In this approach, consumers are first provided assistance in clarifying vocational goals, interests, and abilities. Next, job selection processes are facilitated to enhance the probability of a good job–consumer match. Finally, routine follow-along is provided to assist the consumer in meeting the ongoing challenges of work and disability.

Because the application of supported employment to this population is not yet out of the demonstration phase, measurement of its employment effectiveness has not been adequately achieved. There is also uncertainty about which approach will ultimately prove the most effective and cost-efficient, although Rogers (1997) did a good job of summarizing the available literature in this area.

Physical Disabilities

The direct service technologies used for persons who have physical disabilities closely resemble those used for persons with mental retardation. The major variant is that the use of structural job-site modifications and adaptations is often increased. Prostheses are also more likely to be used with this population. Because of modifications, adaptations, and prostheses, the services of a rehabilitation engineer are frequently used to enhance the employment outcomes of persons with physical disabilities. Yet to be evaluated with this population is the level of ongoing support needed and the cost-effectiveness of supported employment. Again, as with programs designed to serve individuals with traumatic brain injuries and persons with long-term mental illness, systematic documentation of costs and benefits needs to be done.

Corporate Involvement

Approaching corporate chief executive officers to obtain multiple positions (dispersed throughout the organization) is another emerging trend. For example, Pizza Hut, Inc., recently implemented a corporative initiative to bring supported employees into its franchises (Zivolich, Shueman, & Weiner, 1997). This top–down approach may increase both the efficiency with which an adequate number of jobs can be made available and the investment, both programmatic and fiscal, of the employers.

> *Approaching corporate chief executive officers to obtain multiple positions (dispersed throughout the organization) is another emerging trend.*

Population Served

At its inception, supported employment was designed for persons with severe disabilities. With all of the populations served by the individual approach, defining "severe" is an elusive task. For example, if one uses only IQ to determine the severity level of a person with mental retardation (a risky but frequently used application of IQ), supported employment, at this time, is absolutely not meeting the original intent. Findings related to the functional characteristics of individuals in supported employment indicate that persons with severe or profound disabilities continue to represent a small minority of the population served (Kregel, 1995).

The reason for such representations are not clear-cut. The absence of significant numbers of persons with severe disabilities may be the result of inadequate training of vocational rehabilitation counselors and/or service providers.

The service system itself may not yet have been modified adequately to encourage service provision to the most challenging individuals. This current minority status may or may not be able to be changed in the future. Only time will tell.

HOW WELL DOES SUPPORTED EMPLOYMENT WORK?

After over a decade of research, empirical evidence confirms that the majority of individuals with severe disabilities who need relatively permanent employment services fare better in supported employment than in sheltered work or other types of day services. One of the first studies was the *National Employment Survey for Adults with Developmental Disabilities* (Kiernan, McGaughey, & Schalock, 1986), which examined segregated and integrated services and outcomes for more than 85,000 individuals served by 1,119 agencies. Quarterly earnings of sheltered workshop clients were $402.75, compared to $786.01 for individuals in supported employment, with hourly wages averaging $1.31 and $2.59, respectively.

> *Empirical evidence confirms that the majority of individuals with severe disabilities who need relatively permanent employment services fare better in supported employment than in sheltered work or other types of day services.*

Coker, Osgood, and Clouse (1995) studied individuals in sheltered and supported employment who were matched by age, sex, measures of intelligence, primary disability, and secondary disabilities. The average hourly wage of those in sheltered employment was $1.72, compared to $3.95 for those in supported employment; the average annual salary for individuals in supported employment was double that of their matched cohorts in sheltered employment. It should also be stated that these two studies examined only sheltered employment earnings. Many supported employment participants have previously been involved in day support services with little or no remuneration, or were out of the service system altogether, and so their earnings would be even lower.

Longitudinal analyses of persons moving from sheltered to supported employment have also been conducted. Early studies (M. Hill & Wehman, 1983; Lagomarcino, 1986; Vogelsberg, Ashe, & Williams, 1985) established that both service consumers and taxpayers benefited from service movement. More recent evidence continues to affirm these benefits (Helms, Moore, & McSewyn, 1991; Thompson, Powers, & Houchard, 1992). For example, Kregel, Wehman, and Banks (1989) studied 1,550 individuals who transitioned from alternative services to supported employment and found that weekly work hours, hourly salaries, and monthly earnings increased from 280% to 576% across disability groups. Finally, Rehabilitation Services Administration data for fiscal year 1991 show that individuals entering supported employment averaged $0.84 an hour in their previous places of employment (again, primarily sheltered employment and work activities), but were closed from service earning an average of $4.13 per hour.

These data are extremely encouraging, indicating that supported employment is an employment philosophy and technology that works. Thousands of individuals who were previously deemed unproductive by industrial standards and paid accordingly have been assisted to perform work at or above minimum wage in the competitive workforce. However, this option must be used more fully and invested in nationally to affect the historical trends of segregation of persons with severe disabilities.

A STATUS REPORT ON MOVEMENT FROM SEGREGATED TO COMPETITIVE EMPLOYMENT

Despite the growth of the supported employment program, all available evidence indicates that segregated employment services remain the primary service options for the overwhelming majority of individuals receiving long-term employment services (Mank, 1994; McGaughey, Kiernan, McNally, Gilmore, & Keith, 1994). A survey of state mental retardation and developmental disabilities funding systems found that the majority of consumers receiving extended employment services were in sheltered employment (44%) and day activity programs (37%), with only 16% served in supported employment (McGaughey, Kiernan, McNally, & Gilmore, 1993). Additionally, a survey of day programs conducted by McGaughey et al. (1994) found that although the number of persons served in integrated employment increased dramatically from 1986 to 1991, the average number of persons in segregated options also increased by over 28%.

These are critical data to evaluate, especially when one considers the efficacy of supported employment as an alternative strategy for enhancing competitive employment as an outcome. I propose a federally funded competitive employment initiative for those individuals currently and potentially receiving segregated vocational services, as a means of increasing their earnings and reducing dependence on Social Security Administration (SSA) disability programs.

Supported employment programs have been initiated primarily within existing Vocational Rehabilitation–funded rehabilitation facilities with long histories of providing sheltered employment, day activity services, and other segregated services for their caseloads. Those facilities remain the primary points of access to community-based employment services, including supported employment. Major impediments to increasing the numbers of individuals with severe disabilities entering supported competitive employment are the conflicting and counterproductive ways in which federal funds are used by the states and consequently by provider agencies. Recent empirical evidence supports this assertion.

1. The Rehabilitation Research and Training Center on Supported Employment at Virginia Commonwealth University (VCU-RRTC) conducts annual surveys of state-supported employment programs, including the Vocational Rehabilitation (VR) and extended service (mental health, mental retardation, etc.) service agencies. This survey has consistently found that only a small percentage of provider agencies have shifted resources from segregated services to supported employment. In fiscal year 1993, the most recent year for which data have

been collected, respondents indicated that only 15.7% of agencies in their state had downsized segregated services (Wehman & Revell, 1996).

2. The VCU-RRTC also recently completed (August 1995) a national survey of 385 randomly selected supported employment provider agencies in 40 states. Survey respondents were asked if their agencies had downsized staff, consumers, or funds allocated for segregated employment options and increased that of community-based employment services. Only 87 (22.6%) of survey respondents indicated that their agency had shifted resources to community-based employment. Moreover, after an average of 5 years of conversion effort, these agencies as a group continued to allocate most service slots and financial resources to segregated services (VCU-RRTC, unpublished raw data).

3. A national survey of 643 vocational service providers conducted by the Institute for Community Inclusion (McGaughey et al., 1994) requested segregated and integrated service trends for the previous 5 years. Only 18% of agencies reported that they had reduced or discontinued their facility-based programs, with the majority either expanding or keeping constant their consumers in segregated options.

4. The McGaughey et al. (1994) study also requested the number of individuals who had entered facility-based services and community-based employment during the previous year. Respondents reported that more individuals entered segregated programs than entered supported and nonsupported competitive employment combined.

5. Finally, Rehabilitation Services Administration data for fiscal year 1993 indicate that 9,930 individuals were closed rehabilitated in sheltered employment that year, despite the mandates of the 1992 Amendments to the Rehabilitation Act for integrated, competitive employment as the option of choice.

These data reinforce what most consumers, community providers, and funding agencies already know: The first choice of day program options for most people with significant disabilities is not competitive work. Clearly, if individuals with severe disabilities are to enter the competitive workforce to the extent of their capabilities, the agencies that plan and provide services must be encouraged and assisted to reduce the size of segregated work options that consume the majority of program staff, budget, and effort.

CONVERSION FROM SEGREGATED DAY PROGRAMS TO COMPETITIVE EMPLOYMENT

For individuals with disabilities in the United States, the primary source of support is Medicaid, and most states use Supplemental Security Income (SSI) eligibility for determining Medicaid eligibility (Braddock et al., 1995). Of 33.4 million Medicaid beneficiaries in 1993, 3.5% were adults with mental retardation or developmental disabilities, and 11.5% were adults with other types of disabilities. An unknown number of persons with disabilities are also likely to be included under other beneficiary subgroups, such as children, elderly persons, and recipients of Aid to Families with Dependent Children (AFDC). While SSI is a means-tested program, Social Security Disability Insurance (SSDI) requires that an individual meet insured status based on recent work activity. Approximately one third of SSI beneficiaries are also SSDI recipients.

> *Of 33.4 million Medicaid beneficiaries in 1993, 3.5% were adults with mental retardation or developmental disabilities, and 11.5% were adults with other types of disabilities.*

The economic disincentives of employment for SSA beneficiaries have been well documented. As Bowe (1993) noted, SSI and SSDI are "dependence oriented." That is, in order to receive assistance, claimants must prove themselves to be incapable of engaging in substantial gainful activity (SGA), currently defined by SSA as earned income of at least $500 per month. Fear of losing benefits, particularly health care coverage, persuades most beneficiaries to limit their earnings or to not enter the job market at all.

A RATIONALE FOR A CONVERSION STRATEGY

A primary rationale underlying a changeover strategy from predominately segregated work programs to integrated employment is that those individuals who are in segregated work programs are more likely to be dependent on SSA benefits than are those in competitive employment. Obviously, this affirms what supported employment professionals know instinctively. This is a critical rationale because this allocation of trust fund moneys, as well as enormous amounts of local, state, and other federal funds from VR, mental health, and mental retardation agencies, have gone into facility-based services, assuming that these were important training grounds for individuals with disabilities to ultimately enter the competitive workforce.

The long-term data compiled by McGaughey et al. (1994) and other sources show that this has not been the case. Research at the VCU-RRTC strongly suggests that once people enter supported employment, they are more inclined to have their competitive employment work income be their primary source of support, with Social Security being a secondary source (Kregel et al., 1989). National data from the RSA confirm this; at intake, 43% of supported employment participants' primary source of support is SSI or SSDI. Although many supported employees continue to receive a reduced level of benefits at closure, the primary source of support for the majority of participants is their own earnings.

An illustration of reduced SSI dependence from a supported employment consumer would be instructive. Samuel was a young man of 21 years who had moderate mental retardation and cerebral palsy. He attended a local high school and would be graduating in June 1998. Before he acquired his first job, he was receiving $300 a month in SSI benefits. His only activities outside of school were watching sports on TV, listening to the radio, and bowling on Fridays with his family.

Samuel started working with a job coach in September 1994. After spending time with him and discussing his job preferences, the job coach assisted Samuel to obtain a job at a local grocery store as a courtesy clerk and bagger. He worked from 15 to 20 hours per week at $4.50 per hour. After he began working, Samuel's life outside of school changed dramatically. He began socializing more with his nondisabled peers at school, and participated in activities at work, such as contests, incentive programs, and company picnics and parties. After graduation, he would be able to expand his work hours. Samuel's SSI benefit decreased to $169 per month, for an annual savings to the Social Security trust fund of $1,572 per year.

Samuel's case helps to put a human face on this challenging public policy arena. Without the assistance of a job coach, what chance of competitive employment would a person with Samuel's challenges have had? If Samuel's life after school was typical of most individuals with multiple disabilities—that is, graduation to segregated services or to waiting lists for services—what would his SSI benefit have been?

> *Without the assistance of a job coach, what chance of competitive employment would a person with Samuel's challenges have had?*

If only half of the persons currently served in sheltered workshops and activity centers could enter supported employment like Samuel, the savings to the Social Security trust fund would approach $400 million per year. Yet people like Samuel, who are given the chance to work in supported employment rather than in sheltered programs, are the exception. To increase the likelihood that more individuals are afforded this choice, it is critical to tie the funds that day programs receive to the nature of the service and ultimately into the outcomes they deliver. If a day program receives a certain number of program slots and a per diem rate of reimbursement regardless of the nature of the service or outcomes for the consumer (a very common practice in state mental retardation/developmental disability systems), then one should not be surprised if they deliver essentially segregated day program services, which may likely include nonremunerative activities.

SUMMARY

The individual placement approach is the most prevalent approach to providing supported employment services. It is arguably the most normalizing. It certainly results in the highest average wages. The benefit–cost balance of the approach has been demonstrated with some certainty with persons with mental retardation and to a lesser degree with other individuals. Funding, employer involvement, the application of supported employment to a wider variety of persons, and the severity level of persons served are all important and unresolved content areas to be watched in the years ahead.

Is the individual placement approach appropriate for all consumers in supported employment? Certainly not. Should the individual placement approach be the approach of first choice for all consumers in supported employment? Certainly.

REFERENCES

Americans with Disabilities Act of 1990, 42 U.S.C. §12101 *et seq.*

Bond, G. R. (1998). Principles of the individual placement and support model: Empirical support. *Psychiatric Rehabilitation Journal.*

Bowe, F. G. (1993). Statistics, politics, and employment of people with disabilities. *Journal of Disability Policy Studies, 4*(2), 83–91.

Braddock, D., Hemp, R., Bachelder, L., & Fujiura, G. (1995). *The state of the states in developmental disabilities.* Washington, DC: American Association on Mental Retardation.

Coker, C. C., Osgood, K., & Clouse, K. R. (1995). *A comparison of job satisfaction and economic benefits of four different employment models for persons with disabilities.* Menomonie: University of Wisconsin–Stout, Rehabilitation Research and Training Center on Improving Community-Based Rehabilitation Programs.

Federal Register. (1992, June 24). 34 C.F.R. 363, 57 (122), 28432–28442.

Gervey, R., Parrish, A., & Bond, G. R. (1995). Survey of exemplary supported employment programs for persons with psychiatric disabilities. *Journal of Vocational Rehabilitation, 5,* 115–125.

Hayden, M. F., & Abery, B. H. (Eds.). (1994). *Challenges for a service system in transition: Ensuring quality community experiences for persons with developmental disabilities.* Baltimore: Brookes.

Helms, B. J., Moore, S. C., & McSewyn, C. A. (1991). Supported employment in Connecticut: An examination of integration and wage outcomes. *Career Development of Exceptional Individuals, 14,* 159–166.

Hill, J., Seyfarth, J., Banks, P. D., Wehman, P., & Orelove, F. (1987). Parent attitudes about working conditions of their adult mentally retarded sons and daughters. *Exceptional Children, 54*(1), 9–23.

Hill, M., & Wehman, P. (1983). Cost benefit analysis of placing moderately and severely handicapped individuals into competitive employment. *Journal of The Association for Persons with Severe Handicaps, 8,* 30–38.

Kiernan, W. E., McGaughey, M. J., & Schalock, R. C. (1986). *Natural employment survey for adults with developmental disabilities.* Boston: Children's Hospital, Developmental Evaluation Clinic.

Kiernan, W. E., McGaughey, M. J., & Schalock, R. C. (1988). Employment environments and outcomes for adults with developmental disabilities. *Mental Retardation, 26,* 279–288.

Kregel, J. (1995). Personal and functional characteristics of supported employment participants with severe mental retardation. *Journal of Vocational Rehabilitation, 5*(3), 221–231.

Kregel, J., Wehman, P., & Banks, D. (1989). Effects of consumer characteristics and type of employment model of individual outcomes in supported employment. *Journal of Applied Behavior Analysis, 22,* 407–415.

Kreutzer, J., & Wehman, P. (1990). *Community integration following traumatic brain injury.* Baltimore: Brookes.

Lagomarcino, T. R. (1986). Community services: Using the supported work model with an adult service agency. In F. R. Rusch (Ed.), *Competitive employment: Issues and strategies* (pp. 65–95). Baltimore: Brookes.

Mank, D. (1994). The underachievement of supported employment: A call for reinvestment. *Journal of Disability Policy Studies, 5*(2), 1–24.

Mank, D. M., & Buckley, J. (1988). Supported employment for persons with severe and profound mental retardation. In P. Wehman & M. S. Moon (Eds.), *Vocational rehabilitation and supported employment* (pp. 313–324). Baltimore: Brookes.

Marrone, J., Balzell, A., & Gold, M. (1995). Employment supports for people with mental illness. *Psychiatric Services, 46,* 707–712.

McGaughey, M. J., Kiernan, W. E., McNally, L. C., & Gilmore, D. S. (1993). *National perspectives on integrated employment: State MR/DD agency trends.* Boston: Children's Hospital, Institute for Community Inclusion.

McGaughey, M. J., Kiernan, W. E., McNally, L. C., Gilmore, D. S., & Keith, G. R. (1994, April). *Beyond the workshop: National perspectives on integrated employment.* Boston: Children's Hospital, Institute for Community Inclusion.

Murphy, S. T., & Rogan, P. M. (1995). *Closing the shop: Conversion from sheltered to integrated work.* Baltimore: Brookes.

Parent, W., Kregel, J., & Wehman, P. (1992). *The Vocational Integration Index: A guide for rehabilitation and special education professionals.* Andover, MA: Butterworth.

Parent, W., Kregel, J., Wehman, P., & Metzler, H. (1991). Measuring the social integration of supported employment workers. *Journal of Vocational Rehabilitation, 1*(1), 35–58.

Rehabilitation Services Administration. (1992). *Annual report to the President and to the Congress Fiscal Year 1991 on the federal activities related to the Rehabilitation Act of 1973, as amended.* Washington, DC: Author.

Rehabilitation Services Administration. (1994). *Annual report to the President and to the Congress Fiscal Year 1993 on the federal activities related to the Rehabilitation Act of 1973, as amended.* Washington, DC: Author.

Rogers, S. E. (1997). Cost–benefit studies in vocational service. *Psychiatric Rehabilitation Journal, 20*(3), 25–33.

Schuster, J. W. (1990). Sheltered workshops: Financial and philosophical liabilities. *Mental Retardation, 28,* 233–239.

Stapleton, D. C. (1996, July 17). *Research needed on employment of individuals with disabilities.* Draft paper prepared for the Long Range Plan Steering Committee of the National Institute on Disability and Rehabilitation Research, U.S. Department of Education.

Test, D. W., & Wood, W. M. (1996). Natural supports in the workplace: The jury is still out. *Journal of The Association for Persons with Severe Handicaps, 21,* 155–173.

Thompson, L., Powers, G., & Houchard, B. (1992). The wage effects of supported employment. *Journal of the Association for Persons with Severe Handicaps, 17,* 87–94.

Vogelsberg, R. T., Ashe, W., & Williams, W. (1985). Community based service delivery in rural Vermont: Issues and recommendations. In R. Horner, L. M. Voeltz, & B. Fredericks (Eds.), *Education for learners with severe handicaps: Exemplary service strategies* (pp. 29–59). Baltimore: Brookes.

Wehman, P., & Kregel, J. (1985). A supported work approach to comprehensive employment of individuals with moderate and severe handicaps. *Journal of The Association for Persons with Severe Handicaps, 10,* 3–11.

Wehman, P., Parent, W., Wood, W., Kregel, J., & Inge, K. (1989). From school to competitive employment for young adults with mental retardation: Transition in practice. *Career Development for Exceptional Children, 12*(2), 97–105.

Wehman, P., & Revell, G. (1996). Supported employment: A national program that works. *Focus on Autism and Other Developmental Disabilities, 11*(4), 235–243.

Wehman, P., Revell, G., & Kregel, J. (1998). Supported employment: A decade of rapid growth and development. *American Rehabilitation, 24*(1), 31–43.

Wehman, P., West, M. D., Kregel, J., Sherron, P., & Kreutzer, J. S. (1995). Return to work for persons with severe traumatic brain injury: A data-based approach to program development. *Journal of Head Trauma Rehabilitation, 10*(1), 27–39.

Zivolich, S., Shueman, S. A., & Weiner, J. S. (1997). An exploratory cost–benefit analysis of natural support strategies in the employment of people with severe disabilities. *Journal of Vocational Rehabilitation, 8*(3), 211–221.

Chapter 5

◆ ◆ ◆ ◆ ◆ ◆ ◆ ◆ ◆ ◆ ◆ ◆ ◆ ◆ ◆ ◆ ◆ ◆ ◆ ◆

Vocational Training

Paul Wehman

The community-based vocational program is an educational experience conducted under the supervision of school personnel. A variety of community-based work experiences are provided to allow the student to learn how to work. It is the culmination of the outcomes from community-based vocational training, exploration, and assessment that will help identify the student's future vocational support needs and guide the search for employment.

During vocational training, the business environment becomes an extension of the classroom (Pumpian, Shepard, & West, 1988), and the primary goal is to help prepare students with severe disabilities for employment by the time of graduation. Decisions on where these activities will occur, or the curriculum, require careful consideration, as it is imperative that these be reflective of the local labor scene. Many educators have reported feeling overwhelmed with the idea of creating a community-based program and instead opt for creating school-based training. Although this type of activity may be acceptable during early years, prior to age 14, the final years in school should include real community-based experiences (Moon, Kiernan, & Halloran, 1990). Furthermore, whenever possible, students should be encouraged to become employed during their final year of school.

The steps in developing community-based vocational training sites are basically the same as setting up community-based assessment sites, as outlined in the previous chapter. Some of the other similarities include the following:

1. The vocational training experiences must represent future work; if not, the students may have difficulty with their transition from school to work.

2. The goals and objectives must be outlined in the Individualized Education Plan (IEP) or the Individual Transition Plan (ITP).

3. Written agreements that detail specific activities for the vocational training experiences must exist between the student, parent, employer, and school personnel.

Under no circumstances should the student be placed in a work area not specifically outlined in the written agreement. However, teachers should note that initial goals and objectives in the IEP can be written broadly enough to include these experiences so that the team will not have to reconvene multiple times. Whenever the student becomes an employee of the business, an employment relationship will ensue, and it can no longer be considered a training experience.

Teachers must make themselves aware of the specific Department of Labor (DOL) regulations that must be met. The school systems must adhere to the rules and guidelines of the Fair Labor Standards Act (FLSA) administered through the United States DOL (Inge & Wehman, 1993). The guidelines must be incorporated in community-based vocational programs for students with disabilities. The primary intent of the regulations is to ensure that people are not exploited in the workplace. To satisfy the DOL requirement, the relationship between the student and the employer should be one for training purposes only, and activities completed by the student do not result in an immediate advantage to the business. The length of time a student is allowed to participate in vocational training is 120 hours per job experienced.

> *To satisfy the DOL requirement, the relationship between the student and the employer should be one for training purposes only, and activities completed by the student do not result in an immediate advantage to the business.*

Eventually, however, the student may accept a paid employment offer from the employer. The student would then become an employee of the business, and the employer would be responsible for full compliance with the FLSA, including payment of fair wages and overtime pay. The school system must assume the responsibility for adhering to the guidelines and developing a community-based training policy. For answers to common questions that teachers may have, the reader is referred to Inge and Wehman (1993).

A vocational training program, as well as job-site training for a new employee, involves the direct instruction of job duties and related nonvocational skills (Moon, Goodall, Barcus, & Brooke, 1986). Systematic instruction usually begins on the first day of a student's vocational training experience or paid employment and is provided by the teacher or a job coach.

The major objective of vocational skills training is the instruction and utilization of natural supports, which enable the student to perform the required job duties accurately, with decreasing amounts of assistance from the teacher. Factors such as the complexity of the job, the teacher's instructional skill level, and the student's experience will have an impact on the effectiveness of the instruction and ultimately the success of the student. This chapter describes strategies and techniques critical for the teacher to understand and consider when implementing systematic instructional programs in integrated employment settings.

> *The major objective of vocational skills training is instruction and the utilization of natural supports, which enable the student to perform the required job duties accurately, with decreasing amounts of assistance from the teacher.*

TECHNIQUES

Instructional techniques are what most teachers use to instruct students to perform job tasks, such as folding laundry, polishing silverware, washing windows, or dry mopping floors, and related skills, such as use of public transportation, communication with co-workers, and appropriate use of meal and break time. When selecting and using instructional techniques, the teacher should always consider and respect the dignity of the student. The teacher must identify the student's initial performance level on all job skills prior to implementing the instructional plan. Instruction should be modified as determined by ongoing assessment of the student's progress in learning to perform the job tasks. Effective response prompts and cues, along with response chains, must be identified through careful analysis of instructional data records. Finally, all instructional procedures should include the systematic fading of intervention by the teacher.

Determining Initial Job Performance Level

It is imperative for the teacher to determine the initial job performance level of the student. One of the best ways to do this is through task analytic assessment. The critical element of this assessment is providing the student with the opportunity to perform the job-task steps independently, without providing the student with feedback, prompting, or reinforcement. Data should be collected at least once a week and always prior to beginning a training period. Probe data are recorded simply with a plus sign (+) for a step done correctly and a minus sign (–) for a step done incorrectly. This lets the teacher know when the new student is performing a specific task correctly and independently. The teacher should consider a job task learned when all steps in the task analysis are performed independently by the student for three or four consecutive probe trials. One way to ensure correct performance is to continue to collect probe data at least once a week after training has begun. If the student becomes employed, this type of assessment can be completed as the teacher visits the job site long after he or she is no longer present on a daily basis. The task analyses presented in Part II of this book provide ample illustrations of the content necessary for this type of assessment.

> *If the student becomes employed, job performance level assessment can be completed as the teacher visits the job site long after he or she is no longer present on a daily basis.*

The Task Analysis Record Sheet shown in Figure 5.1 shows probe data collected for washing trays at a cafeteria. The teacher collected probe data on tray washing three times during the first day of vocational training for a student named Nick. The probe checks were scattered throughout the workday for an accurate picture of Nick's performance during the entire workday. The teacher began the assessment by asking Nick to wash the trays without providing any assistance; then he discontinued collecting the probe data as soon as Nick made an error. The data for this task indicate that Nick initially performed 3 steps out of a total of 14 necessary to complete the task of washing trays independently.

Response Prompts

Prompts used during acquisition training to facilitate correct responses include verbal instructions, gestures, modeling, and physical assists. Any one of these

Task Analysis Record Sheet

Teacher: Mr. Smith
Student: Nick
Job Site: Snack Bar

	Probe	Probe	Probe	Probe	Prompt	Prompt	Prompt	Prompt	Prompt
1. Go to counter.	+/	+/	+/	+/	+/1	+/1	+/1	+/1	+/1
2. Put spray bottle on counter.	+/	+/	+/	+/	+/1	+/1	+/1	+/1	+/1
3. Put cloth on tray.	+/	+/	+/	+/	+/1	+/1	+/1	+/1	+/1
4. Pick up trays.	-/	+/	-/	-/	P/1	P/1	P/1	M/1	M/1
5. Go to other counter.	-/	-/	-/	-/	M/1	M/1	M/1	M/1	M/1
6. Pick up trays.	-/	-/	-/	-/	P/1	P/1	P/1	M/1	M/1
7. Go to other counter.	-/	-/	-/	-/	M/1	M/1	M/1	V/1	V/1
8. Pick up trays.	-/	-/	-/1	-/1	M/1	M/1	M/1	M/1	M/1
9. Go to kitchen.	-/1	-/	-/	-/	M/1	M/1	M/1	M/1	M/1
10. Wash trays.	-/	-/	-/	-/	P/1	P/1	P/1	P/1	P/1
11. Put trays away.	-/	-/	-/	-/	P/1	P/1	P/1	P/1	P/1
12. Wash cloth.	-/	-/	-/	-/	P/1	P/1	P/1	P/1	P/1
13. Wash hands.	-/	-/	-/	-/	M/1	M/1	M/1	M/1	M/1
14. Go to dining area.	-/	-/	-/	-/	M/1	M/1	M/1	M/1	M/1
Total Steps Correct	3	4	3	3	3	3	3	3	3
Percent Correct	21%	28%	21%	21%	21%	21%	21%	21%	21%

Instructional Code

+ = Correct
- = Incorrect
P = Physical prompt
V = Verbal
M = Model or gestural prompt

Distance Code

1 = within 3 feet
2 = 3–10 feet
3 = beyond 10 feet

Figure 5.1. Task Analysis Record Sheet for initial performance data.

techniques can be used during job-site training. However, the most important factor to consider when choosing prompts is selecting those prompts that most naturally occur within a specific work environment. For example, if a student is working in an industrial laundry facility, model prompts may be most natural, because the student can usually watch others use the machines, fold laundry, or put clean items away. Before any prompts can be used effectively, the job duty must be task analyzed. After this has been completed, the teacher may try various types of prompts on each step to determine which is the most effective. Generally, the least amount of prompting necessary should be used. A description of each type of prompt follows.

> *If a student is working in an industrial laundry facility, model prompts may be most natural, because the student can usually watch others use the machines, fold laundry, or put clean items away.*

Verbal Instructions

Verbally instructing the student is usually the most natural form of assistance provided in the work setting, since verbal directions from a supervisor or co-worker often serve as cues for workers. Instructions for individuals with special needs should be direct and related to each step in the task analysis.

Gestures

Pairing a verbal prompt with a gesture, such as pointing in a desired direction, is another form of assistance given to a student in the workplace. Gesturing is a form of communication that allows students to participate in work and social interactions with supervisors and co-workers. Gestures can involve pointing, tapping, or touching the correct choice (e.g., touching the appropriate sanitizing agent for rinse water).

Models

Modeling a step of the task involves demonstrating that step and waiting for the student to copy that behavior. Modeling should always be performed alongside the student rather than across from or in front of an individual. This allows the student to view the job skill as it is to be performed and does not require him or her to reverse the direction of the modeled step.

Physical Assists

Physical assists (i.e., hands-on assistance) may be required for some students to complete portions of a task. For example, when instructing a student to sweep the floor, physical prompting may require that the teacher stand behind the student, place his or her hand with the student's on the broom, and move it in the appropriate sweeping pattern. Fast-paced or crowded work environments are not the best place for this type of assistance.

Table 5.1 shows examples of response prompts used by teachers. These prompts (verbal instructions, gestures, modeling, physical assists) have been used in various employment settings to facilitate student performance of job tasks.

Table 5.1. Examples of Response Prompts Used in Employment Settings

Verbal Instructions

Teacher says, "Clean the tables."

Teacher says, "Mop the floor."

Teacher says, "Clean the windows."

Gestures

Teacher touches the stack of aprons to prompt the student to put on an apron.

Teacher points to the time clock to remind an individual to punch in before work.

Teacher taps a wristwatch to prompt the student to take a lunch break.

Models

Teacher gives cue, "Fold the towels," and simultaneously demonstrates folding a towel.

Teacher gives cue, "Clean the window," and simultaneously squirts window with cleaning solution.

Teacher gives cue, "Turn on the water," and simultaneously turns faucet handle.

Physical Assists

Teacher uses his or her own hands over the student's hands to guide the student in sweeping a floor mat.

Teacher touches the student's elbow to guide him or her to pick up a cleaning rag.

Teacher grasps the student's hand and places it on a plate simultaneously with the cue "Pick up the plate."

Least Intrusive Prompts

One way to systematically fade the response prompts needed during initial training is to use a system of least intrusive prompts. This allows the teacher to progress from verbal to model or gestural to physical prompts on each step of a task not performed correctly until one type of prompt stimulates the correct response. Most important, the student is not given the opportunity to make an error. The teacher should always be ready to interrupt the beginning of an error or, in the case of no response, be ready to give the next prompt in the system of least intrusive prompts. Guidelines for training using a response prompt hierarchy are included in Table 5.2.

Cueing

Cueing is a method of prompting similar to model prompts and involves directing the student's attention to appropriate materials without using physical contact. Cueing during job-site training normally means pairing one or more dimensions of color, shape, or size—which are redundancy cues—with the correct choice. One example of this is the student who has to select his or her time

Table 5.2. Guidelines for Using a Response Prompt Hierarchy

1. Have the student move to the appropriate work area unless movement is part of the task analysis (TA).

2. Stand behind or beside the student so that you can provide prompts quickly when necessary.

3. Provide a cue to begin the task (e.g., "Wash the mirror").

4. Wait 3 to 5 seconds for student's self-initiation of Step 1 in the TA.

5. If the student completes the step independently, proceed to Step 2 of the TA.

6. If the student is incorrect or does not respond within 3 to 5 seconds, provide a verbal prompt specific to Step 1 in the TA (e.g., "Pick up the cleaner").

7. If the student completes the step independently, reinforce and move to Step 2.

8. If the student is incorrect or does not respond within 3 to 5 seconds, repeat the verbal prompt (e.g., "Pick up the cleaner") and simultaneously model the response (by picking up cleaner yourself).

9. If the student completes the step independently, reinforce and move to Step 2.

10. If the student is incorrect or does not respond within 3 to 5 seconds, repeat the verbal prompt ("Pick up the cleaner") and physically guide the student through the response (guide the student's hand to the cleaner).

11. Reinforce and move to Step 2.

12. Repeat the procedure for each step in the TA until the job duty is completed.

13. Always immediately interrupt an error with the next prompt in the least prompt system.

---

card from a rack that holds the cards of 60 students. Attaching a sticker of a specific color to the student's time card may be all that is needed for him or her to identify the correct card. An example of a permanent cue was used to assist a student named Tina in remembering the correct sequence for hanging rubber curtain dividers inside a dishwasher. The teacher made a small color drawing of the correct order of curtains and taped it to the dishwasher. This picture cue allowed Tina to complete the step without teacher assistance. Eventually Tina no longer needed the picture, but the supervisor asked to keep the picture posted for the students on the two other shifts who experienced difficulty with the same task.

> *Cueing during job-site training normally means pairing one or more dimensions of color, shape, or size—which are redundancy cues—with the correct choice.*

Matching-to-sample is also a type of cueing that can be used easily during job-site instruction. When instructing using the matching-to-sample method, the teacher cues the correct response by showing the learner a sample of the correct choice. For example, when the student is required to stack clean dishes on a dish dolly, the teacher can place a sample piece of dinnerware into each appropriate compartment on the dolly. The student is then able to match the dishes to be stacked with the sample of dinnerware already in each compartment. Other match-to-sample ideas that have been used on job sites include (a) a picture of silverware placed next to slots on a cafeteria silverware holder, (b) a red mark on a scale indicating the appropriate weight for counting forms in lots of 50, and (c) a piece of tape on the wall marking the height for stacking 20 towels.

Forward and Backward Chaining

Nearly all vocational tasks can be classified as response chains, because in order for the student to learn the next step of the task analysis, he or she must have attended to the previous step in the sequence. The steps of this chain (the task analysis) must be performed in sequence, but they can be taught in a forward or backward progression. Additionally, the entire sequence for a task can be taught during a training session.

Simultaneous training on all steps in the task analysis (teaching the total task) is the preferred strategy, since the student can practice each step as it naturally occurs. With this method, response prompting techniques, such as the system of least prompts or time delay, can be applied easily. However, in some cases a forward chaining technique may be necessary.

Forward Chaining

When beginning instruction using the forward chaining method, the teacher instructs the student to perform the first step of the task analysis. No other instruction takes place until the student is able to perform this step of the task analysis independently. Once the student performs Step 1 independently, the teacher begins instruction on Step 2, but requires the student to continue performing Step 1. As the student learns to perform each new step independently, the chain of performance is lengthened until the student can complete all steps in the task analysis independently.

Backward Chaining

When using the backward chaining method of instruction, the teacher completes or assists the student in completing all the steps in a task analysis and then instructs the student to complete the last step in the chain. No other instruction takes place until the student is able to independently perform this step. Once the student is performing the last step independently, the teacher begins instruction on the next step, working backward in the chain (Snell, 1987). The student is required to independently perform the steps learned as instruction progresses from the last step to the first step in that task analysis.

The teacher should decide whether to teach all steps of a task simultaneously or to use a forward or backward chaining method *after* reviewing the results of the probe data. If the assessment data reflect correct performance consistently across the steps of the task, the teacher can consider teaching all steps simultaneously. However, if the first few steps of the task are critical to the entire task (e.g., latching the sink drains to begin pot scrubbing) or if the data reflect very low performance, then a forward chaining method may be more appropriate.

REINFORCEMENT PROCEDURES FOR JOB-SITE TRAINING

Before job-site training, the teacher will spend time investigating the student's likes and dislikes. Specific reinforcers can be identified to be included in the instructional program for training a new job skill. It is hoped that only natural reinforcers, such as verbal praise or, if employed, receiving a paycheck, will be necessary; however, other options may be needed during the initial phases of training.

Timing

The timing of reinforcement delivery is critical when attempting to increase the probability of a behavior's recurring. All reinforcement should be given quickly and immediately following the occurrence of the desired behavior. For example, the teacher for a student named Mario immediately told him, "Good using two hands!" when he simultaneously picked up a glass in each hand. By immediately praising a specific skill, rather than waiting until break time to tell Mario that he had done a nice job, the teacher was more likely to see an increase in the particular behavior praised.

Sometimes it is not feasible to deliver a reward immediately. This is especially true if a tangible reward, such as a cup of coffee or a magazine, has been selected for use at the job site. The teacher would not want to provide a sip of coffee each time the individual exhibited a desired behavior. Instead, the use of exchangeable reinforcers would be necessary. These might include tokens, points on a card, checks on a calendar, and so forth. The tokens, points, or checks would be exchanged later for an item or activity that the student previously selected.

There are several advantages to using exchangeable reinforcers. First, like tangible rewards, they can be delivered immediately and can alert the individual that the preferred item will be available soon. A student may receive a token for each independent response made during pot scrubbing. If the student earned 10 tokens, he or she would then be able to exchange them for a preferred, more tangible reinforcer at a convenient time.

Another positive feature of using exchangeable tokens is that reinforcement can be gradually faded as other, more naturally occurring events become reinforcing to the student. For example, the teacher should always provide verbal praise for a job well done when reinforcing the student with tokens. As the student becomes more independent, verbal praise should become a stronger or more powerful reinforcer than the tangible item, which would be faded gradually. Tokens can also easily be faded by requiring the student to complete an increasing amount of work before receiving the tangible item. For example, initially 10 tokens would have to be earned before receiving the cup of coffee. This number could be increased gradually until the student was working a full day before receiving the item.

> *The teacher should always provide verbal praise for a job well done when reinforcing the student with tokens.*

Delivery Reinforcement

Setting up a schedule of reinforcement to plan frequency of delivery is another important component of the student's instructional program. The teacher must decide between two types of reinforcement schedules: a continuous reinforcement schedule or an intermittent reinforcement schedule. During initial instruction of a new skill, a continuous reinforcement schedule generally is used. This means that the student receives reinforcement for each step in the task that is completed correctly. As the student's independent performance increases, the amount of reinforcement is gradually decreased to an intermittent schedule. Intermittent reinforcement involves the delivery of a reinforcer after a predetermined number of correct responses or a predetermined period of time. When reinforcement is delivered based on a predetermined period of time, an interval schedule of reinforcement is being used. If reinforcement occurs after a predetermined number of correct responses, a ratio schedule is being used.

Establishing the Paycheck as a Reinforcer

Many individuals with severe handicaps have had little exposure to money or the idea that a paycheck represents money for work completed. This will present a problem to the teacher since the paycheck typically is a naturally occurring reinforcer that has the potential for providing a strong motivation for work. There are many different ways to teach a person the meaning of a paycheck. Some individuals may quickly benefit from simply going with the teacher to immediately cash the check and use some of the money to buy a desired item. Another person may grasp the concept of a paycheck by marking off days on a calendar with the teacher indicating that payday will be approaching and that money will be used to buy an item. Still other individuals may understand the concept of a paycheck if a graph is made showing how many dollars were earned every day.

FADING TEACHER PRESENCE FROM THE IMMEDIATE WORK AREA

Students in community-based training settings are to be monitored at all times. However, how closely a student needs monitoring must be determined on an individual basis. The teacher may gradually fade his or her physical proximity to a student as the student begins to independently perform the steps of the task analysis for a job duty. If the student becomes an employee, the teacher must remove his or her presence from the immediate work area in which the job duty is performed and eventually from the job site altogether. The removal of the teacher's physical presence from the immediate work area must be systematically planned and based on the performance of the student or new worker.

> *The teacher may gradually fade his or her physical proximity to a student as the student begins to independently perform the steps of the task analysis for a job duty.*

Initially the teacher should be located beside the student in a position to provide direct instruction. When the student is independently performing approximately 80% of the steps in the task analysis for the job duty and the remaining 20% with a verbal prompt, the teacher should move 3 to 6 feet away from the student. At this time, if it is necessary for the teacher to prompt the student on a step, he or she should move up to the student to give the prompt. Once the student initiates the appropriate response, the teacher should move back to the designated distance. This distance should be maintained until the student performs the task for at least three consecutive probe trials with no more than 20% of the task requiring verbal prompts.

At this point, the teacher's distance from the student should be increased to 6 to 10 feet and maintained until the student performs the task for three consecutive probe trials with no more than 10% of the task requiring verbal prompts. Again, if an instructional prompt is necessary, the teacher moves to the student and gives the prompt while beside him or her.

Next, the teacher's distance from the student should be increased to across the room (10 to 20 feet) and maintained until the student performs the task independently for three consecutive probe trials. At this point, the teacher should leave the immediate work area and continue to monitor the student's performance of the job duty, if the goal is to assess ability to work independently or master the vocational skill. As long as the student's performance is maintained, the teacher should stay out of the immediate work area in which the duty is performed.

If a different agency or person (e.g., job coach) helps deliver these educational services, it remains the public school's or educational agency's primary responsibility to ensure that the guidelines for general supervision are understood and met.

JOB-SITE MODIFICATIONS

Modifications in the work setting and/or the use of adaptive devices can enable a student to complete job duties successfully. Wood (1988) suggested that modifications can be made (a) to the equipment, (b) to the method or sequence of the task, or (c) to improve student interaction in performance of the task. The necessity for and the type of job modification should be based on an analysis of a student's progress through a review of the instructional data for the specific job duty. A plateau at a certain instructional level, such as the student's performing the steps of the task analysis only following gestural prompts, should alert the teacher to the possible need for (a) a change in the task analysis, (b) a change in the instructional program, (c) a modification or adaptation to the work environment, or (d) a change in the student's job responsibilities or work environment.

Change in Task Analysis

At times the task analysis of the selected task behaviors is not sufficiently detailed enough. A greater number of components may help the student learn more quickly if the teacher provides instruction on a smaller number of units. Also, the task may be confusing and need rework or redesign.

Change in Instructional Program

Initially the teacher designs a systematic instructional program to teach a job duty and implements the training program. This plan includes (a) a training schedule; (b) an individualized job duty analysis specifying the sequential, teachable job skills involved in each major duty; (c) the specific instructional techniques, including prompting methods and reinforcement procedures; (d) the data collection procedures used for monitoring the student's progress; and (e) procedures for fading instruction.

In some instances, the initial instructional plan does not result in the student's learning the job tasks. If this is the case, the teacher must revise the instructional plan based on the student's progress. The data collected on the instructional program will allow the teacher to select a revised format that may result in the student's acquisition of the necessary job skills.

For example, a teacher initially selected an instructional format of total task presentation using a least intrusive prompting system. After 1 week of instruction with Robert, it became evident that he was performing individual steps of the job task only upon receiving a model prompt. The teacher considered Robert's instructional data and decided to change the instructional format to a total task format using a time-delay procedure with a model prompt. After 2 weeks of instruction using the revised format, Robert was performing all steps of the task independently.

Adaptations to the Work Environment

If a student can perform a job duty effectively and efficiently without specialized equipment or modification to the work environment, he or she should be expected to do so. However, in some instances, use of adaptive devices, such as a stepstool, tilt table, or specialized chair, and/or modification to the work environment, such as rearrangement of the position of equipment, use of permanent visual or auditory cues, or changes to the sequence of the task, can enable a student to complete a job task successfully. The teacher's job is to find ways to simplify task demands and identify modifications or adaptive devices that meet the student's needs. Some teachers may be skilled in identifying and designing modifications and/or adaptive devices, but many teachers may need the assistance of other professionals, such as an occupational therapist or a rehabilitation engineer (Wood, 1988).

> *If a student can perform a job duty effectively and efficiently without specialized equipment or modification to the work environment, he or she should be expected to do so.*

Change in the Worker's Responsibilities

In spite of efforts to change the instructional format, modify the work environment, or provide adaptive devices, sometimes a newly employed student still has difficulty with parts of a job duty. In this instance, it is necessary to determine if there is a co-worker who could share the job duty. Another alternative is to identify a co-worker's job duty that is of equal responsibility and duration to the task that is difficult for the student. It may be possible to switch job duties with that individual as long as the supervisor and the co-worker approve of the change. The employer, the worker, and the job coach should meet to discuss what, if any, alternatives are acceptable to everyone concerned. In some situations, the employer may not be amenable to changes in the student's responsibilities and may request that the worker resign from the position. However, employers frequently are willing to change students' responsibilities and will explain what alternatives they are willing to implement. The employer and the worker should agree on and specify the course of action and determine when the change is to be effective. A change in an employee's responsibilities will require the development and implementation of an instructional plan for training the worker in performance of the new responsibilities.

> *Another alternative is to identify a co-worker's job duty that is of equal responsibility and duration to the task that is difficult for the student. It may be possible to switch job duties with that individual as long as the supervisor and the co-worker approve of the change.*

There are a few legitimate reasons for termination of training and removal of a student from a vocational training site or an employee from a job. Possible reasons for termination of training are (a) removal of the student or employee by family members, (b) the student or employee refusing to perform the particular job, (c) the student's or employee's health, and (d) the student's or employee's involvement in action at the job site that warrants his or her resignation (e.g., stealing). Inability to perform job tasks independently soon after training is not an acceptable reason to terminate training activities. Teachers must remember that most individuals will not initially possess all of the work- and non–work-related skills necessary to perform the job independently. Supported employment, which uses the teacher or a job coach to provide on-the-job-site skills training using systematic instructional strategies, can be implemented.

REFERENCES

Inge, K. J., & Wehman, P. (1993). *Vocational options project: Designing community-based vocational programs for students with severe disabilities.* Richmond: Virginia Commonwealth University, Rehabilitation Research and Training Center on Supported Employment.

Moon, S., Goodall, P., Barcus, M., & Brooke, V. (Eds.). (1986). *The supported work model of competitive employment for citizens with severe handicaps: A guide for job trainers.* Richmond: Virginia Commonwealth University, Rehabilitation Research and Training Center.

Moon, M. S., Kiernan, W., & Halloran, W. (1990). School-based vocational programs and labor laws: A 1990 update. *Journal for The Association for Persons with Severe Handicaps, 15*(3), 177–185.

Pumpian, I., Shepard, H., & West, E. (1988). Negotiating job-training stations with employers. In P. Wehman & M. S. Moon (Eds.), *Vocational rehabilitation and supported employment* (pp. 177–192). Baltimore: Brookes.

Snell, M. E. (Ed.). (1987). *Systematic instruction of persons with severe handicaps.* Columbus, OH: Merrill.

Wood, W. (1988). Supported employment for persons with physical disabilities. In P. Wehman & M. S. Moon (Eds.), *Vocational rehabilitation and supported employment* (pp. 341–364). Baltimore: Brookes.

Chapter 6

◆ ◆ ◆ ◆ ◆ ◆ ◆ ◆ ◆ ◆ ◆ ◆ ◆ ◆ ◆ ◆ ◆ ◆ ◆

Living in the Community

Paula K. Davis and Ernest L. Pancsofar

One of the most important decisions people make is where they are going to live. Where people live influences virtually every aspect of their lives: where they will work, what they will do in their leisure time, who their friends will be, and what community resources will be available to them (Heward & Orlansky, 1992). Historically, there were few residential options for people with severe disabilities. If they did not live at home, they often were placed in large public residential facilities. In the 1960s, these institutions came under severe criticism because they were not providing services in a humane and normalized environment (Blatt & Kaplan, 1966; Wolfensberger, 1969).

Normalization is defined as "making available to [people with disabilities] patterns and conditions of everyday life which are as close as possible to the norms and patterns of the mainstream of society" (Nirje, 1969, p. 181). Large institutions, due to their physical and organizational structure, are not normalized living arrangements. A complementary principle to normalization is *deinstitutionalization,* which includes discharging people with disabilities out of large institutions into smaller community living arrangements (Heward & Orlansky, 1992). As a result of the deinstitutionalization movement and the normalization principle, people with mental retardation and other disabilities have been moving into smaller community-based settings, such as group homes, foster care, supervised apartments, semi-independent living, and independent living (Beirne-Smith, Patton, & Ittenbach, 1994). Current best practices in community living emanate from a person-centered approach in which homes and supports for individuals with disabilities mirror the homes and supports available for most citizens in a community (Racino, Walker, O'Connor, & Taylor, 1993).

The purpose of this chapter is to provide an overview of residential alternatives for people with severe disabilities. In the first section, the traditional residential continuum approach to preparing people for community living is presented and contrasted to the supported living approach, which assists people to live in residential arrangements of their choice. The second section of the chapter discusses person-centered planning. It provides strategies for identifying the lifestyle preferences of people with severe disabilities and discusses how to evaluate a person's lifestyle. Finally, two case studies are presented that illustrate person-centered community living.

RESIDENTIAL OPTIONS

The Continuum Approach

In the 1960s through 1980s, new school programs, employment options, and residential services for persons with developmental disabilities were developed. The guiding principle behind the development of these options was the least restrictive environment (LRE), sometimes called the least restrictive alternative (LRA). Typically the LRE is viewed as a continuum of options that range from those that are most restrictive to those that are least restrictive. Alternatives listed on the restrictive end of the continuum are considered to be the least integrated and least normalized, and as providing the most intensive services, whereas those on the less restrictive end of the continuum are considered to be the most integrated and most normalized, and as providing the least intensive services (Taylor, 1988). The assumption is that persons with developmental disabilities will receive services from the option on the continuum that meets their needs and will progress along the continuum as they develop new skills.

As applied to residential options, the concept of LRA has included independent living on the least restrictive end of the continuum and institutions for large groups of people on the most restrictive end. Between the two options are placements that represent varying degrees of restrictiveness. Options that have historically been included on the continuum include large group facilities (e.g., public and private institutions, nursing homes), group homes of various sizes, foster homes, semi-independent living, and independent living (Beirne-Smith et al., 1994; Taylor, 1988). The living arrangements, ordered from more to less restrictive, are described briefly in Table 6.1.

> *The concept of least restrictive alternative has included independent living on the least restrictive end of the continuum and institutions for large groups of people on the most restrictive end.*

The residential options listed in Table 6.1 vary along a number of dimensions, including number of residents, location of the residence, degree of privacy and independence available to residents, opportunities for making choices, degree of control that residents have over rules and policies of the residence, and opportunities to participate in activities of daily living such as cooking, shopping, and doing laundry. One assumption of the continuum approach is that persons with developmental disabilities enter the continuum according to the skills they possess and the services they need. However, in recent years there has been a strong move toward helping all individuals with severe disabilities be supported in community-based living situations.

Although viewing residential options along a continuum is tempting because it seems logical and systematic, and it appears to imply that people will move through the continuum, it also has a number of problems (Taylor, 1988). First, a continuum approach implies that options on the more restrictive end of the continuum are legitimate and necessary alternatives for some people, resulting in at least some infringement of their freedoms. Thus, the very principle designed to protect people's rights also legitimizes at least some denial of those rights for some people, who are most likely to be those people with the most severe disabilities.

Table 6.1. Residential Options in Traditional Continuum

Large Group Facilities: A common type of large group facility is the public institution, a state-operated facility that provides services to a large group of people with disabilities in one location (Heward & Orlanksy, 1992). The average size of state operated institutions in the United States in 1988 was 309 residents (White, Lakin, & Bruininks, 1989). Nursing homes and private institutions are much like state-operated institutions. Although some may be somewhat smaller, most serve large numbers of people and are usually not homelike. The nursing home may serve people both with and without mental retardation and may focus primarily on medical services. Like public institutions, private institutions and nursing homes are placed on the more restrictive end of the continuum because they do not meet the standards of a normalized living arrangement and often offer only limited opportunities for community integration. They are viewed by some as less restrictive than state-operated facilities because of their community location, but in all other ways may be nearly identical.

Group Homes: A group home is the form of community living most often used by people with developmental disabilities (Beirne-Smith, Patton, & Ittenbach, 1994). The term group home has been used to include residential options that vary greatly in number of people who live in the home and the amount of services and supports provided in the home. Some of the homes are small (e.g., 3 people), but they may have as many as 15 residents. Some of the homes have live-in counselors, whereas others have staff who work shifts. Some homes are established to be the permanent home of the residents, and others are established as training sites to increase residents' independence so that they may move to less restrictive options. Group homes are considered less restrictive than the large group facilities because of their smaller size and their community-based location.

Foster Homes: A foster home is one in which a person with developmental disabilities lives with a family in the family's home (Heward & Orlanksy, 1992). Foster homes are placed on the less restrictive end of the continuum because of the homelike nature of the arrangement. The person with the disability interacts with family members in a home rather than with paid staff members, goes on regular family outings into the community, and receives attention from the same small number of people on a 24-hour-a-day basis rather than according to a work schedule.

Semi-Independent Living: A variety of options fall into the category of semi-independent living (Beirne-Smith et al., 1994; Heward & Orlanksy, 1992). In general, it refers to people with developmental disabilities living in a home or an apartment, either alone or with one or two roommates, with support or supervision provided as dictated by the needs of the individuals with disabilities. Heward and Orlansky (1992) described three common variations of these arrangements. One variation is the apartment cluster arrangement in which people with disabilities live in a small number of apartments in an apartment complex. Staff who supervise and support the residents with disabilities live in another apartment in the complex. People without disabilities live in the remaining apartments, which may foster social interactions. In another variation of semi-independent living, persons with and without disabilities live together. The duties of the person without the disability depend on the needs of the person with the disability. In some situations, the arrangement may be primarily supportive; in others, more intensive supervision and assistance may be provided. Another variation of semi-independent living is one in which the person with disabilities lives in a home or apartment alone or with one or two others with disabilities. As in the other models of semi-independent living, the residents of the home receive the degree of support needed to allow them to maintain their lifestyle in the community. They usually have the skills necessary to take care of their basic daily living needs but may need daily, weekly, or occasional assistance for tasks that are difficult (e.g., cooking dinner) or that occur infrequently (e.g., paying monthly bills).

Independent Living: On the opposite end of the continuum from institutions is independent living. Independent living has been achieved when formal services and supports are no longer required to maintain community placement. Historically, independent living has been the goal for people with disabilities (Taylor, 1988).

A second problem is that the intensity of services aspect of the continuum is often confused with the segregation versus integration (institution vs. community) aspect of the continuum (Taylor, 1988). Intensity of supports available is often determined by the degree of segregation of the home. More segregated, facility-based options provide more supports and services; less segregated options provide fewer supports and services. As a result of this perspective, people who need the most supports are relegated to living in more segregated residences (i.e., institutions). Intensity of supports and the degree of segregation of the home, however, are two different dimensions of the home. People can live in integrated arrangements and receive intensive supports to assist them in doing so.

> *As a result of the continuum perspective, people who need the most supports are relegated to living in more segregated residences.*

The readiness trap is a third problem associated with the residential continuum (Taylor, 1988). Using the readiness model, which is implicit in a continuum approach, people move to a less restrictive option as they develop skills required by the next placement. Unfortunately, in many of the living arrangements, it is difficult to develop the skills required of the next option on the continuum. For example, if persons live in an institution in which someone else cooks the meals and does the laundry, and the only money they can handle is $1.00 given to them daily by a staff member, it is not very likely that they will learn how to live in the community where they may be at least partly responsible for those activities. Perhaps equally difficult will be the contrast between the highly regimented structure often found in large congregate care facilities and the opportunities for decision making and responsibility for filling one's own time found in smaller, community-based living arrangements. Furthermore, it is possible that some people will not master all of the skills deemed necessary to move to a community-based program. If a specified set of skills is mandatory for movement into the community as the readiness concept dictates, the people who do not acquire the skills will never be permitted to live in a less restrictive living arrangement.

> *If persons live in an institution in which someone else cooks the meals and does the laundry, and the only money they can handle is $1.00 given to them daily by a staff member, it is not very likely that they will learn how to live in the community where they may be at least partly responsible for those activities.*

From a humanistic viewpoint, one of the most troubling aspects of the continuum approach may be that people with disabilities who are successful in becoming more independent must pay a price for that achievement: They must move from their homes (Taylor, 1988). In fact, the more successful people are, the more times they must leave friends, neighbors, and the security and comforts that go with being established in any living arrangement. The end result is that the very model that was developed to assist people with disabilities establish a more desired lifestyle may also be the model that is most dehumanizing because it ignores the feelings associated with being uprooted from one's life.

> *The more successful people are, the more times they must leave friends, neighbors, and the security and comforts that go with being established in any living arrangement.*

The continuum approach to residential services was a step in the right direction. It resulted in the development of a variety of residential alternatives that provided some people with developmental disabilities opportunities to move out of large institutions or to avoid institutions altogether. After more than 20 years of providing services in this fashion, however, the flaws of the continuum became apparent and new ways of supporting people in the community began to emerge.

> *After more than 20 years of providing services within the continuum approach, the flaws of the approach became apparent and new ways of supporting people in the community began to emerge.*

Supported Living

Supported living has been proposed as an alternative way of looking at residential options for people with disabilities. It is characterized by people "living where and with whom they want, for as long as they want, with the ongoing support needed to sustain that choice" (Fredericks, as cited in Bellamy & Horner, 1987, p. 506). In contrast to the continuum approach in which people move to more independent living arrangements as they demonstrate skills, in the supported living model people live in the residential arrangements of their choice with supports provided to enable them to be successful. Instead of assuming that people with the most severe disabilities must live in options on the more restrictive end of the continuum while people with mild disabilities live in options on the least restrictive end, the supported living model puts forth the idea that, regardless of the severity of the disability, people should have the option of living anywhere they choose. To enable that to happen, supports need to be tailored to the individual rather than requiring the individual to demonstrate a particular skill level before moving to a less restrictive option.

> *Instead of assuming that people with the most severe disabilities must live in options on the more restrictive end of the continuum while people with mild disabilities live in options on the least restrictive end, the supported living model puts forth the idea that, regardless of the severity of the disability, people should have the option of living anywhere they choose.*

Key elements necessary to foster the supported living model have been outlined (Boles, Horner, & Bellamy, 1988). Perhaps the most important element of supported living is that there must be accountability for the lifestyle outcomes of people with disabilities. Often the focus of programs for people with disabilities has been on preparing them for their future. Much effort is expended preparing people to move to a less restrictive lifestyle. Unfortunately, when the focus is entirely future oriented, little or no consideration is given to ensuring that people are enjoying their current lifestyle.

If service providers embrace the idea that they must be accountable for the current lifestyle of the people for whom they work, they must be prepared to develop a diverse array of residential options, the second key element of supported living (Boles et al., 1988). It will no longer be acceptable to have three or four prescribed living arrangements in which people must fit. The options available must be as individualized as the people choosing the options. A diversity of residential options will require that a broad array of supports be available to help people obtain their chosen lifestyles and the supports provided must be individually determined.

In a typical approach to residential programming, a prescribed series of placements is available as described in the continuum model. Each of those placements provides specific services. People are placed in the option that provides the services they need. In the supported living model, the residential placement preferred by an individual is determined first. After determining the preferred placement, the supports that would be necessary to achieve the chosen lifestyle are arranged. Supports and the residence are viewed as two separate and independent entities. People receive supports tailored to their needs regardless of the specific living arrangement they have chosen. Supports that people may need to maintain their chosen lifestyles may be quite diverse and include those not typically provided in the community.

Supports for Community Living

The supported living model eliminates the relationship between service and facility by providing supports needed in all residential options. The types and amount of support needed to obtain and maintain a chosen lifestyle will be different for different people. What two people with the same disability need, in all likelihood, will not be identical. Furthermore, each person's needs and preferences are likely to change with time so that a support needed at one time may not be needed later. As a result, a variety of supports need to be available (Walker & Racino, 1993). Some people may need assistance in various aspects of daily living, such as bathing, cooking, meal planning and grocery shopping, and budgeting money. Some people may need partial assistance in performing these tasks, whereas others may require total assistance. Some people with disabilities may wish to acquire skills to be more independent in areas of daily living. In those cases, skills training should be provided. As stated above, however, independent task performance should not be a prerequisite for living in any particular arrangement.

Another area in which support may be needed is accessing and using a wide variety of community services, such as the public assistance office, Social Security, legal services, vocational rehabilitation, medical and dental services, banks, shopping malls, post office, library, and recreational facilities such as parks and the YMCA. Assistance may be needed to call the agency or business, complete paperwork, schedule appointments, respond to correspondence, arrange transportation, and use the agency or facility.

Specialized or adaptive equipment and materials may also be necessary to allow someone to live a chosen lifestyle. These may be very simple adaptations or materials, such as picture cookbooks, color-coded measuring cups, communication boards with pictures or words, telephones programmed with emergency numbers, or a stamp with one's name imprinted on it for signing documents.

Other people may need more sophisticated pieces of equipment, such as emergency cords in apartments that are connected to the apartments of support staff, telecommunications equipment (TDD/TTY), computer-driven communication devices, and robotics.

> *Specialized or adaptive equipment and materials may be necessary to allow someone to live a chosen lifestyle.*

Other supports also might be beneficial to people with disabilities living in the community. These include involvement in a formal or informal peer support group, assistance in making friends and spending time with them, support in making decisions in social and problem situations, assistance obtaining and maintaining employment, ongoing education (e.g., junior college, adult education), and assistance in developing intimate relationships that may include marriage and family.

As these examples illustrate, the supports that an individual may need or want can be quite extensive. In some situations, the individuals with the disabilities or their families may arrange the supports. Other people may choose to use the services of a case coordinator or case manager to arrange the timely and coordinated delivery of services. Case coordinators typically do not provide the needed services, but rather they assist the person in accessing them. They work to ensure that the services and supports are provided in a comprehensive, integrated fashion.

Support Providers

The supports described previously may be provided by different sources who have varying relationships with the person with disabilities (Walker & Racino, 1993). In some situations, the assistance may be provided by a paid staff member of an agency working with the individual. In other instances, the support may be delivered by a private individual hired by the person with the disability to assist with activities such as personal care, medical care, or housekeeping duties. Commonly available community services may also be accessed by a person with disabilities. For example, Meals on Wheels could be arranged, as well as regular home delivery of groceries from a nearby store. Another option for support is a live-in roommate who may or may not be paid to assist with various aspects of living. In still other cases, a volunteer, an advocate, a friend, a family member, or a neighbor may provide the assistance.

Some people with disabilities may receive supports from a variety of sources simultaneously. For example, a person may have (a) a paid staff member who visits the apartment daily to assist with preparing meals and budgeting money, (b) a family member who calls every morning and evening just to talk and see how things are going, (c) a family friend who invites the person to dinner once or twice a month, (d) a volunteer who visits or takes the person out once a week, (e) a co-worker who provides transportation to and from work daily, and (f) a neighbor who informally checks on the person daily. Additionally, the person may have several friends with whom to spend leisure time at home or in the community. As these examples illustrate, some of the supports may be formal and involve paid services, whereas others are informal, less structured, and do not involve payment.

> *Some people with disabilities may receive supports from a variety of sources simultaneously.*

Separation of Supports and Residence

Often the physical building in which persons with disabilities live and the supports they receive are provided by the same agency. That is, the agency owns or leases the home in which the person with disabilities lives and agency staff provide the services needed by the person who lives there. The agency is compensated for both the housing and the support services. Although this arrangement may work in some situations, it may also create problems (Racino & Taylor, 1993). One possible disadvantage is that if an agency owns homes and apartments, the agency will need to keep them filled in order to balance the budget. If the person living in the home chooses to move out, there is the potential for a conflict of interest. The agency that is concerned with the best interests of the person with disabilities must also be concerned with the agency's income. An empty apartment or house may result in the loss of dollars for the agency.

Another drawback to the agency-as-landlord model is that the persons living in the agency-owned home may not feel the same sense of responsibility or control that they would feel if they were dealing directly with a community property owner. A third problem may arise if the person with disabilities no longer needs or is eligible for services from the agency that owns the housing. In that scenario, the person may be forced to move from his or her home, or may be required to receive supervision and support that is no longer necessary. Finally, agencies may become tied to particular service models when they own the homes. They may be more likely to make people with disabilities fit the structure of their programs and less likely to be creative in meeting the needs and desires of the people who receive support.

To ensure that decisions affecting people with disabilities are responsive to their desires, new housing options are being developed that separate the physical housing from the support needed to live there. Two novel approaches to this are described briefly. One is for people to own their own homes. In New Hampshire, the Home of Your Own project was developed to foster home ownership by people with disabilities ("Extending the American Dream," 1995). The U.S. Department of Health and Human Services' Administration on Developmental Disabilities provided a 3-year grant to the Institute on Disability/University Affiliated Program at the University of New Hampshire to assist 21 people with disabilities to find homes, secure financing, and develop appropriate supports necessary for home ownership (e.g., home maintenance, paying bills, problem-solving assistance).

> *To ensure that decisions affecting people with disabilities are responsive to their desires, new housing options are being developed that separate the physical housing from the support needed to live there.*

The project showed that creative, nontraditional sources of income could be developed to assist people who often have no savings or credit history to qualify for loans. In addition to personal resources of the people with disabilities, federal, state, and local agency funding was used to make down payments, pay closing costs, make renovations, and pay for ongoing maintenance. Using this alternative approach, the agency no longer owns or leases the house; the person with disabilities does. The agency's efforts go into assisting the person in finding and purchasing the home, and in planning and providing ongoing individualized supports necessary for community living.

Another creative approach is the use of housing cooperatives (O'Connor & Racino, 1993). In a housing cooperative, members do not own their apartment or home, but belong to a cooperative corporation that provides them with a living unit. Members are expected to work for the cooperative, which results in affordable housing. The Madison, Wisconsin, Mutual Housing Association (MHA) established the MHA Cooperative, which is an example of the use of this alternative for people with disabilities (Racino, 1993). More than 400 people reside in 206 small scattered sites, including single-family homes, apartments, mobile homes, and group homes that form part of the Madison MHA. One of the goals of the MHA is to provide housing to as diverse a group of people as possible, varying by age, income, racial and ethnic backgrounds, and abilities. As of July 1990, about 10% of the residents had disabilities of various types. The MHA views housing and supports as two separate entities so that access to housing is not dictated by a service provider.

Three community organizations provide support services to people with disabilities (and people who are older) living in the Madison MHA housing. These services include, but are not limited to, helping find personal care attendants, providing peer support, providing transportation, providing home health care, assisting with chores, delivering meals, and teaching independent living skills. Additionally, the support staff assist the people with disabilities in developing good relationships with their neighbors and in performing the volunteer chores and responsibilities required of their cooperative membership.

The Home of Your Own project and the Madison MHA illustrate the separation of support from physical structure. As the two examples demonstrate, creative options can be developed that provide opportunities to live in the community in ways that allow people to experience lifestyles based on personal choices and needs.

PERSON-CENTERED PLANNING

It Starts with a Vision

One of the values underlying supported living is often described as person-centered planning. The basic tenet of this approach is to help the individual with the disability (i.e., the focus person) identify a vision of the future that he or she is striving to attain. The vision or dream originates from the focus person's perspective of what he or she wants. This is in sharp contrast to the traditional program planning approach which identifies skill deficits and weaknesses that must be overcome with appropriate training. Person-centered planning follows the spirit of several other processes, including Futures Planning (Mount, 1995), Circles of Support (Wertheimer, 1995), and Career Planning (Powell et al., 1991).

In its simplest form, person-centered planning means that preconceived projections about the supports suited for an individual are not made based on that individual's membership in a group identified with a diagnostic label (e.g., mental retardation, autism, cerebral palsy). Decisions and plans are made only after members of a planning team have an accurate profile of the person's vision, which includes an identification of outcomes that signify an enhanced quality of life for him or her. To help the person achieve the desired outcomes, supports are then developed that build upon his or her capacities, talents, and competencies and are not based on the deficiencies and shortcomings of the person. Table 6.2 contains a further explanation by Mount (1995) of the contrast between traditional program plans and plans developed with a person-centered focus.

> *In its simplest form, person-centered planning means that precon-*
> *ceived projections about the supports suited for an individual are not*
> *made based on that individual's membership in a group identified with*
> *a diagnostic label (e.g., mental retardation, autism, cerebral palsy).*

One way to conceptualize a person-centered approach to planning is to use a template similar to the one in Figure 6.1. This Mandala-type diagram contains the focus person's name in the middle surrounded by the outcomes that bring satisfaction to his or her life. Adjacent to each outcome is a further clarification of what that outcome means to the focus person. Even though the diagram contains only a brief sketch of the person's desires and quality of life outcomes, it

Table 6.2. Contrast Between Traditional Program Plans and Plans Developed with a Person-Centered Focus

Characteristics of Traditional Program Plans	Characteristics of Person-Centered Program Plans
• Goals focus on specific negative behaviors of the focus person to *decrease.*	• Images of the future contain specific, concrete examples of positive activities, experiences, and life situations to be *increased.*
• The plan identified program categories and service options that are often *segregated.*	• Ideas and possibilities reflect specific *community* sites and settings and citizenship contributions within those settings.
• Many goals and objectives reflect potentially *minor accomplishments* that can be attained within existing programs without making any changes.	• Some ideas will seem far out, unrealistic, and impractical, and will require *major changes* in existing patterns such as: funding categories, service options, how staff spend their time, where people live and work, and the reinterpretation of rules and regulations.
• These plans look *similar* to the plans and ideas written for other people.	• These plans will reflect the *unique* interests, gifts, and qualities of the person, and the unique characteristics, settings, networks and life of the local community.
• These plans will probably *not mention personal relationships* or community life.	• These ideas will emphasize creative ways to focus on the development and *deepening of personal relationships* and community.

Note. From *Capacity Works: Finding Windows for Change Using Personal Futures Planning* (p. 23), by B. Mount, 1995, Manchester, CT: Communitas. Copyright 1995 by Beth Mount. Reprinted with permission.

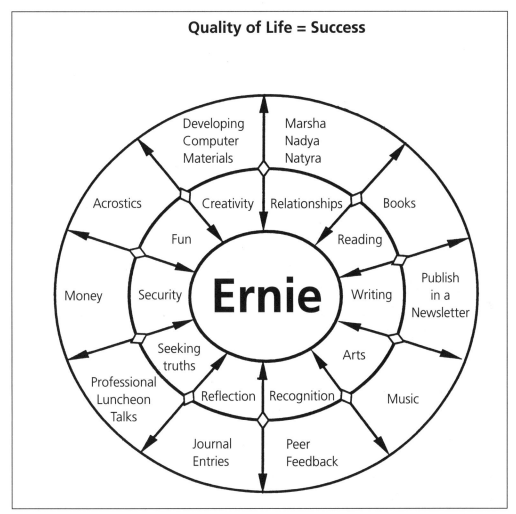

Figure 6.1. This person-centered template contains 10 outcomes of satisfaction for one of the authors. The focus person's name is in the middle surrounded by words that define quality in his life. The outer circle contains examples of activities that assist in obtaining a sense of satisfaction relative to how quality is defined for Ernie.

represents a good point of departure from which team members can discuss supports that impact the ability of the focus person to achieve those outcomes. Figure 6.1 illustrates the use of the diagram with one of the authors. The middle ring of the figure reveals 10 important outcomes for Ernie. The outer ring contains activities that would assist Ernie in attaining satisfaction with each of those 10 outcomes.

Deciding Where To Live

In a person-centered approach to quality of life, one of the most important components of the vision will focus on where the person with the disability will live. For people with disabilities, residential placement decisions are often based on the preferences of the person's parents or legal guardians, on the preferences of the staff members of the person's current residential placement, or on availability of an opening at a home. In a person-centered approach, the desires of the person are of utmost concern in making such decisions.

There are a variety of ways to find out about the preferences of people with disabilities (Racino & Walker, 1993). The most obvious and perhaps most underused approach is simply to ask people what they want or like. Unfortunately, even when people are asked about their wishes, their comments are often not considered when decisions are made. Additionally, some people may not be able to communicate their desires. Spending time with the person is another way to determine what a person's preferences are. Watching what people do, with whom they spend time, and what their reactions are to situations all provide insights into their likes and dislikes.

> *There are a variety of ways to find out about the preferences of people with disabilities. The most obvious and perhaps most underused approach is simply to ask people what they want or like.*

A third way of learning about a person's preferences is to provide the person with opportunities to experience the choices available. It is important to remember that if people have had limited experiences, they may not know whether they would like some options. For example, if someone has never had the opportunity to participate in shopping for clothes, the person may not realize that he or she enjoys it. Similarly, a person who has never been permitted to help with meal preparation may not indicate that activity as a high priority in choosing where to live unless given the chance to experience cooking. Therefore, it is important that people be given as many experiences as possible to allow them to make more meaningful choices.

A final way of ensuring that the preferences of the person are considered when making decisions about residential placement is to involve the people who know the person best in the decision making. In addition to the person with the disability, others who may also have important information about the likes and dislikes of the person include family members, friends, and the staff members who have been working most closely with the person.

Regardless of how the preferences of the person with disabilities are determined, it seems likely that people's satisfaction with their living arrangements will be higher if their opinions and preferences are solicited prior to the residential placement. Two studies have demonstrated how this can be done systematically (Faw, Davis, & Peck, in press; Foxx, Faw, Taylor, Davis, & Fulia, 1993). Institutionalized adults with mental retardation were assessed to determine what characteristics of community homes were important to them. A list of 30 preferences regarding community living was developed by reviewing a variety of quality of life questionnaires. For each of the 30 preferences, an either–or question was developed with pictures that corresponded to the two choices. The assessor described the two contrasting pictures and then asked the person which option was preferred. For example, one question was developed to determine whether a person preferred a private room or preferred to share a bedroom with roommates. To determine the person's preference, the person was shown a picture of a room with one bed and a picture of a room with two beds while the options were explained. The person was then asked in which home he or she would rather live. All 30 items were presented in this fashion, resulting in 30 expressed preferences.

> *Regardless of how the preferences of the person with disabilities are determined, it seems likely that people's satisfaction with their living arrangements will be higher if their opinions and preferences are solicited prior to the residential placement.*

To determine the person's strongest preferences of the 30 items, each of the 30 preferences was paired randomly against another of the 30 preferences. For example, a person who indicated a preference for a private bedroom and for having pets would be shown the corresponding photos, would be reminded of what each photo represented, and then would be asked which was more important. The forced choice testing was done three times with different items paired against each other on each test. Any item chosen all three times was considered a strong preference.

After the preference testing was completed, all of the people with disabilities received small photo albums that had pictures of their strongest preferences. Using the photo albums as prompts, they were taught to go on group home tours and ask questions about the availability of their preferences in the homes, to report that information to their social workers when they returned to the institution after the tours, and to decide if that home was a good place to live. Social workers, parents, and others involved in the placement process can use such information to help people with disabilities make decisions about where to live.

The studies were designed to show how preference information can be used to assist people to choose where they would like to live. Such preference information could also be used to help people obtain a more satisfying lifestyle in their current living arrangement. For example, a top preference for someone might be to have a pet. Although many group homes and apartment complexes say they do not allow pets, the rules may apply only to dogs and cats but not to other forms of pets, such as fish, gerbils, or birds. Or, possibly the person's desire for a pet could be met by volunteering at the local humane society. In another example, a person who lives in a shared apartment or group home may have a strong preference for privacy when using the restroom. If a private restroom is not feasible, an alternative way for ensuring privacy could be developed, such as placing a lock on the bathroom door or hanging an "in use" sign on the door.

These two examples illustrate that it may be possible to provide for a person's preferences in creative ways. It should also be remembered that some preferences may take time, some may take money, and others may not be possible because they are out of the control of the person with the disabilities and support providers (Smull, 1995). Nevertheless, an important step in providing a quality lifestyle to people with disabilities is to be aware of their preferences, to provide those that can be provided, to negotiate reasonable compromises if the provision of the preferences is not currently possible, to continue to explore creative ways of meeting a person's desires, and to evaluate preferences and satisfaction on a continuous basis because a person's desires are likely to change with time and experience.

Evaluating the Lifestyle

In addition to considering a person's preferences and satisfaction when he or she is choosing a place to live, it is also important to ensure that the person's lifestyle is evaluated on an ongoing basis. Several approaches to lifestyle satisfaction can be used. One way is to use an adaptation of the Mandala template described previously. Figure 6.2 shows one for Angie, a person with a severe disability. In this example, the people who know Angie best have identified four words to describe satisfaction in her life: comfort, attention, humor, and relationships. Each of these areas is more clearly defined by providing examples of what each means to Angie as illustrated in the center ring. The outer ring of the circle is used to identify activities that would enhance the opportunities for Angie to experience quality of life outcomes in those four key areas. When Angie experiences one of those activities, people who are responsible for her supports are asked to evaluate how satisfied they think Angie was using the Likert-type scale shown at the bottom of the figure. This method of looking at activities and events in Angie's life is not intended to be free of bias, but rather to be a focal point of discussion about how community experiences can bring satisfaction to Angie's life as observed by the people who know her best.

> *In addition to considering a person's preferences and satisfaction when he or she is choosing a place to live, it is also important to ensure that the person's lifestyle is evaluated on an ongoing basis.*

Another way to use a person-centered approach to documenting the connection between supports and satisfaction with lifestyle is found in Figure 6.3. This form enhances the likelihood that the desired quality of life outcome will be defined from the perspective of the focus person and that his or her satisfaction with the supports will be determined with his or her definition in mind. In this example, an important component of a satisfactory lifestyle for Sam is good relationships. From Sam's perspective, "good relationships" is defined by such things as a mutual interest in rock music and going to concerts together.

A comprehensive system for evaluating a person's lifestyle, Residential Outcomes System (ROS), has been developed by Robert H. Horner and his colleagues (Newton et al., 1994). The ROS was developed as part of a residential program model designed to provide the supports people with severe disabilities need to experience a desired lifestyle. When used properly, the ROS serves not only as a measurement system for evaluating outcomes for people with disabilities, but also as a blueprint for improving supports to assist people in achieving their chosen lifestyles.

Instead of being skill based as is typical in a traditional approach to assessment, the ROS begins by focusing on activities that a person currently performs or would like to perform. Activity preferences are determined by using the Lifestyle Assessment, which contains a listing of the activities typically available in most homes and most communities. The Lifestyle Assessment is completed by the person with the disability and a staff member who knows the person well. For each activity, several pieces of information are recorded, including whether it is an activity preferred by the resident, how many times the resident performed the activity in the past month, and how much assistance was required for the resident to participate in the activity. A parallel form is com-

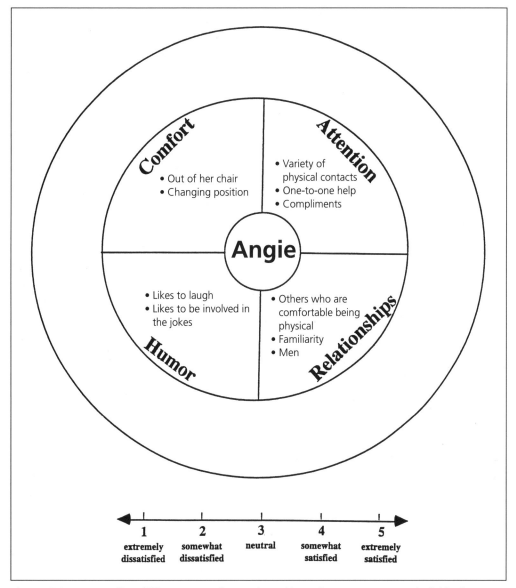

Figure 6.2. Four quality of life outcomes for Angie and how these outcomes are individually defined from her sense of satisfaction. Activities and supports are entered in the outer circle and a level of satisfaction is obtained from Angie's perspective.

pleted by the person's parents or advocate. Information obtained through the inventories is then reviewed to determine which activities should be recommended for the person's individualized plan.

After the plan has been developed, it is reviewed to ensure that it is balanced in several areas. One area of balance is between activities done in the home and those done in the community. Additionally, both personal management and leisure activities should be included. Personal management activities are those required by the environment such as self-care, shopping for and preparing food,

---

Person-Centered Strategies

Focus Person: Sam Johnson

Quality-of-Life Dimension: Relationships

Area of Investigation: Memberships in clubs/organizations

Today's Date: March 15, 1996

Words that define _good relationships_ **from** _Sam_ **'s perspective**

- with people his own age
- mutual interest in rock music
- activities are inexpensive
- not very far to travel

- meets once a month or so
- share CDs/music
- go to concerts together
- can be loud if I want

On a scale from 1 to 5, satisfaction with _good relationships_ **from** _Sam_ **'s perspective would be:**

| 3.5 |

| 1 | 2 | 3 | X | 4 | 5 |
| extremely dissatisfied | somewhat dissatisfied | Neutral | | somewhat satisfied | extremely satisfied |

Describe supports/experiences you have/do not have that influenced your rating.

The community center has been used as a place for Sam to frequent. There are announcements for clubs and common interests among participants but he hasn't found something interesting yet.

There is a computer club that meets every 2 weeks and the members are all interested in talking about music, using the Internet for talking to people, and talking about bands in the area. Sam is going to inquire about going to the next meeting.

Figure 6.3. A feedback form on which a person can define a quality of life outcome and provide a sense of satisfaction if the current supports are promoting its attainment. An advocate or family member could also use this form if the focus person is unable to communicate his or her satisfaction in an understandable way.

domestic chores, and budgeting. In contrast, leisure activities are those that are available in the environment but that are not required for survival. These are often thought of as free time activities (e.g., listening to music, watching videos, participating in games, visiting with friends).

Additionally, the activities should represent a balance between participation activities and training activities because, as mentioned above, the focus of a lifestyle should be not solely on increasing independence through formal instruction, which is the purpose of the training activities, but also on including objectives that ensure that the person has frequent opportunities to engage in preferred activities. In contrast to training activities, participation activities do not involve formal training. Instead, staff members support the person in accessing and participating in the activities. Finally, the activities included on the plan should also be balanced between those selected by the person with the disability and those recommended by others.

As an illustration, the plan for a young man might include the following activities: purchasing grooming items, using a vending machine, playing video games, going to movies, shaving, fixing a sack lunch, and doing laundry. Some of these activities are done in the community and others are done at home. These activities represent both the personal management domain (purchasing grooming items, shaving, fixing a lunch, doing laundry) and the leisure domain (using a vending machine, playing video games, going to movies). Some have been targeted for instruction, whereas others are participation activities to ensure that he has opportunities to engage in desired and meaningful valued activities. Finally, in this scenario, the person may have chosen the activities to fix lunch, purchase grooming aids, and play video games, but others may have chosen the laundry and shaving activities because these skills would provide him with increased opportunities for independence.

In addition to providing a systematic mechanism for developing an individual plan, the ROS is a data management system that measures four primary outcomes associated with a desirable lifestyle: physical integration, social integration, activity frequency, and activity variety. Physical integration is defined as the performance of valued activities outside of the home environment in the community. Social integration occurs when the person performs a valued activity in the company of someone other than a paid staff member or another resident of the home. Activity frequency is measured by recording the total number of valued activities that a person performs in a given time period. Activity variety refers to the number of different types of activities performed. The ROS provides operational definitions and examples of these outcomes, rules for recording their occurrence, management forms for planning the occurrence of activities, and data collection forms and graphs for recording and evaluating activities and outcomes.

The ROS presents a comprehensive approach to individualized planning that ensures that the most important people (i.e., the consumers) are involved in the selection of activities, that the activities are preferred or important to the lifestyle of the person with the disabilities, and that the person receives support to participate in highly preferred activities whether or not training is provided. (More information about the ROS may be obtained from The Neighborhood Living Project, Specialized Training Program, 1235 University of Oregon, Eugene, OR 97403-1235.)

REGULAR PEOPLE WITH REAL LIVES

To illustrate the variety of people with disabilities who are living successfully in the community, the lives of Emma and Bob will be explored. Emma is autistic, mildly to moderately mentally retarded, and hyperactive (Lucyshyn, Olson, & Horner, 1995). She had lived in an institution for persons with developmental disabilities for over 7 years. Her history of severe problem behaviors, including serious self-injury, was the reason she had not previously been considered for community placement. To determine the best community environment for Emma, several assessments were conducted prior to her move into the community. These included (a) a meeting to determine Emma's preferences, to explore her family's vision of her future, and to determine members of her support network; (b) a medical assessment; (c) interviews with family and staff to determine critical features to be included in her residential situation to make it safe and appropriate; and (d) assessment of her problem behaviors to determine what factors might be reinforcing her behavior and to develop an extensive behavioral support plan. Based on information obtained through these assessments, plans for supporting Emma in the community were developed. Emma moved into a three-bedroom house in a residential neighborhood that she shared with a roommate who was profoundly mentally retarded. Emma received one-to-one support during the day; at night a staff person who did not sleep provided supervision and support to the two women. With the support of a job coach, Emma worked 4 hours per week as a produce sorter at a warehouse.

Qualitative and quantitative data were collected over a 2½-year period after Emma moved into the community. Quantitative data included frequency of self-injury and aggressive acts per week, medication use, and activities per week. The qualitative data included interviews with her family members and staff members who had worked with Emma for over 2 years. Additionally observations were made of interactions between Emma and her staff or her friends. The data revealed that Emma became more frequently involved in activities, engaged in more varied activities, and participated in more preferred activities after moving into the community.

Reliable data on self-injury prior to the move were difficult to obtain. After moving to the community, her self-injurious behavior continued, but there were long periods in which she engaged in the behavior at very low rates. Staff reported that during times of increased rates of self-injury, the behavior was less intense and less harmful than previously. Additionally, Emma's medication was gradually reduced throughout her time in the community.

Qualitative data revealed that her family and staff noticed improved physical health, a more active lifestyle, and increased verbal communication and social skills. In summary, major improvements were noted in Emma's behavior, community involvement, and social relationships. Emma's story reveals how a complex support system can be developed to assist someone with severe disabilities to obtain a chosen lifestyle.

> *The data revealed that Emma became more frequently involved in activities, engaged in more varied activities, and participated in more preferred activities after moving into the community.*

There are others like Emma. The Illinois Planning Council on Developmental Disabilities published a book providing the stories of six people with developmental disabilities who moved to the community after years of living in institutions (Sandidge & Ward, n.d.). One of those people is Ed, a 54-year-old man with developmental disabilities, who lived at home until he was 29. When he was a child, his parents tried to obtain special education services for him, but they were told he was not "educable." His mother worked and often had to leave Ed alone. Although they did not want to, his parents decided to place him in a state-operated institution where he lived with 100 other men and received no education or training. Eventually Ed's mother was able to move Ed into a home for 15 adults where he received vocational training, learned to ride the bus, and had increased opportunities to socialize.

Although the home was better than the institution, it had its disadvantages. For example, there was only one washer and dryer for everyone, the residents had little say in their day-to-day lives, and all 11 men shared a single bathroom. Additionally, Ed was not happy about the noise that goes with living with many people. Now Ed lives in a ranch-style house that he shares with two other people. He takes a bus to his job at a community motel and does his share of the chores at home. One of the things he and his roommates like best about the new living arrangement is being able to decorate the house themselves. Both Ed and his mother are happy with Ed's lifestyle.

Ed and Emma are only two examples of lifestyle changes that can accompany community living. They illustrate that no two people are alike and that no two people want the same things out of life or need the same supports to achieve their desired lifestyles. Instead, Ed and Emma show that supports should be individualized to meet each person's unique needs and preferences and that the supports should be modified when desired and as needed by the person receiving the support. As the cases of Ed and Emma reveal, with appropriate personalized supports, the lifestyles of individuals with severe disabilities can be enhanced so that they may live in the community with full presence and active participation.

REFERENCES

Beirne-Smith, M., Patton, J. R., & Ittenbach, R. (1994). *Mental retardation* (4th ed.). New York: Merrill.

Bellamy, G. T., & Horner, R. H. (1987). Beyond high school: Residential and employment options after graduation. In M. E. Snell (Ed.), *Systematic instruction of persons with severe handicaps* (3rd ed., pp. 491–510). Columbus, OH: Merrill.

Blatt, B., & Kaplan, F. (1966). *Christmas in purgatory: A photographic essay on mental retardation.* Boston: Allyn & Bacon.

Boles, S., Horner, R. H., & Bellamy, G. T. (1988). Implementing transition: Programs for supported living. In B. L. Ludlow, A. P. Turnbull, & R. Luckasson (Eds.), *Transition to adult life for people with mental retardation: Principles and practices* (pp. 101–117). Baltimore: Brookes.

Extending the American dream: Home of Your Own project in New Hampshire. (1995, May). *TASH Newsletter, 21,* 8–11.

Faw, G. D., Davis, P. K., & Peck, C. (in press). Increasing self-determination: Teaching people with mental retardation to evaluate residential options. *Journal of Applied Behavior Analysis.*

Foxx, R. M., Faw, G. D., Taylor, S., Davis, P. K., & Fulia, R. (1993). "Would I be able to . . . ?" Teaching clients to assess the availability of their community living lifestyle preferences. *American Journal on Mental Retardation, 98,* 235–248.

Heward, W. L., & Orlansky, M. D. (1992). *Exceptional children* (4th ed.). New York: Merrill.

Lucyshyn, J. M., Olson, D., & Horner, R. H. (1995). Building an ecology of support: A case study of one young woman with severe problem behaviors living in the community. *Journal of The Association for Persons with Severe Handicaps, 20,* 16–30.

Mount, B. (1995). *Capacity works: Finding windows for change using personal futures planning.* Manchester, CT: Communitas.

Newton, J. S., Anderson, S. A., Ard, W. R., Jr., Horner, R. H., LeBaron, N. M., Sappington, G., & Spoelstra, R. J. (1994). *A residential outcomes system operations manual.* Eugene: University of Oregon, Center on Human Development.

Nirje, B. (1969). The normalization principle and its human management implications. In R. B. Kugel & W. Wolfensberger (Eds.), *Changing patterns in residential services for the mentally retarded* (pp. 179–195). Washington, DC: President's Committee on Mental Retardation.

O'Connor, S., & Racino, J. A. (1993). "A home of my own": Community housing options and strategies. In J. A. Racino, P. Walker, S. O'Connor, & S. J. Taylor (Eds.), *Housing, support, and community: Choices and strategies for adults with disabilities* (pp. 137–160). Baltimore: Brookes.

Powell, T. H., Pancsofar, E. L., Steere, D. E., Butterworth, J., Itzkowitz, J. S., & Rainforth, B. (1991). *Supported employment: Providing integrated employment opportunities for persons with disabilities.* New York: Longman.

Racino, J. A. (1993). Madison Mutual Housing Association: "People and housing building communities." In J. A. Racino, P. Walker, S. O'Connor, & S. J. Taylor (Eds.), *Housing, support, and community: Choices and strategies for adults with disabilities* (pp. 253–280). Baltimore: Brookes.

Racino, J. A., & Taylor, S. J. (1993). "People first": Approaches to housing and support. In J. A. Racino, P. Walker, S. O'Connor, & S. J. Taylor (Eds.), *Housing, support, and community: Choices and strategies for adults with disabilities* (pp. 33–56). Baltimore: Brookes.

Racino, J. A., & Walker, P. (1993). "Whose life is it anyway?": Life planning, choices, and decision making. In J. A. Racino, P. Walker, S. O'Connor, & S. J. Taylor (Eds.), *Housing, support, and community: Choices and strategies for adults with disabilities* (pp. 57–80). Baltimore: Brookes.

Racino, J. A., Walker, P., O'Connor, S., & Taylor, S. J. (Eds.). (1993). *Housing, support, and community: Choices and strategies for adults with disabilities.* Baltimore: Brookes.

Sandidge, R., & Ward, A. (n.d.). *A message for policy makers: What people with disabilities are saying about living in the community.* Algonquin, IL: Creative Core.

Smull, M. W. (1995). After the plan. *AAMR News & Notes, 8,* pp. 5, 8.

Taylor, S. J. (1988). Caught in the continuum: A critical analysis of the principle of the least restrictive environment. *Journal of The Association for Persons with Severe Handicaps, 13,* 41–53.

Walker, P., & Racino, J. A. (1993). "Being with people": Support and support strategies. In J. A. Racino, P. Walker, S. O'Connor, & S. J. Taylor (Eds.), *Housing, support, and community: Choices and strategies for adults with disabilities* (pp. 81–106). Baltimore: Brookes.

Wertheimer, A. (1995). *Circles of support: Building inclusive communities.* Bristol, England: Circles Network UK.

White, C. C., Lakin, K. C., & Bruininks, R. H. (1989). *Persons with mental retardation and related conditions in state-operated residential facilities: Year ending June 30, 1988 with longitudinal trends from 1950 to 1988* (Report No. 30). Minneapolis: University of Minnesota, Center for Residential and Community Services.

Wolfensberger, W. (1969). The origin and nature of our institutional models. In R. B. Kugel & W. Wolfensberger (Eds.), *Changing patterns in residential services for the mentally retarded* (pp. 59–71). Washington, DC: President's Committee on Mental Retardation.

Chapter 7

◆ ◆ ◆ ◆ ◆ ◆ ◆ ◆ ◆ ◆ ◆ ◆ ◆ ◆ ◆ ◆ ◆ ◆ ◆ ◆

Job Retention and Natural Supports

Michael D. West

The explosive growth of supported employment providers, services, and funding during the 1980s and 1990s has created employment opportunities for individuals who had previously been considered unemployable beyond the sheltered workshop or activity center, including persons with significant mental retardation, physical disabilities, traumatic brain injury, deaf–blindness, and multiple disabilities. The supported employment initiative has also generated a number of policy and implementation problems, issues, and concerns, not the least of which involve how to most effectively and efficiently provide extended support services that enhance consumers' job retention. How can agencies determine which clients will need ongoing support services to maintain employment? How does an agency plan and fund the types and amounts of extended services that its consumers will need? Why do supported employees lose their jobs despite intensive ongoing support services?

This chapter examines some of the major issues, strategies, and techniques related to the provision of ongoing support services within a program of supported employment. Emphasis is given to two programmatic trends that will likely receive increasing attention in the supported employment literature and in direct services: (1) the development of strategies by which supported employees can monitor and alter their own task-related and social behaviors at the worksite, and (2) incorporating cues, consequences, and change agents found naturally in the work environment into a plan of follow-along services. First, extended services and the need for extended services will be operationally defined, and funding and cost issues explored.

DEFINING EXTENDED SERVICES AND NEED FOR ONGOING SUPPORT

The distinguishing characteristic between supported employment and traditionally time-limited vocational services is the provision of postemployment support services by a rehabilitation professional, often referred to as a job coach or employment specialist. Whereas time-limited vocational services may incorporate supportive and follow-along methods, a program of supported employment, by necessity, includes interventions at the job site due to the nature of its service consumers. The initial regulations for supported employment programs (*Federal Register,* August 14, 1987) state,

> The need for job skills reinforcement under this program distinguishes supported employment from other rehabilitation programs where job accommodations or independent living services, such as readers, transportation, or housing may be the only needed postemployment services . . . individuals with severe handicaps, with the exception of the chronically mentally ill, would be inappropriate candidates for supported employment if they do not need job skill training at least twice monthly. (p. 30549)

The regulations indicate that those persons with mental illness can receive supported employment funds for transitional employment services (p. 30551). This is the only disability with this preference.

Moreover, individuals targeted for supported employment programs would be expected to require ongoing support services for the duration of their employment (p. 30546). Traditionally time-limited postemployment services, by statutory definition, do not extend beyond 18 months from the date of employment (p. 30551). Although many individuals with even severe disabilities are able to obtain and sustain employment through time-limited services alone, many cannot without regular intervention and support.

This leads to a dilemma that provider agencies frequently face: how to determine from the beginning the need for extended services and, by extension, appropriate candidates for supported employment. In some cases, this has led to conflicts between the provider and the funding agency, when individuals identified for supported employment prove able to function adequately with little or no follow-along services, or when those identified for time-limited services evidence a need for extended support. Client screening, for either supported employment services or transitional services only, should be done on an individual client basis that requires consideration of the types and severity of disabilities, the presence of unusual or dangerous behaviors, functional skills and limitations, prior work and employment service history, motivations and aspirations for work, and the personal social support networks that already exist. To some extent, the agency must also consider the generic services and supports that are available to the client and family members, the types of jobs or work settings that have been targeted for the individual, and the overall level of integration and acceptance of persons with severe disabilities within the community at large. The difficulty of prior selection also underscores the need for state policies that have some flexibility in terms of client placement, funding, and movement between transitional and supported employment services.

> *Client screening, for either supported employment services or transitional services only, should be done on an individual client basis that requires consideration of the types and severity of disabilities, the presence of unusual or dangerous behaviors, functional skills and limitations, prior work and employment service history, motivations and aspirations for work, and the personal social support networks that already exist.*

Client screening, for either supported employment services or transitional services only, should be done on an individual client basis that requires consideration of the types and severity of disabilities, the presence of unusual or dangerous behaviors, functional skills and limitations, prior work and employment service history, motivations and aspirations for work, and the personal social support networks that already exist.

The types of activities authorized by the Rehabilitation Act Amendments of 1992 as extended services are on-site and off-site interventions, with authorization for off-site interventions conditional on provision of on-site interventions. These interventions will be explained more fully later in this chapter.

FUNDING EXTENDED SERVICES

Coordination of Funding Sources

Time-limited vocational training services for supported employment consumers are generally funded by state vocational rehabilitation agencies, following the identification of an appropriate state or private nonprofit funding source for extended services (*Federal Register*, 1992). The coordination of funding from time-limited services to ongoing support has often been problematic for supported employment providers, resulting in either the absence of follow-along services or the abandonment of the supported employment concept. In a recent national survey of supported employment provider agencies conducted by West, Johnson, Cone, Hernandez, and Revell (1997), nearly 10% of supported employment agencies reported that they had no formal sources of extended services funding, and were instead covering those costs through other sources such as subcontract funds, case management funds, and so on.

Extended services funding may be even more problematic for individuals with primary disabilities other than mental retardation or long-term mental illness, who may not fall under the traditional state mental health/mental retardation funding "umbrella." Early state surveys of supported employment systems bore this out. For example, in a survey of 27 states receiving supported employment systems change grants, Kregel, Shafer, Wehman, and West (1989) found that 9 or fewer had mandated extended services and identified public funding sources for persons with cerebral palsy, other physical disabilities, traumatic brain injury (TBI), and hearing and visual impairments. In contrast, all 27 states had identified resources for persons with mental retardation, and over 75% for persons with persistent mental illness.

The Vocational Rehabilitation (VR) system at the state and federal levels has recognized this as a significant barrier to expanding supported employment to all eligible populations. Several states have set up special pools of funds for funding extended services to individuals who have no formal source. In addition, the Rehabilitation Act Amendments of 1992 promoted the use of "natural supports" as a means of ensuring the availability of extended support. Natural supports are discussed in greater detail later in this chapter, but the immediate point is that natural supports can be a low-cost or no-cost solution to the absence of a funding source.

Problems with obtaining follow-along funds have also inspired many supported employment providers to approach private agencies or groups to ensure ongoing funding. These sources have included private insurance carriers, the United Way, civic groups, corporate or private foundations, and individual donations. Another alternative has been to have the consumer set aside his or her own resources for later follow-along activities and utilizing the Plan for Achieving Self-Support (PASS) income exclusion offered for Supplemental Security Income (SSI) recipients. Under a PASS, earned and unearned income is set aside for current or future expenses of work-related training, equipment, services, or supports. West, Wehman, and Revell (1996) found that the primary use of the PASS was transportation; however, nearly 20% of supported employment provider agencies nationwide use PASSes to help consumers pay for either time-limited or extended services. The researchers concluded that the PASS had become a much-utilized resource for accessing necessary supports for individuals who otherwise might not qualify for services.

> *Problems with obtaining follow-along funds have also inspired many supported employment providers to approach private agencies or groups to ensure ongoing funding.*

Time and Money for Follow-Along Services

Although state mental retardation/developmental disability and mental health agencies are the primary sources of extended service funds, provider agencies often use a broad array of funding sources and methods for extended services, including state agency funds, local funds, private nonprofits, and the Medicaid Home and Community-Based (HCB) Waiver programs (West, Johnson, et al., 1997). Until October 1, 1997, these funds could be used for providing supported employment to only a very limited and clearly defined group of individuals who met funding restrictions imposed by Medicaid policies—that is, a history of institutionalization (which was imposed on no other HCB Waiver-funded service) and inability to access services through the primary agency (i.e., the VR system). Given the restrictive nature of this funding source, the number of agencies using it as a primary source for extended services was substantial, about 9.5%. The removal of the prior institutionalization restriction will hopefully be a factor in bringing more Medicaid consumers into supported employment, but that remains to be seen.

According to the West, Johnson, et al. (1997) study, contractual or slot-based agreements are the primary method of reimbursing agencies for providing extended services, reported by 44.3% of agencies. Under this type of reimbursement agreement, agencies are paid a daily, weekly, or monthly rate for each filled service slot. The slot rate can be either fixed for all providers, or negotiable between each provider agency and the funding agency based on who is served, where, and how well. Unfortunately, in many states the slot rates are the same regardless of the quality or nature of the service provided. This can produce a financial disincentive for agencies to provide more costly or intensive services.

Fee-for-service agreements were reported by 27.3% of agencies surveyed by West, Johnson, et al. (1997). Under a fee-for-service agreement, providers are reimbursed a fee rate for a defined service. The vendor receives payment of an agreed-upon fee for the time an employment specialist is engaged in providing services to an individual. This method breaks down the unit of service into small increments, frequently an hour, and tracks the length and intensity of service provided to each participant. As with slot rates, fees for service can be either fixed or negotiable.

All other funding methods accounted for 28.4% of the respondents. This latter response rate reflects the sometimes nontraditional or patchwork funding arrangements used for extended services as compared to time-limited services (Revell, West, & Cheng, 1998).

Perhaps the most significant findings of the West, Johnson, et al. (1997) study relate to the impact of funding methods and sources on service quality, particularly consumer choice and movement from segregated to community-based services. There has been much speculation regarding this interrelationship of these variables (cf. Mank, 1994; Wehman & Kregel, 1995; West, 1995) but no empirical validation. In this study, respondents who were reimbursed using statewide fixed hourly rates indicated that this method (a) was less responsive to consumer choice and (b) discouraged movement of consumers and resources from segregated to community-based programs.

With regard to consumer choice, the Rehabilitation Act Amendments of 1992 emphasize the importance of consumer choice in the establishment of job and career goals and the selection of services. Vendors of extended services have a responsibility to respond positively to choices made by consumers and particularly those regarding job changes, an essential component of career development (Pumpian, Fisher, Certo, & Smalley, 1997). However, the use of fixed hourly rates may present financial disincentives for providers in assisting individuals to make voluntary job changes for the purpose of career advancement or simply locating a better job match.

> *With regard to consumer choice, the Rehabilitation Act Amendments of 1992 emphasize the importance of consumer choice in the establishment of job and career goals and the selection of services.*

With regard to movement from segregated programs to supported employment, the Rehabilitation Act Amendments of 1992 unambiguously endorse competitive employment as the option of choice for all individuals regardless of the extent of their disabilities. Yet supported employment staffing and consumers remain small in comparison to segregated, facility-based services (McGaughey, Kiernan, McNally, Gilmore, & Keith, 1995). The staff and funds currently committed to supporting center-based, work-related services segregated from the competitive labor force represent a substantial potential resource for expanding supported employment opportunities.

Funding methods are needed that encourage and support service providers to expand community-based service capacity. For example, flexible rate systems can be designed to cover excess costs to providers for serving individuals with more intensive support needs or employment barriers, or to provide incentives for assisting consumers to achieve more positive outcomes in terms of job choice, wages, benefits, and integration. The findings of the West, Johnson, et al. (1997) study confirm that negotiable rate systems are preferable to fixed rate systems in encouraging this expansion. When providers are able to negotiate higher rates for services with more valued outcomes, such as community-based employment, they will be more likely to expand those options for their consumers.

> *Flexible rate systems can be designed to cover excess costs to providers for serving individuals with more intensive support needs or employment barriers, or to provide incentives for assisting consumers to achieve more positive outcomes in terms of job choice, wages, benefits, and integration.*

How much time and money are required for extended services? This answer is not purely empirical; it depends to a large degree on reimbursement method, consumer needs, and agency philosophy. Studies by the Rehabilitation Research and Training Center on Supported Employment at Virginia Commonwealth University (VCU-RRTC) have looked at time and money required for extended services using Virginia's regulations for transition from time-limited to extended services and beyond (West, 1992). The transition point in Virginia is defined as 4 weeks after the individual's required intervention time falls below 20% of the individual's work time (i.e., 2 hours of intervention for every 10 hours of work). Although states have different funding systems, the Virginia method was one of the first methods developed and has been adopted in whole or in part by many other states.

On average, supported employment consumers studied by West (1992) stabilized in their jobs by week 12. Post-stabilization intervention time thereafter averaged 5% of client work time. Because these consumers worked an average of 27 hours per week, on average they received approximately 1.45 hours of extended services per week. At the time these data were reported (1992), the average hourly rate for extended services was $28 per hour, so the annualized cost of extended services was $2,111 per client.

The types and amounts of intervention time required for job maintenance appear to be influenced by the primary disabilities of clients. McDonald-Wilson, Revell, Nguyen, and Peterson (1991) compared interventions for persons with chronic mental illness with those of all other persons in the program, primarily persons with mental retardation. They found that supported employees with chronic mental illness, on average, required less time to reach job stabilization and less time for job maintenance. West, Callahan, et al. (1991) studied intervention patterns for persons with severe physical impairments compared to all participants and found that, for those with severe physical impairments, proportionally less time was spent for training and more in program development time (including job modifications) and advocacy efforts both at the job site and off-site. The difference was most profound for job-site advocacy time, evidencing the need to nurture and support employers and co-workers as well as the client.

West, Wehman, et al. (1991) studied intervention patterns for supported employment clients with severe traumatic brain injury (TBI). They found that clients with TBI required more time and expenditures than other supported employment participants to reach stabilization and to maintain their jobs. Ongoing services required 1.64 hours per week, at an annual cost of $2,476. They found tremendous variability in transitional service needs, but on a per client basis, average weekly extended service needs were 1 to 2 hours per week.

Kregel, Hill, and Banks (1987) compared supported employment clients who had mild or borderline mental retardation with those who had moderate or severe mental retardation. There was no significant difference between the two groups on total intervention time required for the first year of employment. The group with moderate or severe retardation required more initial training time but required fewer hours of extended services.

Those studies, however, report gross averages from highly variable data. This is where reimbursement method, consumer needs, and agency philosophy come into the picture. First, many states reimburse extended services on a fixed daily or monthly rate and not by the hour of contact time (West, Johnson, et al., 1997). Thus, extended services will "cost" whatever that rate happens to be, regardless of the amount of time expended in providing services.

Second and more important, there is a widely held presumption based on the previously cited research that each individual in supported employment will need only a small amount of intervention in a week or month to maintain employment. In reality, individuals vary in their support needs, and many will require more or less than the average. In addition, each supported employee will have crisis periods during which additional time will need to be expended on them. Yet provider or funding agencies may be resistant to allotting additional time and money because they conceptualize the *average* level of intervention as a cap on hours or a standard measure for appropriateness for services.

> *There is a widely held presumption based on the previously cited research that each individual in supported employment will need only a small amount of intervention in a week or month to maintain employment. In reality, individuals vary in their support needs, and many will require more or less than the average.*

As an example of this resistance, the West, Johnson, et al. (1997) survey asked respondents to estimate the percentage of their supported employment consumers who received no more than the minimal number of monthly contacts per month (two). Agencies reported that 6 of 10 supported employees received only the minimal number of contacts, and a sizable proportion (about 20%) of respondents stated that their agency did not provide more than two contacts per month to *any* consumer. Clearly, many supported employment providers have either strayed from or never adopted the belief that individuals with severe disabilities should receive the types and levels of support they need to maintain their jobs.

ISSUES RELATED TO PROVIDING EXTENDED SERVICES

Why Do Supported Employees Lose Their Jobs?

Prior to describing strategies for helping supported employees keep their jobs, I explore the reasons they may lose their jobs. There is considerable evidence that a significant percentage of individuals who enter a supported employment position will be separated, most within 6 months of placement (Lagomarcino, 1990). Within the VCU-RRTC Supported Employment Information System (SEIS), a database of over 2,600 supported employees, only about 62% remain employed in their first placement after 6 months, and fewer than half remain in their first position after 1 year. The primary reason for job separation is employee-initiated resignation from the position (44.5%), followed by termination (37.5%), layoff (16.7%), and extended leave of absence (1.1%). From the available literature, specific factors that contribute to separation can be related to (a) the worker's production, (b) the worker's physical or mental health status, (c) economic factors, (d) the worker's responsibility to the job, and (d) other external factors.

Production Factors

Production problems typically relate to the worker's speed or quality of work, inability to perform certain tasks, or need for continual prompting to initiate or complete work. Within the SEIS (VCU-RRTC, 1990), these are given as the primary reasons for 17.5% of all separations. In a study by Lagomarcino (1990), production factors accounted for 12% of separations.

Production factors may be mitigated early in the placement process through careful job analysis and client–job matching. Job demand should be assessed under the conditions in which the supported worker will be expected to perform specific tasks. Initially, supported workers need not be able to perform the job as expected, of course, but employment specialists should be realistic about differences between client capabilities and job expectations and the extent to which training, adaptation, and support can lessen these differences over the long term.

Changes in production speed, work quality, or self-initiation during the follow-along phase may signal several things, including boredom with the job, supervisor, or co-workers.

Physical and Mental Health Factors

Physical and mental health factors contribute substantially to job separations of persons with traumatic brain injury (Sale, West, Sherron, & Wehman, 1991) and chronic mental illness (Lagomarcino, 1990; McDonald-Wilson et al., 1991). These disabilities frequently require intermittent hospitalization or absence from work for active psychiatric impairment, for medical or health problems, or for receiving other rehabilitative treatments. Interestingly, in the Lagomarcino (1990) study, medical reasons also accounted for 9% of terminations for persons with mild mental retardation, which may be due to the presence of other disabling conditions, such as epilepsy.

If occasional hospitalization or other prolonged absence from work for physical or mental health reasons can be foreseen, the provider agency can negotiate with the employer to job-share a position. When the regular worker is absent, a substitute (with training by the employment specialist) will be provided by the agency to fill in.

Economic Factors

Economic factors account for 16.7% of all separations in the SEIS and for 17% of separations in the Lagomarcino (1990) study. Typically, these separations occur because the company is terminating or laying off workers because of slow business. This category also includes seasonal layoffs during slow times of the year, which are anticipated at the time of hire.

The types of jobs targeted for supported employment consumers are frequently entry-level, high-turnover jobs in service-related businesses, largely because they are usually the easiest points of access for supported workers to the

competitive work world. Unfortunately, they are also the positions most suscep-
tible to cuts when business is slow. If the skills and interests of the individual
client warrant placement in such a position, the agency should be prepared for
occasional job changes. Agencies should also examine their local labor market to
identify industries and specific businesses in which economic layoffs are likely.
In addition, Lagomarcino (1990) recommended caution in placing supported
employees in new businesses, which tend to fail at higher rates than older, established businesses.

> *The types of jobs targeted for supported employment consumers are
> frequently entry-level, high-turnover jobs in service-related businesses,
> largely because they are usually the easiest points of access for sup-
> ported workers to the competitive work world. Unfortunately, they are
> also the positions most susceptible to cuts when business is slow.*

Job Responsibility

An absence of job responsibility is a significant contributor to job separation
across disability groups, but particularly for persons with mild mental retardation (Hill, Wehman, Hill, & Goodall, 1986) or chronic mental illness (Lagomarcino, 1990). A substantial group of supported employees simply decide that they
no longer desire to be employed. In addition, problems with attendance, punctuality, and general attitude toward the job are frequently given as reasons for
separation. As with production problems, absence of job responsibility may be
outward signs of dissatisfaction or boredom with the job.

Other External Factors

A number of other external factors contribute to job separation. These include
problems with transportation to and from work, parental or spousal interference, potential loss of government benefits, or the client's moving away. Also in
this category are positive separations, such as the supported employee finding a
better job or retiring.

From the previous discussion, it should be apparent that supported employment providers need to be diligent about maintaining close contact with the supported employee, the family, the employer, and other service providers or
involved parties, and be prepared to respond to any and all threats to the job
security of their clients. It should also be apparent that agencies should attempt
to proactively plan extended service needs by identifying a client's potential
problems in each of the above areas, anticipating methods of intervention, and
considering the individuals responsible for each anticipated intervention. Ideally, the follow-along plan should be written and developed jointly by all involved
participants, describing in concrete terms how each problem will be addressed.
Although no follow-along plan will identify every future problem, or ensure that
a problem will be addressed as planned, a written plan is the agency's first and
best assurance that problems affecting employment will come to their attention
and that there is a commitment to solve them before a separation occurs.

> *It should be apparent that supported employment providers need to be diligent about maintaining close contact with the supported employee, the family, the employer, and other service providers or involved parties, and be prepared to respond to any and all threats to the job security of their clients.*

Although many of the cited studies related to job separation attempted to isolate single causes, it is unlikely that a job separation truly has a single, discrete cause. Separation is more likely the culmination of any number of events, attitudes, and decisions on the part of both the employee and the employer—in the words of Sale et al. (1991), "more a process rather than an event" (p. 211)—with the end result being that either the employee or the employer decides the employment situation is not worth pursuing further. As an elementary example, an individual may have been terminated because he was repeatedly absent from work. He may have been absent because he had no reliable transportation, which resulted because his parents, who originally agreed to provide transportation, failed to do so. Yet, if the job paid more, they might have been more likely to follow through with their commitment. Yet again, if the job were more interesting and reinforcing to the employee, he might very well have pushed his parents harder or made other arrangements for getting to work.

Viewing separation as a process has positive connotations for a supported employment program. First, the separation process can be reversed if the client and employer have mutual feelings that the placement can be saved and is worth saving. Second, incidents, behaviors, or production deficits need not lead to separation if the employee is able to compensate by being a worthwhile employee in other ways.

Given the nature of supported employment consumers (the severity of their disabilities, their historical exclusion from vocational preparation and other adult services, their limited competitive work experience, etc.) and the entry-level jobs into which they are frequently placed, it should not be too surprising that many eventually lose their jobs. Perhaps the larger issue facing the field is not that many supported employees are separated, but what happens to them afterward. While many are placed again (and many again and again), an approximately equal number are either discharged from the program or returned to waiting-list status without replacement. For many supported employees and their families, the promise of long-term support lasts only as long as the first job. The reasons for this phenomenon, including the influence that providers, funding agencies, consumers, and families have in the decision to terminate supported employment services after a separation, require further scrutiny.

Family Involvement and Job Retention

Without full support from the family, long-term job retention is unlikely. This support is usually manifested in agreements to monitor medication, to report health or psychological status, to provide transportation, to ensure that the supported employee is adequately prepared to go to work, and to provide emotional support and encouragement. Depending on his or her age and level of dependency, a supported employment consumer may require these or other supports as part of a job retention plan. It is also helpful for family members to understand the difference between active involvement in job retention and overprotection. In some cases, this may involve agreements to not engage in certain activities, such as unnecessary contact with the employer or supervisor, "covering" for the supported employee, and so forth.

> *Without full support from the family, long-term job retention is unlikely. This support is usually manifested in agreements to monitor medication, to report health or psychological status, to provide transportation, to ensure that the supported employee is adequately prepared to go to work, and to provide emotional support and encouragement.*

Service providers should also be attuned to the psychological health of family relationships, particularly for clients with emotional or behavioral disabilities associated with chronic mental illness or traumatic brain injury. In some cases, family-based therapeutic intervention may be vital to achieving employment success. Support programs for these families will need to focus attention on three areas that directly influence job placement and retention:

1. Helping the parents or spouse develop realistic vocational and independent living goals

2. Helping families develop mechanisms and skills for relieving family stress and dysfunction, and to access needed therapeutic services

3. Helping family members understand and prepare for the financial implications of full-time or part-time employment, such as the loss or reduction of Social Security suport, Medicaid, or other entitlements

Importance of Choice in Job Retention

Consumer participation and choice in identifying and selecting from vocational options during the placement phase is the first step toward long-term job retention. In recent years, consumer choice has become a focus of much discussion and research in the disability field (see Wehmeyer & West, 1995). This initiative has largely been pressed by individuals with disabilities themselves, who often find themselves patronized, ignored, or labeled behaviorally challenged when they are vigorous in expressing their views, desires, and expectations.

In some cases, a focus on consumer choice may mean balancing the desires and expectations of the consumer and his or her family with the constraints of the local labor market or realistic expectations for achieving specific occupational goals. It also may involve an attitude adjustment on the part of service providers, who frequently explore available jobs first and consumer skills and aspirations afterward. Consumers may be advised to take the available job now (even if it presents no challenge or gratification), until the job they want comes along. As with any member of the general population, a supported employee who feels that his or her job is trivial, dead-end, uninteresting, or beneath or out of line with his or her level of skill or education will not likely be motivated to alter behaviors or increase productivity in order to keep that job.

> *In some cases, a focus on consumer choice may mean balancing the desires and expectations of the consumer and his or her family with the constraints of the local labor market or realistic expectations for achieving specific occupational goals.*

A study by West (1995) illustrates this point. He examined aspects of the workplace as predictors of long-term job retention. Using the *Vocational Integration Index* (Parent, Kregel, & Wehman, 1992), a measure of workplace supports and integration opportunities, he found that supported employees with traumatic brain injury who held their jobs for at least 6 months were placed into jobs that offered

- Opportunities for work-related social interaction (shared break and lunch times, close proximity to co-workers, etc.)

- Opportunities for nonwork social interaction (recognizing special occasions, group outings, etc.)

- Opportunities for advancement or regular raise reviews

- Paid vacation and sick leave

- Employer-sponsored medical benefits

West (1995) concluded that these individuals succeeded in their jobs because they had been assisted in locating positions that were worth getting and keeping. The positions offered a "sense of belonging," as well as financial motivation that promoted good work habits, satisfaction, and a desire to stay.

Once a desirable position has been found and obtained, the decision to remain in the position is also a matter of choice for the supported employee. The myth of the worker with disabilities who toils away year after year in an entry-level or monotonous job, just happy to be working, is fast giving way to reality. Although many individuals with disabilities do, indeed, stay with these types of jobs for many years, the relative size of this group is probably not much different from that found in the general workforce. Persons with disabilities, like most members of the workforce, need to be given the opportunity to make voluntary career moves upward, downward, or laterally; to change scenery; or to begin anew. When such times arise, job terminations should not necessarily be viewed as a failure on the part of the consumer, the employment specialist, the employer, or the program, but as evolutionary stages in the development, growth, and self-determination of the consumer.

PLANNING SERVICES FOR ENHANCING JOB RETENTION POTENTIAL

Fading from the Job Site

Fading of the employment specialist from the job site is perhaps the most difficult adjustment period for both the supported employee and the employer. Fading too rapidly may result in a loss of skill and behavioral gains that had been previously made; fading too slowly may increase employee and employer dependence on the employment specialist. The determination of the rate of fading must be made on an individual basis, using all the available client data (supervisor's evaluations, production rates, etc.) as guides.

Fortunately, there are strategies that the employment specialist can employ to mediate the effects of fading. Two approaches that are particularly relevant to the discussion of follow-along services, self-management strategies and the use of co-workers as providers of support, are reviewed here.

Developing Self-Management Strategies

The most powerful antecedents and consequences to behavior are those that occur in natural vocational, social, or academic environments (Stokes & Baer, 1977). When the learner seems unable or unwilling to respond to natural antecedents and consequences, alternative strategies, such as self-management procedures, need to be developed. Self-management involves training the learner to (a) recognize his or her own problem, (b) translate problems into behaviors to be altered, (c) locate or contrive natural contingencies, and (d) arrange contingencies to promote behavioral change. Self-management procedures have been used successfully in the instruction of children and adults with developmental disabilities in social, academic, daily living, and vocational situations. Wacker and Berg (1986) described the use of self-management within an employment situation. Although they specifically addressed strategies for workers with mental retardation, as do the overwhelming majority of self-management studies, similar strategies may be useful for workers with other primary disabilities, who have deficits of memory, concentration, or disinhibition. By teaching self-control of behavior, the employment specialist is closer to ensuring that the worker can function in the workplace in the absence of external guidance and instruction.

Lagomarcino, Hughes, and Rusch (1989) described the steps that employment specialists should follow in developing a self-management program to promote job independence for workers with disabilities:

1. Identify the problem through routine work performance evaluations. Self-management programs can be developed for problems with both productivity and social skills.

2. Verify the problem by direct observation of the worker and interviews with the supervisor and co-workers.

3. Establish a range of acceptable behavior based on observations of co-workers and negotiations with the employer.

4. Assess the work environment for naturally occurring cues and reinforcers to prompt and maintain behavior. Natural cues can be in the form of clocks or timers, employee checklists, whistles, and actions or statements of co-workers or supervisors, and natural reinforcers can be food items from a vending machine, supervisor praise, preferred tasks, and so on. If no natural cues or reinforcers are present, or if natural cues and reinforcers are not sufficient for the individual worker, then socially acceptable, artificial cues and reinforcers must be developed.

5. Select a self-management procedure that will be compatible with specific job requirements and that will not draw negative attention to the worker. A few examples of these procedures are described later in this chapter.

6. Teach self-management skills using techniques based on established learning principles (fading, shaping, modeling, etc.), which gradually withdraw external assistance from the trainer.

7. Evaluate the effects of self-management training by comparing the worker's performance before and after training, and comparing post-training performance with that of co-workers.

Self-management strategies are grouped as those that rely on self-administered cues and those that rely on self-administered consequences. These may be used in isolation or in any combination.

Self-Administered Cues. Wacker and Berg (1986) described three methods of self-cuing. The most frequently used form is self-instruction, in which the worker is first taught to perform the task, and then to produce self-generated verbal prompts to initiate and complete the task. For example, after instructing a motel housekeeper in the various tasks associated with room cleaning, the employment specialist might train the employee to initiate each task with an instruction (i.e., "First, clean the bathroom. Next, dust the furniture") immediately prior to the performance of each step. Self-instruction might also be used for initiating social contacts on the job, (e.g., lunch or break behavior, greeting the supervisor or co-workers) or responding appropriately to stressful situations.

Agran, Fodor-Davis, and Moore (1989) used a similar procedure, which they termed verbal training, to teach workers with mental retardation to increase their productivity in sheltered work tasks. These workers were instructed to tell themselves that they needed to work faster with positive results, with no instruction specifically given in improving speed or efficiency. Although this particular strategy was used in a sheltered workshop, where workers verbally motivating themselves may be socially accepted, this type of behavior might go unnoticed or be acceptable in some competitive settings.

A strategy similar to self-instruction is verbal labeling, in which tools, workpieces, or aspects of a job are made more concrete and salient by the worker verbalizing their name or label. For example, in a data-entry position, which requires separate entry formats for various forms or lists, the employment specialist might instruct the worker to verbally name each form prior to entry. This verbal cue then triggers the appropriate response, in this case, the selection of the appropriate format.

> *A strategy similar to self-instruction is verbal labeling, in which tools, workpieces, or aspects of a job are made more concrete and salient by the worker verbalizing their name or label.*

The third method of self-cuing is the use of a permanent prompt, such as a written list of duties or task sequences, or picture prompts bound into a book or posted in an unobtrusive place. For example, a dining room attendant in a fast food restaurant may have a picture sequence of duties taped on the inside of the door to a utility room or on the lid of a garbage bin. The worker can refer to this picture prompt regularly to ensure that tasks are not neglected.

Another permanent prompting system, one that might be less stigmatizing to the supported worker, is the use of taped instructions and a portable cassette player with earphones (Berg & Wacker, 1983). The worker is instructed to start and stop the tape at appropriate times in order to receive task or sequencing instructions. In many work environments, personal cassette players are acceptable and common among workers, and this adaptation will not call attention to itself or to the worker. For example, personal cassette players might be acceptable in a motel setting for room cleaners or laundry workers, but not for desk clerks or accountants.

Self-Administered Consequences. Training workers with disabilities to self-administer reinforcement and/or punishments has two potential benefits. First, by self-administering reinforcement, the worker has the opportunity to receive greater amounts of reinforcement when natural reinforcement is scarce. Second, an employee who self-reinforces or self-punishes is less likely to be affected by disruptions at the job site, such as changes in supervision (Wacker & Berg, 1986).

Self-administered reinforcements and punishments at the job site are an individual determination, based on the likes and dislikes of the worker and the level of tolerance at the job site. For example, as reinforcement for completing assignments or responding appropriately to his or her co-workers, a supported employee may be trained to allow himself or herself a special treat at break periods. This type of self-reinforcement would be easily tolerated at almost any job, whereas allowing extra break periods might not be.

> *Self-administered reinforcements and punishments at the job site are an individual determination, based on the likes and dislikes of the worker and the level of tolerance at the job site.*

SUPPORTED EMPLOYMENT AND NATURAL SUPPORTS

The enhancement and individualization of natural supports for persons with disabilities has received much attention in recent years (Bradley, Ashbaugh, & Blaney, 1994; Nisbet, 1992). *Natural supports* refers to the resources inherent to community environments that can be used for habilitative and supportive purposes (Kiernan, Schalock, Butterworth, & Sailor, 1993). Using natural supports has been advanced as a cost-effective means of achieving maximum integration at school, work, and other community settings for individuals with severe disabilities (Nisbet, 1992; Nisbet & Hagner, 1987).

The use of natural supports has added significance for individuals receiving services under the federal/state VR program. The Rehabilitation Act Amendments of 1992 endorse natural supports as a source of extended services for individuals receiving supported employment (Sec. 635[b][6][C][iii]). As noted previously, many groups of potential supported employment participants, particularly those with disabilities acquired in adulthood, had limited access in part because no source of funding for extended services was available at the time of VR enrollment.

Natural supports within the VR service context was intended to be a broad term meant to include (a) individuals at the job site, such as employers, supervisors, or co-workers; (b) friends or family members who provide supportive roles; or (c) volunteers or mentors from work or the community (Rehabilitation Act Amendments of 1992). Recently, several writers in the field have further broadened the context of natural supports to include other types of community and workplace resources, such as employee assistance programs, transportation providers, community service organizations, recreational and social associations, and governmental supports that are not limited to persons with disabilities, such as subsidized housing, income tax assistance, and so forth (Albin & Slovic, 1992; Parent, Unger, Gibson, & Clements, 1994; Rheinheimer, VanCovern, Green, Revell, & Inge, 1993; Rogan, Hagner, & Murphy, 1993).

> *Natural supports within the VR service context was intended to be a broad term meant to include (a) individuals at the job site, such as employers, supervisors, or co-workers; (b) friends or family members who provide supportive roles; or (c) volunteers or mentors from work or the community.*

The role of employers and co-workers in supporting employees with severe disabilities has emerged with potential to improve supported employment outcomes. However, there is little data about the impact of natural supports. In a comprehensive review of research literature on the effectiveness of natural supports in supported employment, Test and Wood (1996) found that (a) the concept of natural supports is often poorly defined or not defined at all, (b) natural support strategies are often nebulous and difficult to replicate, and (c) little empirical evidence exists to justify the widespread use of natural supports and the incorporation of the concept into federal employment policy.

The available information to date about natural supports in supported employment is almost exclusively qualitative information and case studies. These case studies offer an appealing array of what is possible in the typical employment of people in supported employment and the roles that employer personnel can play in supporting the employment of people with severe disabilities. These studies (e.g., Hagner & Dileo, 1993; Murphy, Rogan, & Fisher, 1994) show an increase in the integration and stability of supported employment participants when co-workers are involved with the employees with severe disabilities.

At the same time, however, some professionals (e.g., Test & Wood, 1996) are concerned that the available quantitative information on the efficacy of natural supports does not provide a sound empirical basis for policy and program decision making. Only recently has quantitative information begun to be available about typical features of employment and natural supports. Mank, Cioffi, and Yovanoff (1996a, 1996b) have constructed a database of nearly 500 individuals (from eight states) in supported employment placed in jobs by programs thought to be implementing natural supports in the workplace. These data show a positive relationship between high wages, higher patterns of interaction with employees without disabilities, and the "typicalness" of the features of their employment (when compared to co-workers without disabilities). This data set provides one of the first broader, quantitative data sets that can provide useful information to consumers, community rehabilitation providers, and policy makers on the efficacy of natural support strategies.

Some professionals have expressed caution about the directions that the natural supports initiative might take. Kregel (1994) and West and Parent (1995) noted that natural support methods are being advanced as alternatives to the traditional "job coaching" model of supported employment, when in fact coworker and supervisor involvement has been a component of "best practices" since the program's inception. The controversy over the use of natural supports in supported employment has significant implications for the long-term future of the program (DiLeo, 1995; West, 1992). Wehman (1993) and West (1992) both expressed concern that the research base on social acceptance of persons with disabilities in the workplace does not support programmatic dependence on coworkers and supervisors.

Clearly, if natural supports strategies are to become the foundation of employment service delivery for individuals with significant disabilities in supported employment, then investigations into the nature and effectiveness of supported employment strategies must be expanded. In that vein, West, Kregel, Hernandez, and Hock (1997) undertook a large-scale examination of the current use of natural support technology in supported employment operated by local community rehabilitation programs throughout the United States. Among their major findings are these:

1. Over 85% of respondents indicated that their agency emphasized natural supports in the delivery of supported employment services.

2. Natural supports were used with most consumers in all stages of service, including job development and placement, time-limited services, and extended services.

3. Over 80% of respondents indicated that they had found natural supports to be a viable support option for every member of their caseload.

4. For those indicating otherwise, the primary reason that natural supports were not viable were related to conditions at the worksite (i.e., fast-paced, highly competitive, or unfriendly workplaces), and secondary reasons were characteristics of consumers (disability labels, learning or behavioral problems, etc.).

5. Despite the benefits of this strategy, more than half had experienced difficulties in utilizing natural supports, such as resistance from coworkers, difficulty in locating natural support agents, and reduced program effectiveness and efficiency.

These findings give clear and powerful support to the argument made by Test and Wood (1996) that the lack of a clear and concise definition of natural supports makes it difficult to conduct research into the effectiveness of these important strategies. When 85% of all programs indicate that they "emphasize the use of natural supports" in service delivery, the dichotomy of "natural supports versus the job coach" of supported employment is no longer relevant. It is unequivocally clear that virtually all programs are using and perhaps have always used natural supports in the design and delivery of services.

PLANNING AND IMPLEMENTING EXTENDED SERVICES

As mentioned previously, the identification and provision of appropriate support services should, to the greatest extent possible, be a proactive rather than a reactive process. Potential problem areas, antecedents, and consequences should be identified during the job stabilization phase, and a prescriptive, written follow-along plan developed by the employment specialist, the employer, the co-workers, the family members, the consumer, and any other concerned parties. For the benefit of both the client and the employer, response to crisis or requests for assistance should be immediate and according to the agreed plan.

Effective follow-along utilizes both informal and formal strategies of problem analysis and data collection. Informal methods include discussions with the supervisor or co-workers at the job site, discussions with family members, accessing community support services, and other direct and indirect consumer-related activities. Formal methods are used to collect outcome data that are used for ongoing assessment of work performance or data that is aggregated for the purpose of evaluating program effectiveness.

Informal Follow-Along Strategies

On-site Intervention

Following job stabilization, contacts with employers typically involve site visits or telephone contacts concerning the employee's job performance. In most cases, the site visit will elicit the most useful information about the employee's adjustment to the workplace, to the supervisor, and to the co-workers. Retraining activities may be necessary in the event that the employee's work quality or speed diminishes over time or if job duties change (Brooke, Inge, Armstrong, & Wehman, 1997).

For an employee with persistent mental illness or traumatic brain injury, another vital concern may be monitoring the employee's emotional stability. Disinhibition, temper outbursts, and other inappropriate behaviors are often latent responses to employment stress (Kreutzer & Morton, 1988) and may not be predictable, especially if the client has little or no other employment experience. Employers will need to be informed of any known symptoms of an impending flare-up and appropriate means of supervisory response, including time-out procedures, suspensions, or calling the employment specialist for crisis intervention. In some instances, part of the initial negotiations between the employer and the employment specialist may be obtaining permission for "psychosocial first aid" (Ford, 1995) to be administered at the job site by the employment specialist or a qualified therapist if the employee's behaviors escalate beyond the supervisor's control.

It should be evident from the preceding discussion that many individuals with severe production deficits or emotional or behavioral anomalies will require sympathetic and understanding employers for placement to be successful. It is vitally important that employers know what to expect from the employee, both in terms of productivity and potential problems, and the degree to which the employment specialist and other crisis intervention staff or consultants may be used as resources in correcting problems in either area.

Off-site Intervention

As mentioned earlier in this chapter, family members are often vital to employment success by providing direct assistance, emotional support, or both. The employment specialist's contacts with family members should focus on aspects of home life that are likely to impinge upon the work environment. These would include the ongoing assessments of the consumer's emotional stability; use or abuse of prescription and nonprescription drugs, including alcohol; and problems related to finances, health, and family functioning. The employment specialist should perform educational and referral functions, such as informing the consumer and family members of treatment programs (i.e., residential services, Alcoholics Anonymous, respite care) and other services and entitlements (i.e., Social Security benefits) that are available in their community and helping them to access these services.

> *Family members are often vital to employment success by providing direct assistance, emotional support, or both. The employment specialist's contacts with family members should focus on aspects of home life that are likely to impinge upon the work environment.*

A comprehensive retention plan also includes advocacy efforts with related service personnel or other individuals on behalf of the consumer. These might include progress or status reports to the consumer's vocational rehabilitation counselor, neuropsychologist, or physician. For individuals who reside in supervised apartments or group homes, changes in work schedule or problems with dress, medication, or finances need to be communicated to the appropriate staff. Individuals who live independently or semi-independently may require an intermediary for dealing with a landlord or creditor. In short, any problem that may affect the individual's job placement becomes the concern of the employment specialist.

Scheduling Follow-Along Contacts

Although a number of writers have addressed the types of activities that constitute follow-along, little direction has been given as to the frequency and intensity of contacts. The determination of sufficient or necessary contacts to maintain employment has generally been left to the discretion of the employment specialist, provided that legal minimum levels are met.

Rusch (1986) described two types of schedules, the adjusted schedule and the fixed schedule. The adjusted schedule varies with the consumer's success in meeting the employer's expectations for progress. If an employer cannot tolerate this arrangement, then a predetermined, or fixed, schedule of follow-along contacts is negotiated.

One problem with using a fixed schedule of contact is that job duties, production demands, co-workers, and even supervisors may vary according to the day or time of day. An obvious example is restaurant work, where peak hours are during lunch and dinner rushes. For restaurants located in business districts, weekday lunch periods will likely be more hectic than weekend lunches; week-end dinner volume may be greater than weekdays; or the employee's work schedule may bridge two shifts with different co-workers or supervisors. On a fixed schedule of visits based on employer request or convenience of the program staff, subtle and overt differences in work demands, the atmosphere of the workplace, and acceptance of the supported employee may go unnoticed.

> *One problem with using a fixed schedule of contact is that job duties, production demands, co-workers, and even supervisors may vary according to the day or time of day.*

As much as the setting allows, the employment specialist should obtain a variety of opinions regarding the performance and social adjustment of the supported worker. The observations and opinions of the supervisor are of paramount importance, as are those of any designated helper. But other co-workers (or possibly regular customers) may also have made observations or have valid opinions, which the supervisor should be encouraged to share with the program staff.

The Support Group

The job retention support group for workers with disabilities (Fabian & Wiedefeld, 1989; West & Hughes, 1990) can be a valuable medium for assisting and monitoring ongoing adjustment to employment, particularly for individuals with severe traumatic brain injury or psychiatric impairment. Members of the support group meet voluntarily to discuss problems or stresses associated with work and to provide mutual emotional support. Through these exchanges, supported employment staff are also able to monitor the emotional stability of the group members and to identify potential problem areas at the job site or at home.

Formal Follow-Along Strategies

In this section, I describe formal data collection methods and instruments that can be completed as part of the follow-along process. In addition, I describe schedules for completion of the forms.

Supervisor's Evaluations

Formal supervisor evaluations provide insight into not only the work performance of a supported employee but also the expectations and priorities of the supervisor. For example, Shafer, Kregel, Banks, and Hill (1988) examined scores on the VCU-RRTC's Supervisor's Evaluation Form (see Figure 7.1) for initial and terminal evaluations for 125 workers with mental retardation. They found that employees who eventually were separated from their job tended to score lower than successful placements in the areas of attendance, punctuality, and timeliness of lunch and breaks. They concluded that employers may be willing to lower performance standards of speed and quality for a dependable, loyal worker. Although these findings have yet to be generalized to other disability

---

Supervisor's Evaluation Form

Using the following scale, please circle one number to the right of each question that *best* represents your opinion about this employee's present situation:

1 Extremely dissatisfied
2 Somewhat dissatisfied
3 Satisfied
4 Very satisfied
5 Extremely satisfied

How satisfied are you with this employee's

1. timeliness of arrival and departure from work?	1 2 3 4 5
2. attendance?	1 2 3 4 5
3. timeliness of breaks and lunch?	1 2 3 4 5
4. appearance?	1 2 3 4 5
5. general performance as compared to other workers?	1 2 3 4 5
6. communication skills?	1 2 3 4 5
7. consistency in task performance?	1 2 3 4 5
8. work speed?	1 2 3 4 5
9. quality of work?	1 2 3 4 5
10. overall proficiency at this time?	1 2 3 4 5

Additional Comments:

Figure 7.1. Items from the Supervisor's Evaluation Form.

groups, supervisor evaluation forms have utility for examining worker–supervisor relationships in both aggregated data and individual cases.

In the VCU-RRTCs data collection schedule, the Supervisor's Evaluation Form is completed by the employee's job-site supervisor, ideally with the employment specialist and the employee present, at a minimum of 1 month, 3 months, and 6 months postplacement, and every 6 months thereafter. The evaluation form is also completed immediately following job termination. If deemed necessary and feasible, employment specialists may request evaluations from the supervisor on a more frequent schedule. Because the work performance evaluations often used in businesses and industries are usually not sufficiently expansive or behavioral for supported employment purposes (Rusch, 1986), employers are requested to use the RRTC's Supervisor's Evaluation Form in addition to any other employee evaluation forms or methods that they would normally use.

Consumer Self-Evaluation

The VCU-RRTC's project for consumers with traumatic brain injury also developed a self-evaluation form that mirrors the Supervisor's Evaluation Form in its content (refer to Figure 7.1). At the time that the job-site supervisor completes an evaluation, the consumer completes an identical form, assessing his or her own work performance. This procedure has two related functions. First, it provides the employment specialist insight to the consumer's perceptions of his or her own strengths and weaknesses. Second, it may reveal areas of dissonance between the consumer's and the supervisor's perceptions, thus providing the employment specialist with general areas in which to concentrate intervention.

The Job Update Form

The Job Update Form (Figure 7.2) is used to collect data related to changes in job elements, such as wages, work hours, and level of integration with customers or co-workers. The Job Update Form is completed by the employment specialist at 3 and 6 months postplacement, every 6 months thereafter, and at job termination.

Consumer Update Form

The Consumer Update Form (Figure 7.3) collects data related to the supported employee's level of independence. The areas of interest include the employee's (a) vocational rehabilitation case status, (b) residential situation, (c) mode of transportation to and from work, and (d) government financial aid and entitlements. The form is completed on the same time schedule as the Job Update Form. Because this information is also collected either prior to or at initial placement, changes in the employee's status, as a direct result of employment, can be tracked over time. Thus, this form provides significant information necessary for consumer-level benefit–cost analysis.

Consumer Satisfaction Surveys

With the growing emphasis on rehabilitation clients as customers or consumers has come an increased emphasis on assessing consumer satisfaction with the services they receive. The Rehabilitation Act Amendments of 1992 require that state VR systems incorporate consumer satisfaction surveys as a component of

Job Update Form

1. Type of service/employment for this report (check one):
   ☐ Work activity or sheltered employment
   ☐ Entrepreneurial
   ☐ Mobile work crew
   ☐ Enclave
   ☐ Supported job
   ☐ Supported competitive employment
   ☐ Time-limited (no ongoing services anticipated)
   ☐ Other (specify: _____)

2. Type of update: Ongoing ☐   Final ☐

3. Job title: _____

4. Current hourly wage (or last wage in this position): _____

5. Did a wage change occur since the last Job Screening or Job Update?
   Yes ☐   No ☐

6. If yes, then complete this section:
   Hourly rate changed from $ _____ to $ _____ on ___/___/___
   Hourly rate changed from $ _____ to $ _____ on ___/___/___

7. Number of hours worked per week: _____

8. Number of months worked per year: _____
   If less than 12 months per year, what months is the job not available:_____
   _____

9. Number of employees in this company at this location: _____
   Number without disabilities in immediate area (50' radius): _____
   Number of other employees with disabilities: _____
   Number in immediate area (50' radius): _____
   Number of other employees in this position: _____
   During the same hours: _____

10. Level of social contact (check one):
    ☐ 0 Employment in a segregated setting in which the majority of interactions with persons without disabilities are with caregivers or service providers.

    ☐ 1 Employment in an integrated environment on a shift or position that is isolated. Contact with co-workers without disabilities or supervisors is minimal.

    ☐ 2 Employment in an integrated environment on a shift or position that is relatively isolated. Contact with co-workers without disabilities is available at lunch or break.

    ☐ 3 Employment in an integrated environment in a position requiring a moderate level of task dependency and co-worker interaction.

    ☐ 4 Employment in an integrated environment in a position requiring a high degree of task dependency and co-worker or customer interaction.

Figure 7.2. Items from the Job Update Form.

Consumer Update Form

1. Current Vocational Rehabilitation (VR) case status for this consumer (enter Department of Rehabilitative Services code): _____
   If never served by VR, enter "none" in the space provided.

2. Current residential situation (check one only):
   ☐ Independent
   ☐ Supported living arrangement
   ☐ Sponsored placement (foster care)
   ☐ Domiciliary care apartment (home for adults)
   ☐ Supervised apartment
   ☐ Parents
   ☐ Other relatives
   ☐ Group home/halfway house
   ☐ Other (specify: _____)

3. Current primary mode of transportation to work (select one only):
   ☐ Independent use of public transportation
   ☐ Walks/rides bike or moped
   ☐ Dependent use of public transportation (needed bus training)
   ☐ Arranged car pool
   ☐ Parent/friend drives
   ☐ Handicapped transportation
   ☐ Taxi
   ☐ Drives own vehicle
   ☐ Other (specify: _____)

4. Financial aid received by consumer at present or as of last day of work. Circle yes or no for each selection. If yes, write the amount received to the left of the selection.
   _____ Yes / No   None
   _____ Yes / No   Supplemental Security Income (SSI)
   _____ Yes / No   Social Security Disability Insurance (SSDI)
   _____ Yes / No   Medicaid
   _____ Yes / No   Medicare
   _____ Yes / No   Food Stamps
   _____ Yes / No   Public Assistance (Welfare)
   _____ Yes / No   Other (specify: _____)

5. Total income from all government financial aid during the past month:
   _____

Figure 7.3. Items from the Consumer Update Form.

their planning processes. Locally based consumer satisfaction surveys can provide a couple of valuable functions for agencies as well. First, these surveys can be a method by which consumers can become more involved in planning their own careers and services. Second, aggregated satisfaction surveys can aid in evaluating the effectiveness of services in meeting consumers' needs and expectations.

Parent, Kregel, and Johnson (1997) presented findings from a satisfaction survey conducted with 110 supported employment consumers. Their survey contained both Likert-scale and open-ended items requesting levels of satisfaction in the following areas:

- Pay and benefits
- Supervision
- Relationships and teamwork
- Job conditions
- Job satisfaction
- Job coach satisfaction
- Service satisfaction

Satisfaction surveys can provide useful information for making programmatic modifications for individuals or across the scope of services. However, agencies must be prepared to accept the views of their consumers as valid, and to take responsive actions.

SUMMARY

Extended services in supported employment should be prescriptive and proactive. The identification of employment barriers and interventions should occur during the initial phases of client screening, assessment, and placement, and a written plan developed for addressing anticipated training, support, and advocacy needs. Using natural cues, consequences, and supports can increase the supported worker's independence and social integration in the work area and improve the prognosis for long-term job retention. However, if these are inadequate for the particular worker, artificial cues, reinforcers, and supports can be effectively imposed.

Although the ultimate purpose of extended support services is to avoid unnecessary job separations, many individuals in supported employment are separated from their jobs. Job separations are not necessarily undesirable in and of themselves. In fact, job retention should be viewed less as an absolute, static state and more as gradual improvements in the supported employee's ability to function in the competitive workforce. These improvements are frequently dependent upon refinement of the individual's career goals, productive abilities, and social ties, and may involve movement from one employment setting to another, voluntarily or involuntarily. Such a dynamic view of job retention requires that provider and funding agencies be committed to continually provide supported employment services beyond the first separation.

Long-term job retention does not begin with extended services. It begins when agencies listen to the desires and goals of their consumers and plan job development, training, and supports accordingly.

REFERENCES

Agran, M., Fodor-Davis, J., & Moore, S. (1989). The application of a self-management program on instruction-following skills. *Journal of The Association for Persons with Severe Handicaps, 14,* 147–154.

Albin, J., & Slovic, R. (1992). *Resources for long-term support in supported employment.* Eugene: University of Oregon, The Employment Network.

Berg, W., & Wacker, D. (1983). *Effects of permanent prompts on the vocational performance of severely handicapped individuals.* Paper presented at the Association for Behavior Analysis, Milwaukee, WI.

Bradley, V. J., Ashbaugh, J. W., & Blaney, B. C. (Eds.). (1994). *Creating individual supports for people with developmental disabilities: A mandate for change at many levels.* Baltimore: Brookes.

Brooke, V., Inge, K., Armstrong, A., & Wehman, P. (Eds.). (1997). *Supported employment handbook: A customer-driven approach for persons with significant disabilities.* Richmond: Virginia Commonwealth University, Rehabilitation Research and Training Center.

DiLeo, D. (1995). The risks of misapplying natural supports in the workplace. *Supported Employment InfoLines, 6*(8), 4–5.

Fabian, E., & Wiedefeld, M. F. (1989). Supported employment for severely psychiatrically disabled persons: A descriptive study. *Psychosocial Rehabilitation Journal, 13*(2), 53–60.

Federal Register. (1987, August 14). 34 C.F.R. 363. *52*(157), 30546–30552.

Federal Register. (1992, June 24). 34 C.F.R. 363. *57*(122), 28432–28442.

Ford, L. H. (1995). *Providing employment support for people with long-term mental illness.* Baltimore: Brookes.

Hagner, D., & Dileo, D. (1993). *Working together: Workplace culture, supported employment and persons with disabilities.* Brookline, MA: Brookline Books.

Hill, J., Wehman, P., Hill, M., & Goodall, P. (1986). Differential reasons for job separation of previously employed persons with mental retardation. *Mental Retardation, 24*(6), 347–351.

Kiernan, W. E., Schalock, R. L., Butterworth, J., & Sailor, W. (1993). *Enhancing the use of natural supports for people with disabilities.* Boston: Children's Hospital, Training and Research Institute for People with Disabilities.

Kregel, J. (1994). *Natural supports and the job coach: An unnecessary dichotomy.* Richmond: Virginia Commonwealth University, Rehabilitation Research and Training Center.

Kregel, J., Hill, M., & Banks, P. D. (1987). An analysis of employment specialist intervention time in supported competitive employment: 1979–1987. In P. Wehman, J. Kregel, M. Shafer, & M. Hill (Eds.), *Competitive employment for persons with mental retardation: From research to practice* (pp. 84–111). Richmond: Virginia Commonwealth University, Rehabilitation Research and Training Center.

Kregel, J., Shafer, M., Wehman, P., & West, M. (1989). Policy and program development. In P. Wehman, J. Kregel, & M. Shafer (Eds.), *Emerging trends in the national supported employment initiative: A preliminary analysis of 27 states* (pp. 15–45). Richmond: Virginia Commonwealth University.

Kreutzer, J. S., & Morton, M. V. (1988). Traumatic brain injury: Supported employment and compensatory strategies for enhancing vocational outcomes. In P. Wehman & M. S. Moon (Eds.), *Vocational rehabilitation and supported employment* (pp. 291–311). Baltimore: Brookes.

Lagomarcino, T. R. (1990). Job separation issues in supported employment. In F. R. Rusch (Ed.), *Supported employment: Models, methods, and issues* (pp. 301-316). Sycamore, IL: Sycamore.

Lagomarcino, T. R., Hughes, C., & Rusch, F. R. (1989). Utilizing self-management to teach independence on the job. *Education and Training in Mental Retardation, 24,* 139–148.

Mank, D. (1994). The underachievement of supported employment: A call for reinvestment. *Journal of Disability Policy Studies, 5*(2), 1–24.

Mank, D., Cioffi, A., & Yovanoff, P. (1996a). *The consequences of compromise: An analysis of natural supports, features of supported employment jobs and their relationship to wage and integration outcomes.* Manuscript submitted for publication.

Mank, D., Cioffi, A., & Yovanoff, P. (1996b). *Patterns of support for employees with severe disabilities.* Manuscript submitted for publication.

McDonald-Wilson, K. L., Revell, W. G., Nguyen, N., & Peterson, M. E. (1991). Supported employment outcomes for people with psychiatric disability: A comparative analysis. *Journal of Vocational Rehabilitation, 1*(3), 30–44.

McGaughey, M. J., Kiernan, W. E., McNally, L. C., Gilmore, D. S., & Keith, G. R. (1995). Beyond the workshop: National trends in integrated and segregated day and employment services. *Journal of The Association for Persons with Severe Handicaps, 20,* 270–285.

Murphy, S., Rogan, P., & Fisher, E. (1994). Diversity or confusion? National survey of SE natural supports. *Supported Employment InfoLines, 5*(4).

Nisbet, J. (Ed.). (1992). *Natural supports in school, at work, and in the community for people with severe disabilities.* Baltimore: Brookes.

Nisbet, J., & Hagner, D. (1987). Natural supports in the workplace: A reexamination of supported employment. *Journal of The Association for Persons with Severe Handicaps, 13,* 260–267.

Parent, W., Kregel, J., & Johnson, A. (1997). Consumer satisfaction: A survey of individuals with severe disabilities who receive supported employment services. In *Supported employment research: Expanding competitive employment opportunities for persons with significant disabilities* (pp. 128–155). Richmond: Virginia Commonwealth University, Rehabilitation Research and Training Center.

Parent, W., Kregel, J., & Wehman, P. (1992). *Vocational Integration Index: A guide for rehabilitation and special education professionals.* Austin, TX: PRO-ED.

Parent, W., Unger, D., Gibson, K., & Clements, C. (1994). The role of the job coach: Orchestrating community and workplace supports. *American Rehabilitation, 20*(3), 2–11.

Pumpian, I., Fisher, D., Certo, N. J., & Smalley, K. A. (1997). Changing jobs: An essential part of career development. *Mental Retardation, 35,* 39–48.

Rehabilitation Act Amendments of 1992, 29 U.S.C. § 706 *et seq.*

Revell, W. G., West, M., & Cheng, Y. (1998). Funding supported employment: Are there better ways? *Journal of Disability Policy Studies, 9*(1), 59–79.

Rheinheimer, G. B., VanCovern, D., Green, H., Revell, G., & Inge, K. J. (1993). *Finding the common denominator: A supported employment guide to long-term funding supports and services for people with severe disabilities.* Richmond: Virginia Commonwealth University, Rehabilitation Research and Training Center on Supported Employment.

Rogan, P., Hagner, D., & Murphy, S. (1993). Natural supports: Reconceptualizing job coach roles. *Journal of The Association for Persons with Severe Handicaps, 18,* 275–281.

Rusch, F. R. (1986). *Competitive employment issues and strategies.* Baltimore: Brookes.

Sale, P., West, M., Sherron, P., & Wehman, P. (1991). An exploratory analysis of job separations from supported employment for persons with traumatic brain injury. *Journal of Head Trauma Rehabilitation, 6*(3), 1–11.

Shafer, M. S., Kregel, J., Banks, P. D., & Hill, M. L. (1988). An analysis of employer evaluations of workers with mental retardation. *Research in Developmental Disabilities, 9,* 377–391.

Stokes, T., & Baer, D. (1977). An implicit technology of generalization. *Journal of Applied Behavior Analysis, 10,* 349–367.

Test, D. W., & Wood, W. M. (1996). Natural supports in the workplace: The jury is still out. *Journal of The Association for Persons with Severe Handicaps, 21,* 155–173.

Wacker, D. P., & Berg, W. K. (1986). Generalizing and maintaining work behavior. In F. R. Rusch (Ed.) *Competitive employment: Issues and strategies* (pp. 129–140). Baltimore: Brookes.

Wehman, P. (1993). Natural supports: More questions than answers? *Journal of Vocational Rehabilitation, 3,* 1–3.

Wehman, P., & Kregel, J. (1995). At the crossroads: Supported employment a decade later. *Journal of The Association for Persons with Severe Handicaps, 20,* 286–299.

Wehmeyer, M. L., & West, M. (Eds.). (1995). Self-determination and persons with disabilities [Special issue]. *Journal of Vocational Rehabilitation, 5*(4).

West, M. (1992). Job retention: Toward vocational competence, self-management, and natural supports. In P. Wehman, P. Sale, & W. Parent (Eds.), *Supported employment: Strategies for integration of workers with disabilities* (pp. 176–203). Stoneham, MA: Andover Medical.

West, M. (1995). Choice, self-determination, and VR services: Systemic barriers for consumers with severe disabilities. *Journal of Vocational Rehabilitation, 5,* 281–290.

West, M., Callahan, M., Lewis, M. B., Mast, M., Simek-Dreher, S., Rock, R., Sleight, L., & Meravi, A. (1991). Supported employment and assistive technology for individuals with physical impairments. *Journal of Vocational Rehabilitation, 1*(2), 29–39.

West, M., & Hughes, T. (1990). Supported employment phase III: Job retention techniques. In P. Wehman & J. S. Kreutzer (Eds.), *Vocational rehabilitation for persons with traumatic brain injury* (pp. 201–221). Rochville, MD: Aspen.

West, M., Johnson, A., Cone, A., Hernandez, A., & Revell, G. (1997). Extended employment support: Analysis of implementation and funding issues. In P. Wehman, J. Kregel, & M. West (Eds.), *Supported employment research: Expanding competitive employment research for persons with significant disabilities* (pp. 85–97). Richmond: Virginia Commonwealth University, Rehabilitation Research and Training Center on Supported Employment.

West, M., Kregel, J., Hernandez, A., & Hock, T. (1997). Everybody's doing it: A national survey of the use of natural supports in supported employment. In P. Wehman, J. Kregel, & M. West (Eds.), *Supported employment research: Expanding competitive employment opportunities for persons with significant disabilities* (pp. 98–109). Richmond: Virginia Commonwealth University, Rehabilitation Research and Training Center.

West, M., & Parent, W. S. (1995). Community and workplace supports for individuals with severe mental illness in supported employment. *Psychosocial Rehabilitation Journal, 18*(4), 13–24.

West, M., Wehman, P., Kregel, J., Kreutzer, J., Sherron, P., & Zasler, N. (1991). Costs associated with a supported work program for traumatically brain injured individuals. *Archives of Physical Medicine and Rehabilitation, 72,* 127–131.

West, M., Wehman, P., & Revell, G. (1996, August). Use of social security work incentives by supported employment agencies and consumers: Findings from a national survey. *Journal of Vocational Rehabilitation, 7*(1, 2), 117–123.

Part II

◆ ◆ ◆ ◆ ◆ ◆ ◆ ◆ ◆ ◆ ◆ ◆ ◆ ◆ ◆ ◆ ◆ ◆

Vocational Curriculum for Competitive Employment

Pamela Sherron Targett

Part I of this book provides an empirical basis for understanding how to design the vocational curriculum. In Part II the curriculum itself is presented. It is divided into nine sections, each representative of a domain from the *Dictionary of Occupational Titles* (DOT): Building and Related Services, Sales, Production and Stock Clerk, Food and Beverage Preparation, Clerical, Lodging and Related Services, Plant Farming, Information and Message Distribution, Computing and Accounting Related Occupations. The DOT is the most comprehensive source of occupational literature available. The dictionary alphabetically identifies and describes jobs found in the workforce.

Each section in Part II opens with a description of the domain. Next, a cross-section of task-analyzed vocational skills that are found in some of the various jobs within the different occupations represented in the domain are provided. These can be helpful in the process of developing and implementing situational assessments, community-based training programs, and job site skills training for students who become hired. An illustrative case study and sample Individual Transition Plan are also provided for each occupational domain.

The commonly used abbreviations in this section are defined as follows:

CSB—Community Services Board
DOT—Dictionary of Occupational Titles
DRS—Department of Rehabilitative Services
ED—Emotional disturbance
EFE—Education for Employment Program
IEP—Individual Employment Plan
ITP—Individual Transition Plan
LD—Learning disability
MH—Mental health

MR—Mental retardation
PATH—Planning Alternative Tomorrows with Hope
SSA—Social Security Administration
SSDI—Social Security Disability Insurance
SSI—Supplemental Security Income
TBI—Traumatic brain injury
YWCA—Young Women's Christian Association

REFERENCE

U.S. Department of Labor Employment and Training Administration. (1991). *Dictionary of occupational titles* (4th ed., Vol. 1). Washington, DC: U.S. Government Printing Office.

Building and Related Services Occupations

◆ ◆ ◆ ◆ ◆ ◆ ◆ ◆ ◆ ◆ ◆ ◆ ◆ ◆ ◆ ◆ ◆ ◆ ◆

Description of Domain

The *Dictionary of Occupational Titles* defines Building and Related Services occupations as those concerned with the "cleaning and upkeep of building interiors and the conveying of passengers and freight by elevator" (p. 281).

JOB DESCRIPTIONS

1. Pool Cleaner

Time	Sequence of Activities
10:00–10:20 a.m.	Get supplies
10:20–12:30	Clean pool and Jacuzzi deck
12:30–1:00	Lunch
1:00–3:00	Wash pool furniture

Key Related Tasks

A. Cleaning the Pool
   1. Blow leaves and debris off deck if needed
   2. Skim pool if needed
   3. Brush down sides of pool
   4. Vacuum pool or use leafer to pick up big leaves on the bottom of pool
   5. Empty leaf catcher
   6. Backwash/empty skimmers

B. Vacuuming the Pool
   1. Empty leaf catcher if necessary (see instructions below)
   2. Screw in adapter
   3. Assemble vacuum and place in pool
   4. Open vacuum valve/counterclockwise
   5. Close skimmer valve/clockwise
   6. Wait for leaf catcher to clear
   7. Vacuum pool
   8. Open skimmer valve/counterclockwise

9. Close vacuum valve/clockwise
10. Put vacuum, hose, and adapter in maintenance shed
11. Empty leaf catcher

C. Emptying the Leaf Catcher
   1. Turn off pump
   2. Unscrew and remove lid
   3. Empty basket
   4. Put on lid
   5. Turn on pump; if backwashing is the next step, *do not* turn on pump

D. Backwashing the Pool
   1. Turn off pump (if not already turned off)
   2. Close top right valve/clockwise
   3. Open bottom right valve/counterclockwise
   4. Open top left valve/counterclockwise
   5. Close bottom left valve/clockwise
   6. Turn pump on
   7. Backwash for 3 to 4 minutes
   8. Remove and clean three skimmers while backwashing
   9. Turn off pump
   10. Close top left valve/clockwise
   11. Open bottom left valve/counterclockwise
   12. Open top right valve/counterclockwise
   13. Close bottom right valve/clockwise
   14. Turn on pump
   15. Clean remaining skimmers

E. Cleaning Pool with Leafer
   1. Put leafer head on pole
   2. Hook garden hose to spigot and leafer head
   3. Tie leafer bag to leafer head
   4. Submerge leafer
   5. Turn on water just enough to inflate bag
   6. Clean pool
   7. Remove leafer from pool by turning leafer on side and placing it on the deck
   8. Turn off water
   9. Clean and return leafer equipment

F. Draining the Pool
   1. Open top right valve/counterclockwise
   2. Close bottom right valve/clockwise
   3. Turn on pump until water level drops to desired level
   4. Turn off pump
   5. Close top left valve/clockwise
   6. Open bottom left valve/counterclockwise
   7. Clean leaf catcher, if needed
   8. Turn on pump
   9. Clean remaining slammers
   10. Empty garbage if needed

G. Cleaning the Jacuzzi Deck
   1. Get broom from building #3
   2. Sweep Jacuzzi deck

    3. Get materials from Jacuzzi pump room
      a. 7961 ZEP detergent
      b. Scrub brush
      c. Jacuzzi hose
    4. Hose down deck
    5. Distribute detergent randomly around deck
    6. Scrub deck
    7. Rinse deck with hose
      Do Not Splash Detergent in Jacuzzi
    8. Squeegee to remove excess water

H. Washing Pool Furniture
    1. Gather materials

Item	Place
a. Cleanser	Shop
b. Hose	Pump Room
c. Hose nozzle	Pump Room Wall
d. Bucket and rag	Pump Room
e. Handled scrub brush	Jacuzzi Pump Room

    2. Take all materials to pool deck
    3. Sprinkle cleanser, scrub and rinse 4 lounge chairs at one time
    4. Sprinkle cleanser, scrub and rinse 1 table and 4 table chairs at one time
    5. Continue this task until lunch or when it's time to do breezeways
    6. Put materials back in place

2. Janitor

Time	Sequence of Activities
8:00–9:00 a.m.	Clean women's bathroom
9:00–10:00	Clean men's bathroom
10:00–10:15	Break
10:15–Noon	Sweep and mop floors
Noon–12:30	Break
12:30–2:00	Special assignment

Key Related Tasks

A. Cleaning the Toilet
    1. Pick up rag
    2. Dip rag in cleaning solution
    3. Wring out excess water

4. Wipe top of toilet tank with rag
5. Wipe sides of toilet tank
6. Wipe front of toilet tank
7. Wipe handle of toilet
8. Dip rag in cleaning solution
9. Wring out excess water
10. Wipe outside of toilet seat
11. Wipe area between seat and tank
12. Dip rag in cleaning solution
13. Wring out excess water
14. Lift toilet seat
15. Wipe under the seat lid
16. Wipe toilet seat rim
17. Dip rag in cleaning solution
18. Wring out excess water
19. Pick up cleaning powder
20. Sprinkle powder around the inside of bowl
21. Pick up scouring brush
22. Brush around inside of toilet four times
23. Check for stains
24. Brush stain, if needed, until gone
25. Place brush in container beside toilet
26. Flush the toilet
27. Dip rag in cleaning solution
28. Wring out excess water
29. Wipe outside of toilet bowl
30. Dip rag in cleaning solution
31. Move to the next toilet
32. Repeat

B. Refilling the Paper Towel Dispenser
1. Stand facing dispenser
2. Get key ring from pocket
3. Insert key into keyhole
4. Turn key to the right
5. Pull back on key to open dispenser
6. Pick up paper towel package
7. Remove wrapper
8. Turn towels so smooth side faces up
9. Insert needed towels to fill dispenser
10. Close dispenser lid
11. Turn key to the left to lock dispenser
12. Pull out key to remove
13. Place key in pocket
14. Pull out one paper towel from bottom to ensure free flow

C. Cleaning the Mirror
1. Stand in front of the first mirror (nearest to the door)
2. Pick up spray bottle
3. Aim toward top of mirror
4. Place finger on spray button
5. Pump three times
6. Move bottle, aim to middle of mirror

7. Place finger on spray button
8. Pump three times
9. Set spray bottle down
10. Pick up clean dry rag
11. Place rag at top of mirror on left side
12. Wipe left to right, top to bottom, until all cleaner is gone
13. Step back
14. Look for streaks
15. Wipe streaks
16. Move to next mirror
17. Replace wet rag with dry one; if needed, repeat Steps 1–16

D. Damp Mopping the Floor
 1. Go to storage area
 2. Pick up mop
 3. Pick up bucket
 4. Identify cleaning fluid
 5. Pour one capful into the bucket
 6. Take bucket to sink
 7. Place bucket in sink
 8. Turn on hot water
 9. Fill bucket half full
 10. Remove bucket from sink
 11. Take to work area
 12. Place bucket on floor
 13. Place mop in cleaning solution until mop is soaked
 14. Remove mop and wring out excess water by pushing lever down
 15. Mop 6 foot by 6 foot section of the floor
 16. Place mop in cleaning solution
 17. Remove mop and wring out excess water by pushing lever down
 18. Mop 6 foot by 6 foot section of the floor
 19. Continue Steps 13–18 above until entire floor is mopped
 20. Allow floor to dry before walking on it

3. Porter

Time	Sequence of Activities
10:30–11:00 a.m.	Sweep floor
11:00–2:30	Bus tables
2:30–3:00	Vacuum

Key Related Tasks

A. Sweeping the Floor
 1. Get broom and dustpan from closet

2. Go to area to be swept
3. Place dustpan out of the way of sweeping
4. Go to corner of area with left side of body facing toward the center of area to sweep
5. Hold broom with both hands, dominant hand on bottom
6. Sweep floor by bringing broom to right or back toward the center of area
7. Step forward or backward as needed
8. Bring broom back
9. Swing broom forward
10. Step forward or backward as needed
11. Bring broom back
12. Swing broom forward
13. Continue until in the center of area
14. Get dustpan
15. Hold dustpan next to dirt pile
16. Hold broom with dominant hand and push pile of dirt into dustpan
17. Repeat Steps 15 and 16 until all dirt is removed and in the dustpan
18. Pick up dustpan
19. Walk to trash can
20. Empty dustpan into trash can
21. If dirt spills, get broom and sweep spill into dustpan
22. Dump into trash can
23. Get broom
24. Take and store dustpan back in closet

B. Bussing the Tables
1. Take bus pan and rag to table with dirty dishes and without guests
2. Place bus pan on stand adjacent to table
3. Place rag on table
4. Pick up plate and place on top of another plate
5. Repeat until all plates are stacked
6. Pick up plates
7. Place plates in bus pan
8. Pick up two glasses
9. Place glasses in bus pan
10. Repeat until all glasses are in bus pan
11. Pick up silverware
12. Place in bus pan
13. Repeat until all silverware is in bus pan
14. Gather up napkins and trash and place in bus pan
15. Place money to side of table
16. Pick up ashtray with dominant hand
17. Dump ashes into pan
18. Wipe out ashtray until clean
19. Place salt and pepper and sugar off table
20. Pick up rag with dominant hand
21. Wipe table from left to right, top to bottom
22. Wipe and catch crumbs into other hand
23. Dump crumbs into pan
24. Place salt and pepper and sugar back on table
25. Place ashtray back on table

26. Place tip in/under ashtray
27. Visually inspect table top and spot clean as needed
28. Visually inspect chairs and wipe out if needed
29. Visually inspect floor and pick up trash if needed
30. Place clean rag in bus pan
31. If pan is full, take bus pan to dishwashing area
32. If pan is not full, take bus pan to next table

C. Vacuuming the Floor
   1. Get vacuum from storage closet
   2. Take vacuum to area to be cleaned
   3. Pull out cord and insert in nearest electric socket
   4. Remove all items that cannot be maneuvered around or under from area to be vacuumed
   5. Push on switch
   6. Stand away from the edge of area to be vacuumed
   7. Begin at outer edge of area to be vacuumed
   8. Pull vacuum back to self
   9. Step one step to the right
   10. Repeat Steps 6–9 until area has been cleared
   11. Push on switch to turn off machine
   12. Unplug and drop cord
   13. Push rewind button
   14. Take and store vacuum in closet
   15. Put moved objects back in proper place

4. Groundskeeper

Time	Sequence of Activities
8:00 a.m.	Check in with supervisor
8:00–10:00	Perform assigned duties
10:00–10:15	Break
10:15–12:30	Perform assigned duties
12:30–1:15	Lunch
1:15–3:00	Perform assigned duties
3:00–3:15	Break
3:15–4:30	Perform assigned duties
4:30	Check out with supervisor

Key Related Tasks

A. Weeding the Plant Beds
   1. Go to topmost right portion of bed

   2. Put on gloves
   3. Squat down
   4. Identify plant
   5. Look around the plant
   6. Determine if it is a plant or weed
   7. If weed, grasp at bottom
   8. Pull weed up
   9. Shake dirt from weed
   10. Throw weed to side of bed
   11. Move down or to the right
   12. Repeat until entire bed has been inspected
   13. Get rake
   14. Rake weeds into pile
   15. Get trash bag
   16. Open trash bag
   17. Place weeds into trash bag
   18. Tie bag when full and move it to pickup area

B. Mowing the Lawn
   1. Go to shed
   2. Check gas in mower
   3. If needed, fill with gasoline
   4. Wheel mower to appropriate area
   5. Visually scan and walk through area to remove rocks, large objects
   6. Put choke on high
   7. Pull starter cord
   8. Repeat until the mower starts
   9. Lower choke
   10. Adjust control to height of grass
   11. Go to start point of boundary
   12. Grasp mower with both hands
   13. Push mower along boundary to the end
   14. Walk mower around making half circle
   15. Place mower on cutting area overlapping slightly with previously mowed area by no more than 3 inches
   16. Repeat Steps 11–15 until area is mowed
   17. Turn off mower
   18. Wheel back to shed

5. General Utility

Time	Sequence of Activities
8:00 a.m.	Punch in
8:00–9:00	Wipe barstools and table stools (daily)
9:00–10:00	• Dust artifacts (Monday)
	• Clean woodwork (Tuesday)
	• Clean brass (Wednesday)
	• Dust lamps and ceiling tiles (Thursday)
	• Dust plants (Friday)
10:00–10:30	Wipe chairs
10:30–11:00	Mop floor
11:00	Punch out

Key Related Tasks

A. Wiping the Barstools
1. Get small bucket from kitchen
2. Fill ½ inch with blue soap
3. Get rag from brown bucket
4. Dunk rag
5. Go to first stool at bar
6. Wring out rag
7. Wipe seat
8. Wipe inside back
9. Turn seat around
10. Wipe outside back
11. Squat down
12. Wipe top of 4 legs
13. Wipe ring
14. Wipe bottom of 4 legs
15. Go to next stool, and repeat Steps 6–14 above until done

B. Wiping the Table Stools
1. Go to table 1
2. Wipe inside back of stool
3. Turn seat around
4. Wipe outside back
5. Squat down
6. Wipe top of 4 legs
7. Wipe ring
8. Wipe bottom of 4 legs
9. Go to next stool
10. Repeat Steps 2–8 above until all stools are done at table
11. Go to the next table; repeat Steps 2–10 above

C. Dusting the Artifacts
1. Get purple duster
2. Start by bathrooms
3. Dust around edges of anything on wall
4. Go to next artifact
5. Go to sunroom—music
6. Dust around edges of anything on wall
7. Go to next artifact
8. Go to front dining—movies, Marilyn, Elvis, western
9. Dust around edges of anything on wall
10. Go to next artifact
11. Dust around edges of anything on wall
12. Go to next artifact
13. Go to side dining—cars, trains, football, baseball
14. Dust around edges of anything on wall
15. Go to next artifact
16. Go to stained glass—basketball, Coke
17. Dust around edges of anything on wall
18. Go to next artifact
19. Go to kitchen area—circus
20. Dust around edges of anything on wall
21. Go to next artifact
22. Put duster away
23. Water break

D. Cleaning the Woodwork
1. Get small bucket from dishroom
2. Fill about ½ inch with pink soap
3. Put scrub brush in bucket
4. Get rag from brown bucket
5. Start by the bathrooms
6. Sit down
7. Take brush out and scrub walls using up and down motion
8. Wipe down with rag
9. Go on to next area
   a. Bathrooms—famous people, pool, cards, golf
   b. Sunroom—music
   c. Front dining—movies, Marilyn, Elvis, western
   d. Side dining—cars, trains, football, baseball
   e. Stained glass—basketball, Coke
   f. Kitchen area—circus
10. When finished, take bucket and put by dishwasher
11. Rinse out brush
12. Put brush in brown bucket
13. Water break

E. Cleaning the Brass
1. Get clear bucket from kitchen
2. Fill to ½ inch of blue cleaner
3. Drop rag into bucket
4. Go to bathrooms
5. Pull rag out of bucket
6. Wring out rag
7. Wipe name plate of Women's Room

8. Drop rag into bucket
9. Wring out rag
10. Wipe door handle
11. Drop rag into bucket
12. Wring out rag
13. Wipe kick plate at bottom
14. Drop rag into bucket
15. Wring out rag
16. Go to Men's Room door
17. Wipe name plate of Men's Room
18. Drop rag into bucket
19. Wring out rag
20. Wipe door handle
21. Drop rag into bucket
22. Wring out rag
23. Wipe kick plate
24. Drop rag into bucket
25. Wring out rag
26. Go to side exit door
27. Wipe door handle
28. Drop rag into bucket
29. Wring out rag
30. Wipe kick plate
31. Drop rag into bucket
32. Wring out rag
33. Go to ramp by sun room
34. Place rag on railing and walk up ramp
35. Drop rag into bucket
36. Wring out rag
37. Wipe brass fastener
38. Drop rag into bucket
39. Wring out rag
40. Walk down ramp and wipe off ball support
41. Drop rag into bucket
42. Take bucket to kitchen

F. Dusting the Lamps
1. Use purple duster
2. Start at sunroom dining room
3. Go to first lamp
4. Place duster at top of chain
5. Run duster down chain
6. Go to next lamp
7. Work on one side of area at a time
8. Go to next area
9. Repeat Steps 3–8 until all lamps have been dusted

G. Dusting the Ceiling Tiles
1. Get purple long-handled duster
2. Start in bathroom corridor
3. Sweep back and forth (side to side) while walking
4. Clean each tile, especially around vents and intakes
5. Clean all red tiles in dining room
6. Water break

H. Dusting the Plants
   1. Get feather duster from brown supply bucket
   2. Go to sunroom area
   3. Start with 1st plant at 6-top table
   4. Dust top of plant
   5. Dust sides of plant
   6. Dust bottom of plants
   7. Go on to the next plant
   8. Repeat Steps 4–7 until all plants are done

I. Wiping the Chairs
   1. Continue working with bucket, rag, and blue liquid
   2. Dunk rag
   3. Wring out rag
   4. Start in sunroom with 6-top table
   5. Pull chair out from table
   6. Wipe seat
   7. Tilt chair back
   8. Wipe front legs
   9. Tilt chair forward
   10. Wipe back legs
   11. Push chair in
   12. Go to next chair

J. Mopping the Floors
   1. Go to back dock
   2. Get bucket and mop
   3. Check bucket; if water is in it, dump out
   4. Roll mop bucket into kitchen
   5. Put two scoops of powder soap in bucket
   6. Roll bucket around to side sinks
   7. Turn on hot water
   8. Get a plastic pitcher
   9. Fill plastic pitcher
   10. Pour water from pitcher into bucket
   11. Repeat Steps 9–10 until bucket is full (8 pitchers)
   12. Turn off water
   13. Replace plastic pitcher on shelf
   14. Roll bucket into women's bathroom
   15. Lift mop head into wringer
   16. Push down on black handle
   17. Mop entire floor
   18. Replace mop into bucket
   19. Roll bucket into men's bathroom
   20. Lift mop head into wringer
   21. Push down on black handle
   22. Mop entire floor
   23. Replace mop into bucket
   24. Roll mop bucket to front doors of restaurant
   25. Fold doorway mats up
   26. Pick mats up and place on couch
   27. Place mop head into wringer
   28. Push down on black handle

29. Mop entryway
30. Replace mop back into bucket
31. Lift mop head into wringer
32. Push down on black handle
33. Mop waiting area
34. Replace mop into bucket
35. Roll mop bucket to the back dock
36. Lift mop head into wringer
37. Push down on black handle
38. Hang mop up on rack
39. Pull wringer off bucket
40. Dump water out
41. Replace wringer in bucket
42. Roll bucket off to the side
43. Go back into the kitchen

 ## Case Study

Jamal is a 17-year-old male with a moderate mental handicap paired with a mild emotional disability. He also has a mild speech impediment.

Jamal is enrolled in a center-based special education program in a suburban school system. His mother has refused Jamal's transition to his home school due to fears of his peers' ridicule. Jamal has experienced a great deal of success in his Education for Employment (EFE) Program. He works as a custodial assistant in an elementary school. Jamal plans to graduate with an IEP diploma next year. His mother and he have applied for DRS services and are making transition plans with the work coordinator.

Jamal had participated in an informal conversational interest inventory. He had expressed a great deal of interest in the custodial field. In a geographic radius near his apartment, Jamal had indicated interest in three potential employment locations: the local airport, a large hotel, and a local elementary school. The work coordinator developed an employment site with the airport. Jamal was interviewed and hired for a "carved" position. The carved position was a composite of custodial and food services entry-level positions.

The work coordinator and Jamal attended a regular employee orientation and participated in two 4-hour training sessions at the airport. The work coordinator also worked two shifts without Jamal. In an effort to provide increased success, Jamal was paired with a mentor at work. This co-worker provided periodic support throughout the workday, as well as a scheduled meeting once per week.

Jamal has now been working 28 hours per week for the past 3 months. He does not attend school at all; rather, work is his school program. He and his mother have elected to continue this program for the next school year. Jamal will graduate in June with his former classmates.

Individual Transition Plan 1

Student Profile

Jamal is 17 years old with a moderate mental handicap and mild emotional disability. Also, he has a mild speech impediment.

Individual Transition Plan

Student's Name   Jamal F. Fraley
                        First   M.I.   Last

Birthdate 12/15/70   School Rosemount High School

Student's ID No. 5   ITP Conference Date 11/30/97

. . . .

Participants

Name	Position
Jamal	Student
Elizabeth	Mom
Donald	DRS Counselor
Marc	Work Coordinator
Robert	Airport Maintenance Associate

Individual Transition Plan 1

I. Career and Economic Self-Sufficiency

1. Employment Goal	Full-time competitive employment
Level of present performance	Part-time school-sponsored program; independent place-ment with mentor support up to 38 hours per week.
Steps needed to accomplish goal	1. Wean away Work Coordinator support to probe level only. 2. Make application for full-time position.
Date of completion	7/98
Person(s) responsible for implementation	EFE Work Coordinator, Jamal
2. Vocational Education/Training Goal	Jamal has successfully completed this training program.
Level of present performance	Independent placement.
Steps needed to accomplish goal	N/A
Date of completion	N/A
Person(s) responsible for implementation	N/A
3. Postsecondary Education Goal	N/A
Level of present performance	N/A

Individual Transition Plan 1

Steps needed to accomplish goal	N/A
Date of completion	N/A
Person(s) responsible for implementation	N/A

4. Financial/Income Needs Goal	Jamal will apply for SSI and open a bank account.
Level of present performance	Jamal has no health benefits and his sole support is Mom. He can acquire Medicaid benefits through SSI.
Steps needed to accomplish goal	1. Mom, Jamal contact SSA representative. 2. Make application. 3. Open bank account.
Date of completion	5/98
Person(s) responsible for implementation	Jamal, Mom

II. Community Integration and Participation

5. Independent Living Goal	Jamal will live with family indefinitely.
Level of present performance	Jamal and his mother have a supportive extended family. Nieces/nephews will provide support.
Steps needed to accomplish goal	N/A
Date of completion	N/A
Person(s) responsible for implementation	N/A

Individual Transition Plan 1

6. Transportation/Mobility Goal	Jamal will use CARE transportation, a municipal service for persons with disability.
Level of present performance	Jamal rides his bike to the airport.
Steps needed to accomplish goal	1. Make applications to CARE by 1/98. 2. Ride on CARE van with Work Coordinator 3 times. 3. Ride independently at least 1 shift per week by 2/98.
Date of completion	2/98
Person(s) responsible for implementation	Jamal, Work Coordinator
7. Social Relationships Goal	N/A
Level of present performance	Jamal is actively involved with his church. His total social outlet is related to church-sponsored activities.
Steps needed to accomplish goal	N/A
Date of completion	N/A
Person(s) responsible for implementation	N/A
8. Recreation/Leisure Goal	See above.
Level of present performance	N/A
Steps needed to accomplish goal	N/A

Individual Transition Plan 1

Date of completion	N/A
Person(s) responsible for implementation	N/A

III. Personal Competence

9. Health/Safety Goal	Jamal will develop stress management skills through his mental health counselor.
Level of present performance	Jamal cries when frustrated and leaves his worksite (twice in 6 months).
Steps needed to accomplish goal	1. Sign up for group sessions at East End Mental Health Center. 2. Attend all (8) sessions.
Date of completion	4/98
Person(s) responsible for implementation	Jamal, Mom, MH Counselor

10. Self-Advocacy/Future Planning	Jamal has identified employment and social goals.
Level of present performance	N/A
Steps needed to accomplish goal	N/A
Date of completion	N/A
Person(s) responsible for implementation	N/A

Student Career Preference

Utility (maintenance) worker

Individual Transition Plan 1

Student's Major Transition Needs

1. Full-time employment with modified support
2. SSI
3. Mental health maintenance
4.
5.
6.
7.
8.
9.

Additional Notes

Jamal is on his way toward a fulfilling career and social existence.

Sales Occupations

◆ ◆

Description of Domain

The *Dictionary of Occupational Titles* defines Sales occupations as those concerned with "selling real estate, insurance, securities, and other business, financial, and consumer services" (p. 219).

JOB DESCRIPTIONS

1. Customer Assistant

Time	Sequence of Activities
10:00 a.m.	Clock in
10:00–10:10	Review memo board
10:10–Noon	• Remove trash • Straighten shoe sales floor • Reclip shoes together • Make boxed shoe display • Answer phone as required
Noon–12:30	Break
12:30–2:30	• Remove trash • Straighten shoe sales floor • Reclip shoes together • Make boxed shoe display • Answer phone as required
2:30	Clock out

Key Related Tasks

A. Clocking In
1. Retrieve time card from rack in break room
2. Return to clock in front of store
3. Hold card with right thumb over giraffe head
4. Swipe card through clock slot until green button lights up and beeps once; display will read "punch accepted"
5. Put card in rack behind customer service counter

6. Request shoe stockroom key from staff at counter
7. Go to shoe department
8. Open door
9. Begin work

B. Removing Trash
1. After box is emptied of shoe stock, get box cutter from shelf
2. Flatten box with cutter using proper safety measures
3. Collapse box and place it against wall under phone
4. Return cutter to shelf
5. If box is a "do not destroy" box, fold to collapse
6. Put top on box
7. Put box on floor under phone
8. Remove full bag from trash can
9. Tie trash bag
10. Put bag on floor under phone
11. Put new trash bag in can
12. At end of shift or before (if needed), take boxes and bag to receiving area
13. Put cut boxes in dumpster
14. Put "do not destroy boxes" on pallet by door
15. Put bag to right of receiving door
16. Return to stock room

C. Straightening Shoe Sales Floor
1. Go to endcap in front of girls' athletics
2. Remove all shoes hanging improperly
3. Determine correct "reclipping" method
4. Clip shoes back together
5. If a clip is not available, retrieve proper type from shelf in stock room
6. Hang shoes in correct sizing order
7. Repeat until all shoes are hung appropriately
8. Go to endcap in front of girls' dress shoes
9. Repeat Steps 2–7
10. Go to boys' casual front endcap
11. Repeat Steps 2–7
12. Go to boys' athletics/promotional front endcap
13. Repeat Steps 2–7
14. Go to clearance/promotional front endcap
15. Repeat Steps 2–7
16. Go to free-standing fixture
17. Repeat Steps 2–7
18. Go to wall fixture
19. Repeat Steps 2–7
20. Go to clearance/promotional rear endcap
21. Repeat Steps 2–7
22. Go to boys' athletic/promotional rear endcap
23. Repeat Steps 2–7
24. Go to girls' dress shoe rear endcap
25. Repeat Steps 2–7
26. Go to girls' athletics rear endcap
27. Repeat Steps 2–7
28. Go to infant/toddler wall shelving
29. Ensure that each column has a display

30. Rebox shoes (if on floor or found loose on shelf) according to style and size
31. Repeat Steps 29–30 for girls' athletic shelves
32. Repeat Steps 29–30 for girls' dress shoe shelves
33. Repeat Steps 29–30 for boys' athletic shelves
34. Repeat Steps 29–30 for boys' athletic/promotional shelves
35. Repeat Steps 29–30 for clearance/promotional shelves
36. Repeat Steps 29–30 for infant/toddler athletics wall shelves
37. Go to promotional table in front of store
38. Repeat Steps 29–30 for the table
39. Go to promotional table in front of shoe department
40. Repeat Steps 29–30 for the table
41. Go to clearance table between shoe and girls' accessories departments
42. Repeat Steps 29–30 for the table
43. Determine need to put shoes on salvage shelf throughout the straightening task

D. Reclipping Shoes Together
1. Determine clip type needed (toe insert or heel clip)
2. For toe insert, hold clip in left hand with size marker pointing up
3. Hold right shoe in right hand with toe pointing up
4. Insert right side of clip into toe of right shoe
5. Pick up left shoe in left hand (while holding right shoe with clip in it in right hand)
6. Stabilize clip in shoe with thumb of right hand
7. Insert left side of clip into toe of left shoe
8. Grasp top of clip in left hand
9. Hold heels of both shoes in right hand
10. Pull down gently with right hand to align and secure both shoes on hook
11. Return shoes to rack
12. For heel clip, hold bottom center of the clip in left hand with the size marker facing up
13. Pick up right shoe with right hand
14. Put right side of clip on back "lip" of right shoe heel
15. Transfer right hand hold to secure clip on shoe
16. Pick up left shoe in left hand
17. Put left side of clip on back "lip" of left shoe heel
18. Return shoes to rack

E. Making Boxed Shoe Display
1. Choose a size 7 if making a display for infant/toddler; choose a size 18 if the display is for children
2. If the designated size is not available, choose the next higher or lower size
3. Take top off shoe box
4. Place top within arm's reach
5. Remove shoes
6. If shoes are connected with a string, cut the string
7. Determine which shoe is the right shoe
8. Set the right shoe within arm's reach
9. Put left shoe back in box
10. Put top back on box
11. Place box within arm's reach

12. Remove a Velcro "dot" sticker from paper backing with left hand (these are located on a roll in the red bin on the utility shelf of the stock room)
13. Pick up shoe box with right hand
14. Turn box so that stock and price information are facing you
15. Put Velcro dot on top of box lid at end opposite stock and price information
16. Separate top Velcro dot piece from one stuck to box
17. Place box within arm's reach
18. Peel the back from the Velcro dot piece
19. Pick up right shoe
20. Turn shoe over
21. Put Velcro dot on heel of shoe
22. Press dot firmly to ensure adhesion
23. Place shoe on box top, matching the Velcro dots
24. Put display at the top of corresponding shoe column

F. Providing Customer Assistance
1. Pick up phone when requested over the intercom "Shoe Department, call on line"
2. Note which phone line to pick up
3. Pick up phone
4. Press correct line
5. Say, "Shoes, may I help you?"
6. Ask for customer's name
7. Write down customer's name on phone prompt sheet
8. Check off shoe type (e.g., children's/infants') needed on prompt sheet
9. Write down shoe color on prompt sheet
10. Write down shoe size on prompt sheet
11. Write down shoe style on prompt sheet
12. Write down customer's telephone number
13. Tell customer, "Please hold a moment while I check for you."
14. Push hold button on phone
15. Determine availability of stock
16. If available, bring shoes back to the telephone
17. Punch appropriate line button
18. Respond to customer request
19. Determine if stock should be held
20. If customer wants shoes put on hold, complete hold card by writing in information requested and attach shoes
21. If shoes are not to be held, put them back on shelf

G. Clocking Out
1. Retrieve time card from rack behind customer service counter
2. Go to clock in front of the store
3. Hold card with right thumb over giraffe head
4. Swipe card through clock slot until green button lights up and beeps once; display will read "punch accepted"
5. Take card to break room
6. Put card in rack on wall by door

2. Courtesy Clerk

Time	Sequence of Activities
3:00 p.m.	Clock in
3:00–5:00	Bag and deliver groceries
5:00–5:15	Clock out and take break
5:15	Clock in
5:15–7:00	Bag and deliver groceries
	*During slow periods, sweep floor or replace bags.

Key Related Tasks

A. Getting Ready To Bag
   1. Go to checker with groceries at the end of belt
   2. Face the customers entering the store
   3. Ask customer for bag type (plastic or paper)
   4. Get three bags
   5. Look at the customer; if elderly or frail, pack bags light

B. Bagging Items that Are Not Refrigerated, Soap, or Household Cleaning Products
   1. Put no more than two layers of canned items, or hard and large fruits (melons) or vegetables (cabbage, potatoes) in bag bottom to create a base
   2. If melon is cut, place in white plastic bag (wet pack); then place in bag
   3. Put lighter objects (napkins, bread), keeping glass objects apart on top of base
   4. Lift bag to check weight; if heavy, remove items

C. Bagging Frozen and Refrigerated Items
   1. Put one, but no more than two 1-gallon milk containers or other cold hard items in bag bottom to create base
   2. Put lighter frozen or refrigerated items on top of base
   3. If meat or fish, check bottom of package for wetness
   4. If wet, place in plastic bag (wet pack); then place in bag
   5. Check seal on salads; if sealed, place in white plastic bag (wet pack); then place in bag
   6. Lift bags to check weight; if heavy, remove items

D. Bagging Soap and Household Cleaners
   1. Set soap and household cleaning items to the side
   2. Create a base using square or other hard items
   3. Place lighter soap and household cleaning items on top of base

3. Telemarketer

Time	Sequence of Activities
10:00 a.m.	Punch in
10:00–11:45	Set appointments
11:45–Noon	Break
Noon–1:55	Set appointments
2:00	Punch out

Key Related Tasks

A. Making a Telephone Call
   1. Punch in the telephone number on the telephone number pad
   2. Use a pleasant introduction, "How are you today?"
   3. Ask, "Are you a home owner?"
   4. Ask if home is wood or brick
   5. If brick, give siding trim pitch
   6. If siding, give replacement window pitch
   7. If they say they're not interested, use rebuttal script
   8. If they say they've just painted, use rebuttal script
   9. If they ask price, use rebuttal script
   10. If not interested, use no obligation pitch
   11. If get appointment, complete appointment sheet
   12. If no appointment, hang up

B. Making an Appointment
   1. Write in name, address, and telephone number
   2. Ask, "What time can we come to see you when you and your spouse will be at home?"
   3. Record time on appointment sheet
   4. Say, "Thank you, we look forward to seeing you"
   5. Hang up

4. Movie Video Clerk

Time	Sequence of Activities
Shift A	
10:00–10:05 a.m.	Open store
10:05–10:10	Change dates in the computer
10:10–10:25	Remove movies returned in drop box and enter them into computer
10:25–10:30	Return movie boxes to shelves
10:30–10:40	Straighten movie boxes throughout store
10:40–1:30	• Rent movies • Return movies • Sell movies • Set up new customer memberships • Return movies to shelves
1:30–2:00	Break
2:00–4:00	• Rent movies • Return movies • Sell movies • Set up new customer memberships • Return movies to shelves
Shift B	
4:00–7:00	• Rent movies • Return movies • Sell movies • Set up new customer membership • Return movies to shelves
7:00–7:30	Break
7:30–10:00	• Rent movies • Return movies • Sell movies • Set up new customer membership • Return movies to shelves
10:00–10:10	Run daily report
10:10–10:20	Close out register
10:20–10:25	Close store

Key Related Tasks

A. Opening the Store
  1. Turn off alarm
  2. Turn on computer
  3. Adjust pitch to 17
  4. Leave first date as is
  5. Press enter
  6. Move cursor to day
  7. Enter next day a movie will be due back

8. Enter next date a movie will be due back
9. Press enter
10. Press A
11. Enter your customer ID#
12. Type ER
13. Press enter
14. Increase first day shown by 1
15. Increase second day shown by 1
16. Go to main menu
17. Turn on laminator
18. Return movies that were in the drop box
19. Put returned movies on shelves
20. Straighten movies on shelves

B. Returning Movies to Inventory
   1. Press B on computer
   2. Press enter
   3. Type in movie identification number
   4. Answer "Does customer wish to return all?"
      If no, follow Steps 5–6.
   5. Type Y next to films being returned
   6. Type N next to films not yet being returned
   7. If late fee appears, confirm that movies are late
   8. Answer "Is the above fee correct?"
   9. Type N
  10. Enter correct amount
  11. Press enter
  12. Answer "Does customer wish to pay now?" If customer wishes to pay now, follow Steps 13–17
  13. Tell customer amount due
  14. Collect payment
  15. Type amount rendered
  16. Press enter
  17. Give correct change; if customer wishes to pay later, follow Steps 18–26
  18. Write down customer ID#
  19. Write down movie ID#'s fee is due on
  20. Go to main menu
  21. Press C for new customer
  22. Tab down to main comments
  23. Type amount owed
  24. Type movie ID#'s money is owed on
  25. Type your initials
  26. Press enter until main menu is reached

C. Renting Movies to Customers
   1. Press A for rentals
   2. Type customer ID# and proceed to Step 7
   3. If customer doesn't have his or her card, ask to see driver's license and follow Steps 4–7
   4. Press enter
   5. Type customer last name
   6. Scroll to correct name
   7. Press enter
   8. Type ER

9. Press enter 3 times
10. Enter movie ID
11. Answer "Is above price correct?" If no, follow Steps 12–13
12. Enter correct price
13. Press enter
14. Follow Steps 10–13 until all movies are entered
15. Press enter for total
16. Tell customer the total
17. Enter amount of money given by customer
18. Open cash drawer
19. Give customer correct change
20. Tear receipts from printer
21. Ask customer to sign store copy
22. Give customer the receipt copy
23. Put store copy under counter
24. Tell customer when movies are due back

5. Customer Service Representative

Time	Sequence of Activities
8:30–10:30 a.m.	• Answer telephones • Take orders • Enter orders into computer • Xerox machine use • Fax machine use
10:30–10:45	Break
10:45–Noon	• Answer telephones • Take orders • Enter orders into computer • Xerox machine use • Fax machine use
Noon–12:30	Lunch
12:30–2:30	• Answer telephones • Take orders • Enter orders into computer • Xerox machine use • Fax machine use
2:30–2:45	Break
2:45–4:30	• Answer telephones • Take orders • Enter orders into computer • Xerox machine use • Fax machine use

Key Related Tasks

A. Answering the Telephone
  1. Pick up phone
  2. Say, "Good morning, (name of company). May I help you, please?"
  3. If person not in, take the message
     a. Who person wants
     b. What company person is from
     c. Telephone #
     d. Reason calling
     e. Your initials
  4. Place message in appropriate box
  5. If need to transfer to appropriate phone:
     a. Press ICM
     b. Press person's #
     c. Press ICM
  6. If person doesn't answer, take a message (see Step 3)
  7. If customer is placing an order:
     a. Get Department #
     b. Get P.O. #
     c. Get phone #
     d. Get company name
     e. Ask if "ship to" address is same as "sell to" address
     f. Whose attention does the order go to
     g. Get stock item #
     h. Get description
  8. After hang up, look up company's customer # in computer
  9. Give order to Bob or Susan to double check

B. Entering Customer's Order
  1. Turn switch on in back of computer
  2. Type in own operator #
  3. Type in company # (1)
  4. Type in warehouse # (1)
  5. See date, hit return
  6. See menu and hit button #2 for order entry
  7. See O.E. menu and choose sep. (user #2)
  8. Enter customer's account number
  9. If this is the correct customer, hit CR/N
  10. Order source:
     a. 11 walk-in
     b. 21 telephone
     c. 31 mail
     d. 41 requisition outside sales
     e. 51 fax
     f. 99 bids
  11. Enter department #; if no department #, hit RET
  12. Enter P.O.#; if no P.O.#, hit RET
  13. Enter 0 to accept line # to add, or * for help
  14. Punch in Line #11
  15. Enter contact person's name
  16. Enter telephone # and extension

17. Enter one of the following
    a. 0 to accept
    b. line # to change
    c. S to change ship to
    d. B to change billing
18. Enter stock #
19. Enter amount customer wants and correct unit of measure
20. Check pricing
    D–Salesman will give this to you on order sheet, or computer will already have set up as shown with discount
    P–Ditto
    L–List price as computer shows
    O–Override if salesman's price is different from computer's
    C–contract pricing (do not change contract prices)
21. Enter correct pricing
22. Hit RET
23. Is this correct? CR/N
24. Lines added? Y/N
25. Repeat Steps 18–22 if more orders need to be entered
26. Punch in END in place of stock # when last order has been entered; hit RET
27. Write the order # from top right corner of screen down on order sheet
28. Stamp today's date
29. Type END, hit RET
30. Check total pricing and tax
31. 0 to accept, CANCEL to cancel order, or HO to place a hold on the order
32. Repeat Steps 8–31

C. Entering Credit Returns
    1. Type INQ in the customer's # to get menu
    2. Punch in # for credits
    3. See credit menu and punch in credits (#2)
    4. Enter order #
    5. "Is this correct customer?" Hit CR/N
    6. Enter order date, hit RET
    7. Enter source of order, hit RET
    8. Enter department #, hit RET
    9. Enter P.O.#, hit RET
    10. Enter reason code description
        a. 111 damaged merchandise
        b. 222 allied sent wrong
        c. 333 customer ordered wrong
        d. 444 customer changed mind
        e. 555 pricing discrepancy
        f. 666 short shipped
        g. 777 defective merchandise
        h. 888 stockroom buyouts
        i. 999 reason unknown
    11. Hit RET
    12. Enter stock item #, RET
    13. Enter amount, U. of M. (Unit of money), RET
    14. Enter pricing code
    15. Repeat Steps 12–14 if more credits

16. Enter END in stock item # when finished
17. Write down credit memo # from top right corner
18. Stamp today's date
19. Key in END
20. Check pricing and tax for credit
21. Enter 0 to accept HO to hold or cancel to cancel; hit RET
22. Repeat Steps 4–21 if need to

D. Sending Fax
  1. Fill out cover sheet
  2. Number pages to be sent including cover page
  3. Press clear button on fax machine
  4. Punch in the number to be faxed
  5. Place stack of papers face down in slot
  6. When see "communicating," press green fax button
  7. After papers have been faxed, pick up sheets

E. Picking Up Fax
  1. Pick up papers that have been faxed over
  2. Give to whomever the fax has been sent to
  3. If no contact name, give to the receptionist

Case Study

Judi is a 17-year-old with a primary disability of borderline personality disorder and a secondary disability of mild learning disability. She is on grade level in most subjects and is expected to graduate with a regular diploma in June. Judi's mother is very concerned with Judi's inability to maintain a part-time job. Her medications were recently readjusted, and Judi has been stable for 4 months.

Judi is currently enrolled in a suburban high school. Her IEP case manager provides some academic instruction in a resource room setting. Judi attends two collaborative classes as well. Because she has block scheduling, Judi is able to attend academic classes every morning. An interest inventory and formal vocational/career assessment revealed strengths in word processing, organizational skills, and fine motor skills. Severe deficits were noted in interpersonal skills, coping abilities during stressful moments, and general maturity. Judi recognizes that she is not a "people person."

The work coordinator collaborated with the mental health counselor, mother, DRS counselor, and student to develop a position at a local discount retail store. She now rides a vocational school bus to her job at the warehouse clothing store each afternoon after lunch. Her mother picks her up at 6:00 in the evenings.

Judi learned basic stock/inventory skills within the first 3 days of work. Her manager then recommended that Judi be trained to use the computerized pricer. The work coordinator attended the training session with Judi, then slowly weaned her presence at the store from 1 hour daily to one visit per week.

Judi seemed happy and well adjusted at work until she began to observe resentment from former co-workers in the receiving department. Apparently, the floor manager had chosen Judi over another worker to learn the new task. Judi began having crying spells and missed 2 days of school and work over the perceived slights. The work coordinator intervened and, with some assistance from Judi's mental health counselor, was able to develop a coping plan for Judi. Whenever she overheard comments, she was to put her Walkman headset on for up to 15 minutes to "change the subject in her mind." This simple accommodation resolved the issue.

Individual Transition Plan 2

Student Profile

Judi is a 17-year-old with a primary disability of borderline personality disorder and a secondary disability of mild learning disability.

Individual Transition Plan

Student's Name Judith "Judi" Cross
                        First   M.I.   Last

Birthdate 01-06-80   School Midlothian High School

Student's ID No. 634   ITP Conference Date 05-16-97

Participants

Name	Position
Judi	Student
Jane	Mom
Ralph	Work Coordinator
Donna	MH Counselor
Steve	DRS Counselor

Individual Transition Plan 2

I. Career and Economic Self-Sufficiency

1. Employment Goal	Part-time employment with mentor
Level of present performance	Part-time employment, with part-time support
Steps needed to accomplish goal	1. Maintain current position until graduation (June 10). 2. Apply for full-time position in May.
Date of completion	N/A
Person(s) responsible for implementation	Judi, DRS Counselor, Work Coordinator

2. Vocational Education/Training Goal	Judi will maintain cooperative relationships with Work Coordinator.
Level of present performance	Working well in program
Steps needed to accomplish goal	1. Meet with Work Coordinator 1 time per week for 20 minutes. 2. Maintain attendance record (1 absence/month).
Date of completion	6/98
Person(s) responsible for implementation	Judi, Work Coordinator, Mother

3. Postsecondary Education Goal	None at this time
Level of present performance	N/A

Individual Transition Plan 2

Steps needed to accomplish goal	N/A
Date of completion	N/A
Person(s) responsible for implementation	N/A

4. Financial/Income Needs Goal	None at this time
Level of present performance	Judi and her mother prefer to explore financial issues privately.
Steps needed to accomplish goal	N/A
Date of completion	N/A
Person(s) responsible for implementation	N/A

II. Community Integration and Participation

5. Independent Living Goal	Judi will require support for emotional needs residentially.
Level of present performance	Lives with parents.
Steps needed to accomplish goal	1. Explore community options with DRS, MH Workers. 2. Participate in Center for Independent Living Services for Teens.
Date of completion	Ongoing
Person(s) responsible for implementation	Judi, MH Worker, Mother

Individual Transition Plan 2

6. Transportation/Mobility Goal	Judi will call a taxi independently for emergencies by 6/98.
Level of present performance	Judi rides only with her mother or on a school bus.
Steps needed to accomplish goal	1. Ride in taxi with mom. 2. Ride in taxi with friend. 3. Ride in taxi alone.
Date of completion	6/98
Person(s) responsible for implementation	Judi, Mother, MH Worker
7. Social Relationships Goal	Judi will eat one meal per week with co-workers.
Level of present performance	Eats alone at break
Steps needed to accomplish goal	1. Eat with mentor 1 time per week. 2. Eat with co-worker 1 time per week.
Date of completion	6/98
Person(s) responsible for implementation	Judi, MH Worker
8. Recreation/Leisure Goal	N/A (Judi's choice)
Level of present performance	N/A
Steps needed to accomplish goal	N/A

Individual Transition Plan 2

Date of completion	N/A
Person(s) responsible for implementation	N/A

III. Personal Competence

9. Health/Safety Goal	N/A
Level of present performance	N/A
Steps needed to accomplish goal	N/A
Date of completion	N/A
Person(s) responsible for implementation	N/A

10. Self-Advocacy/Future Planning	Judi will make personal requests at work and in the community.
Level of present performance	Judi is dependent upon school and mental health personnel to intercede on her behalf.
Steps needed to accomplish goal	1. Role playing with school personnel. 2. Practice at work with inconsequential requests (Please pass the salt. May I leave my apron on your hook?). 3. Independent requests/monitored by Work Coordinator.
Date of completion	6/98
Person(s) responsible for implementation	Judi, Work Coordinator

Student Career Preference

Part-time competitive employment as a retail sales associate

Individual Transition Plan 2

Student's Major Transition Needs

1. Maintain medication stability
2. Maintain part-time employment
3.
4.
5.
6.
7.
8.
9.

Additional Notes

Production and Stock Clerk Occupations

◆ ◆ ◆ ◆ ◆ ◆ ◆ ◆ ◆ ◆ ◆ ◆ ◆ ◆ ◆ ◆ ◆ ◆ ◆ ◆

Description of Domain

The *Dictionary of Occupational Titles* defines Production and Stock Clerk occupations as those occupations concerned with "compiling and maintaining production records, expediting flow of work and materials, and receiving, storing, shipping, issuing, requisitioning, and accounting for materials and goods" (p. 194).

JOB DESCRIPTIONS

1. Box Packer

Time	Sequence of Activities
7:00 a.m.	Punch in
7:00–10:00	Construct and load boxes
10:00–10:15	Break
10:15–Noon	Construct and load boxes
Noon–12:30	Lunch
12:30–2:30	Construct and load boxes
2:30–2:45	Break
2:45–4:30	Construct and load boxes
4:30	Punch out

Key Related Tasks

  A. Folding the Boxes
    1. Place stopping block on conveyor belt
    2. Get labels for boxes
    3. Identify bag size
    4. Identify box size by dimension
    5. Get box
    6. Open box into square

7. Put box on table with dimension on top facing you
8. Fold left side in flat against box
9. Fold right side in flat against box
10. Fold front in flat against box
11. Fold back in flat against box
12. Flip box over with folded edges at the bottom
13. Fold down front
14. Fold down back
15. Fold down left side
16. Fold down right side
17. Fold front of top outside flat to box
18. Fold back of top outside flat to box
19. Fold left of top outside flat to box
20. Fold right of top outside flat to box

B. Putting the Bag in the Box
1. Get bag off of shelf
2. Open bag/shake out
3. Place corners halfway between each side
4. Grasp open edges at left and right
5. Pull out over front flap
6. Pull box toward body, back flap flat against body
7. Hook bag under front flap
8. Slide bag under right and left side flaps
9. Move box away from body
10. Slide bag under back flap

C. Putting Bundles into Boxes
1. Turn to bundles
2. Push in uneven strips on bundle
3. Grasp bundle from both ends (short ends)
4. Squeeze bundle
5. Pick up bundle
6. Place bundle over box
7. Slide right hand under bundle for support
8. Lower bundle into left side of box
9. Push uneven strips
10. Repeat Steps 1–7
11. Lower bundle on top of bundle on left already in box
12. Push in uneven strips
13. Place cardboard on end up against bundles
14. Repeat Steps 1–7
15. Lower bundle into middle of box
16. Push in uneven strips
17. Repeat Steps 1–7
18. Lower bundle on top of middle bundle already in box
19. Push in uneven strips
20. Place cardboard in end up against bundles
21. Repeat Steps 1–7
22. Gently lower bundle into right side of box
23. Release bundle gently when you no longer lower it
24. Push in uneven strips
25. Repeat Steps 1-7
26. Gently lower bundle onto stack already on right side of box

27. Release bundle gently when you can no longer lower it
28. Fold in left side of bag
29. Fold in right side of bag
30. Fold in front of bag
31. Fold in back of bag
32. Fold in left side of box
33. Fold in right side of box
34. Fold in front of box
35. Fold in back of box
36. Slide box to left
37. Feed box through tape machine

D. Putting Boxes on Pallet
    1. Pick up bundle off conveyor
    2. Carry bundle to pallet
    3. Arrange bundles on pallet
    4. Make sure 10 bundles go in a row, placing bundles side by side in a length–width, length–width pattern
    5. Lay cardboard over bundles
    6. Repeat Steps 1–5 for as many rows as necessary

2. Order Picker

Time	Sequence of Activities
8:00 a.m.	Punch in
8:01–10:00	On the line—filling orders
10:00–10:10	Break
10:10–12:30	Filling orders
12:30–12:31	Punch out for lunch
12:31–1:00	Lunch
1:00–1:01	Punch in
1:01–3:00	Filling orders
3:00–3:10	Break
3:10–5:30	Filling orders
5:30	Punch out
Days: Monday, Tuesday, Thursday, Friday	

Key Related Tasks

A. Breaking Down the Table
    1. Get lead copies from lead box
    2. Place leads on matching magazine

3. Repeat Step 2 until line finished
4. Move to beginning/end of line on next magazine
5. Count magazines in 1st stack; including lead and covers
6. Write it down
7. Count bundles left over
8. Look at bundle count on lead
9. Multiply bundle count × bundle count
10. Add this to written figure
11. Determine total
12. Write total # of magazine on lead copy and circle
13. Move to next magazine
14. Repeat Steps 5–13 until table counted

B. Pulling the Magazine (Front Start Point)
   1. Press right button to display customer account #
   2. Match invoice customer account # to display
   3. If #'s don't match, press left button to check previous account #'s
   4. Match #'s
   5. Move to 1st Computac
   6. Read display/Read invoice
   7. Count magazines needed
   8. Turn face up
   9. Place in invoice box; if full, get new box
   10. Move full boxes in front of invoice box
   11. Move to next Computac
   12. Repeat Steps 6–11 until you meet co-worker
   13. Level magazines
   14. Place invoice in least full box of the order; if posted outside, leave outside
   15. Mark bundles with customer account # and store name
   16. Place bundles in front of invoice box
   17. Send to next station
   18. Repeat Steps 1–17 until you need to restock or breakdown table

C. Pulling the Magazines (End Start Point)
   1. Move to last Computac
   2. Read display
   3. Count magazines needed
   4. Turn titles face up
   5. Stack magazines on belt
   6. Get box if needed
   7. Move to next Computac
   8. Repeat Steps 2–7 until you meet co-worker
   9. Place counted magazines in invoice box until full, then get new box
   10. Level magazines in box
   11. Place invoice in least full box of the order; if invoice outside box, leave it outside
   12. Move invoice box behind any full boxes of the order or bundles
   13. Mark bundles with customer account # and store name
   14. Send cartons to next station
   15. Repeat Steps 1–14 until you restock or break down table

D. Restocking the Table
   1. Identify magazine that needs stocking

    2. Look for magazine directly across from table (if not there, look under table)

    3. Move bundles needed to table

    4. Open with snips

    5. Stock magazines face up/face down

    6. Remove torn/damaged magazines and place in lead box

    7. Throw away trash

    8. Repeat Steps 1–7 until restocked

E. Setting the Table
    1. Pick up lead copy
    2. Read location
    3. Go to designated area
    4. Find the magazine; if not there use the following:
        a. Go to row A
        b. Scan the 1st tier (floor) for the magazine
        c. Go to row B
        d. Scan the 1st tier
        e. Go to row C
        f. Scan the 1st tier
        g. Repeat loop until magazine found; progress up a level (tier) as you repeat
    5. Load magazines (bundles) onto dolly/forklift
    6. Bring back to where lead is located on the table
    7. Move 1 bundle to table
    8. Count the bundle
    9. Match # counted to bundle count on lead
    10. Put lead copy in box
    11. Stock magazine in designated space alternating face up/face down, bound side toward you
    12. Continue stacking until magazine is at right height
        1st = up to Computac
        2nd = midway to first copy
        3rd = one quarter of 2nd copy
    13. Stock leftover bundles directly across from magazines on table
    14. Move to next copy
    15. Repeat Steps 1–14 until table set
    16. Move to beginning/end of line
    17. Match UP # of magazines to UP # on Computac
    18. Move to next copy
    19. Repeat Steps 17–18 until you meet co-worker or finish table

F. Completing the Short Sheet
    1. Place a piece of cardboard where magazine should be
    2. Write name of magazine on cardboard
    3. Get short sheet
    4. Write title of magazine in top left corner of sheet
    5. Write UP # from invoice under title
    6. Write customer account # from invoice in column 1
    7. Write route # from invoice in BPD column
    8. Write # of magazines short in Qty column
    9. Put sheet in slot where magazine should be
    10. Find the magazine short on the invoice
    11. Circle Qty. #

12. Write # of magazine short to right of title on the invoice
13. Return to pulling

3. Warehouse Assistant

Time	Sequence of Activities
10:00 a.m.	Check in with supervisor
10:05–10:10	Locate materials
10:10–Noon	Begin labeling
Noon–12:30	Lunch
12:30–12:35	Replenish materials
12:35–2:25	Resume labeling
2:25–2:30	Secure materials for next day
2:30	Check out with supervisor

Key Related Tasks

A. Folding Boxes
1. Place "Box Maker" on the table approximately 6 inches from the end of the table
2. Place stack of unfolded boxes on the table with brown side facing up (approximately 15 boxes)
3. Take box with top facing to the side and bend the top fold and bottom fold until it fits into the box maker
4. Fold end tabs together until they meet
5. Fold end flap over tabs and press it until it locks into the hole in the bottom of the box
6. Rotate box maker 180 degrees until unfinished end faces you
7. Repeat Steps 4 and 5
8. Stack box squarely on top of the other boxes

B. Adjusting Scale for Plastic Sheets
1. Place box on scale and press button marked zero to set scale for weight of box
2. Press Sample Button one time until scale reads ADD 10
3. Count out 10 pieces of plastic

C. Weighing Plastic Sheets
1. Adjust scale for boxes
2. Place plastic sheets into box until scale reads 100 and green light is above the word "Stable"
3. Close box by placing flap on lid inside front of box
4. If not labeled, place corresponding label on right-hand side of box
5. Place box on palate with label facing toward you

D. Operating the Shrink Wrap Machine
   1. Place stack of plastic sheets on top of metal plate and under top sheet of plastics (place so that the shorter side of sheet is going left to right and longer side is up and down)
   2. Place stack snugly into the top left-hand corner of the plastic
   3. Pull down handle of bag sealer (machine will automatically release)
   4. Carefully slide stack onto heat tunnel conveyor
   5. Retrieve stack at other end of machine

E. Punching the Plastic Sheets
   1. Locate stack of punched plastic sheets
   2. Retrieve approximately 4 sheets (tissue not included)
   3. Place sheets with longer side down into puncher
   4. Ensure tops of plastic are flush
   5. Ensure left side of plastic is flush against the metal stop
   6. Press pedal to operate punch
   7. Stack sheets on piece of cardboard from package of plastic
   8. Align sheets in stack so edges are flush
   9. When all pieces are punched and stacked, place cardboard on top of stack
   10. Stamp top piece of cardboard

F. Punching the Luggage Tags
   1. Remove a pack of luggage tags from box
   2. Carefully remove plastic from luggage tags (plastic will be used later)
   3. Put 4 tags into hole punch machine
   4. Press black button on left side of the front of the machine
   5. When all tags are punched, put them back into the plastic bag and seal the bag
   6. Return pack to box

G. Adjusting the Scale for Sorting Screws
   1. Place funnel on scale and press button zero to set scale for weight of funnel
   2. Press sample button 4 times to set scale to 25
   3. On table, count out 25 pieces of product to be weighed
   4. Place all pieces at one time into the funnel
   5. Count out 5 more pieces on table; then, place in funnel at one time (scale should read 30)
   *NOTE: Scale should be adjusted each time a new product is weighed.

H. Weighing Screws
   1. Adjust scale for product being weighed
   2. Place pieces into funnel until scale reads 100 and green light appears above the word STABLE
   3. Pour pieces into plastic bag
   4. Seal bag just above the pieces
   5. Label bag with corresponding sticker just above seal
   6. Place bag into corresponding labeled box (5 bags per box)
   7. Place box on shelf labeled for those pieces

4. Engraver

Time	Sequence of Activities
7:00 a.m.	Clock in
7:00 –12:30	• Assemble plaques • *or* Cut name plates
12:30	Clock out for lunch
12:30–1:00	Lunch
1:00	Clock in from lunch
1:00–3:30	• Assemble plaques • *or* Cut name plates
3:30	Clock out

Key Related Tasks

   A. Assembling Large Ball Plaques 10½" × 13"
1. Get order and plates from table
2. Take to assembly table
3. Locate 10½" × 13" plaques
4. Get required number
5. Locate large 8 × 10 acrylic
6. Get required number
7. Lay plaques on table with hole on left side
8. Match the numbers on the plate, certificate, and ball
9. Locate smooth tape
10. Cut 4 pieces of smooth tape
11. Put one piece of tape on nameplate on left
12. Put one long piece of tape on nameplate on right
13. Cut 4 very small pieces of rough-edged tape
14. Put 2 pieces on back of certificate
15. Put 2 on back of photo
16. Peel paper off tape
17. Locate cardboard pattern
18. Center pattern in right-hand corner of plaque
19. Match corners and edges
20. Hold pattern with one hand in a steady position
21. Place photo in space at top of pattern
22. Place certificate in space at bottom of pattern
23. Locate a hammer, ratchet, gold nails, and nuts
24. Put one piece of acrylic on the table and peel backing from both sides
25. Wipe off fingerprints with rag
26. Align acrylic holes with bottom of certificate corners
27. Hammer gold nail on top right corner
28. Hammer gold nail in top left corner
29. Hammer gold nail in bottom right corner
30. Hammer gold nail in bottom left corner
31. Put gold pedestal in with white part on top

32. Put a nut in the ratchet
33. Center pedestal on plaque and insert nut
34. Tighten nut while holding plaque and pedestal
35. Peel paper from tape on nameplate
36. Center nameplate and press down
37. Turn plaque over with pedestal at top
38. Pick up correct letter in bag and position in center of plaque with signature facing the right
39. Put 3 pieces of clear tape on the sides and bottom; close top
40. Put ball in box with ball plaque and take to shipper

B. Assembling Dealer Plaques
1. Take order and plates to table
2. Locate 6" × 8" plaques, unbag
3. Get required number
4. Locate round stickers
5. Place one round sticker on back of plate at each corner
6. Peel paper from stickers
7. Center nameplate on plaque
8. Wipe off fingerprints
9. Put plaques in bag
10. Take order to shipper

C. Cutting Nameplates
1. Take completed plates to cutter
2. Place small plate at 5-in. mark, letters facing to the right
3. Cut off excess
4. Place each side at 2½-in. mark
5. Cut off excess
6. Place plate right before 4-in. mark
7. Face names to the right
8. Cut off 1st name
9. Place plate right before 3-in. mark
10. Cut off 2nd name
11. Place plate right before 2-in. mark
12. Cut off 3rd name
13. Place plate right before 1-in. mark
14. Cut off 2nd name
15. Check plates for rough edges
16. Check plates for spacing of letters and edges
17. Stack plates
18. Put with order
19. Put cutter handle down

Case Study

Kim is a 17-year-old who experiences cognitive and speech deficits as the result of anoxia, loss of oxygen to the brain, in a near-drowning accident at age 7. Her significant speech disturbance has entitled her to lifelong speech therapy/IEP support at school. Kim is able to read on a seventh-grade level and do basic, not abstract, math functions.

During an IEP meeting in September, Kim and her parents expressed concerns about Kim's ability to work upon completion of high school. Kim's IEP case manager referred Kim to the school's Rehabilitative Services counselor. Because there are no vocational special needs services in Kim's school, all training will have to occur with parental or agency support.

Kim was referred for a comprehensive vocational evaluation. A situational assessment revealed strengths in understanding verbal instructions, memory, and ability to stay on task for up to 3 minutes. She also displayed good fine motor skills. Kim's weaknesses included loss of verbal fluency, reasoning, and four-step tasks. Reports recommended that she seek part-time employment that does not require frequent changes or active problem-solving abilities. Kim expressed an interest in working in a warehouse or manufacturing setting based on a DRS-sponsored work trial experience. She became very involved in all aspects of her job search, and her IEP case manager provided extra time at school to work on applications and her resume. Kim met with her DRS counselor twice monthly to discuss leads and to visit potential employment sites.

Eight weeks later, Kim accepted a part-time position as an order puller at a distribution company that fills magazine orders for retailers. The setting is a temperature-controlled warehouse located two blocks off the busline. Kim takes the bus to work each afternoon, Wednesday through Friday, and works from 4:30 to 8:30 p.m. Her parents pick her up at night. She also works on Saturdays from 8:00 a.m. to 3:00 p.m. The job requires Kim to keep the magazine inventory stocked and fill customer orders. Kim reached skill acquisition by day 6 and the employer's production standard by day 12. Because Kim experienced some difficulty reaching some magazines on upper shelves during her training, a footstool was provided by her DRS counselor, which alleviated Kim's mild anxiety.

To date, Kim has been working for 6 months. She is still working on her goal to initiate conversations with co-workers. To that end, she has enrolled in a speech therapy support group for teens overcoming speech disorders, which meets at a local college. She has made two friends from the group and incrementally practices simple greetings at work.

Individual Transition Plan 3

Student Profile

Kim is 17 years old and has a severe speech disorder. She attends an urban high school that has no vocational special needs support services.

Individual Transition Plan

Student's Name   Kim L. Smith

First   M.I.   Last

Birthdate 08/08/80   School Foresbridge High School

Student's ID No. 8   ITP Conference Date 9/97

Participants

Name	Position
Kim	Student
Harry and Joan	Parents
Kathleen	IEP Teacher
Joseph	DRS Counselor

Individual Transition Plan 3

I. Career and Economic Self-Sufficiency

1. Employment Goal	Full-time competitive employment
Level of present performance	Kim works part time.
Steps needed to accomplish goal	1. Increase hours to comfortable level until graduation. 2. Wean support, as appropriate.
Date of completion	9/98
Person(s) responsible for implementation	Kim, DRS Counselor
2. Vocational Education/Training Goal	There are no vocational special needs support services at Kim's school.
Level of present performance	N/A
Steps needed to accomplish goal	N/A
Date of completion	N/A
Person(s) responsible for implementation	N/A
3. Postsecondary Education Goal	Kim does not wish to pursue postsecondary educational options.
Level of present performance	N/A

Individual Transition Plan 3

Steps needed to accomplish goal	N/A
Date of completion	N/A
Person(s) responsible for implementation	N/A

4. Financial/Income Needs Goal	Kim will manage her trust fund with assistance.
Level of present performance	Kim was awarded a settlement due to her accident. It is held in trust until her 25th birthday.
Steps needed to accomplish goal	1. Develop budgeting skills through employment/support. 2. Open a personal savings/checking account.
Date of completion	Ongoing until graduation (9/98–9/99)
Person(s) responsible for implementation	Kim, Parents, IEP Teacher

II. Community Integration and Participation

5. Independent Living Goal	Kim will live with friends/partner.
Level of present performance	Kim lives with her parents and younger sibling in a home.
Steps needed to accomplish goal	1. Enroll in support classes at local DRS sponsored Center for Independent Living. 2. Increase responsibilities at home.
Date of completion	9/98
Person(s) responsible for implementation	Parents, Kim, DRS Counselor

Individual Transition Plan 3

6. Transportation/Mobility Goal	N/A—Kim independently accesses community public transportation and will rely on this means in the future.
Level of present performance	N/A
Steps needed to accomplish goal	N/A
Date of completion	N/A
Person(s) responsible for implementation	N/A

7. Social Relationships Goal	Kim will increase socialization skills.
Level of present performance	Kim rarely socializes.
Steps needed to accomplish goal	1. Enroll in Center for Independent Living classes. 2. Enroll in youth group at church. 3. Enroll in extra speech therapy sessions (private).
Date of completion	9/98
Person(s) responsible for implementation	Kim, Parents

8. Recreation/Leisure Goal	Kim will participate in age-appropriate recreational activities.
Level of present performance	Kim likes to stay home, read, knit.
Steps needed to accomplish goal	1. Research teen clubs in area. 2. Attend at least four meetings by 9/98.

Individual Transition Plan 3

Date of completion	9/98
Person(s) responsible for implementation	Kim, Parents

III. Personal Competence

9. Health/Safety Goal	N/A
Level of present performance	Kim is very aware of health/safety issues.
Steps needed to accomplish goal	N/A
Date of completion	N/A
Person(s) responsible for implementation	N/A

10. Self-Advocacy/Future Planning	Kim will advocate for herself as appropriate.
Level of present performance	Kim has been very dependent upon her mother to solve problems.
Steps needed to accomplish goal	Participate in self-advocacy support group with DRS-sponsored group by 6/98.
Date of completion	6/98
Person(s) responsible for implementation	Kim, DRS Counselor

Student Career Preference

Warehouse Stock Clerk

Individual Transition Plan 3

Student's Major Transition Needs

1. Increase Self-advocacy awareness

2. Increase conversational phrases

3. Increase work hours

4. _____

5. _____

6. _____

7. _____

8. _____

9. _____

Additional Notes

The special educator and parents would benefit from heightened awareness regarding vocational special needs services. The director of special education may wish to contact other school districts to begin a collaborative partnership with vocational education.

Food and Beverage Preparation Occupations

◆ ◆ ◆ ◆ ◆ ◆ ◆ ◆ ◆ ◆ ◆ ◆ ◆ ◆ ◆ ◆ ◆

Description of Domain

The *Dictionary of Occupational Titles* defines Food and Beverage Preparation occupations as those concerned with "preparing food and beverages and serving them to patrons of such establishments as hotels, clubs, restaurants, and cocktail lounges" (p. 240).

JOB DESCRIPTIONS

1. Linebacker

Time	Sequence of Activities
7:00 a.m.	Clock in
7:00–10:30	Prepare soups, vegetables, croutons
10:30–10:45	Put the soup out front
10:45–11:15	Break
11:15–12:15	Slice and divide cheeses
12:15–2:00	Slice and weigh the meats
2:00–3:00	Clean the work area
3:00	Clock out

Key Related Tasks

A. Cooking the Soups
   1. Wash your hands
   2. Check walk-in cooler to see if there are any leftover soups that need to be used up
   3. If there are leftover soups, get the soups out of the walk-in
   4. Get the two big soup pots
   5. Put the pots on the burners
   6. Dump the remaining soup in the pots
   7. Turn the burners on high

8. If there are not any leftover soups in the walk-in cooker, go into the freezer
9. Pick out two soups, one cream-based and one red-based
10. Read the directions on the bags of soup
11. Fill the two soup pots with water according to the directions on the bags
12. Put the soup pots on the burners
13. Turn the burners on high
14. Stir the soup every half hour
15. At 10:00 a.m., turn the burners off
16. Take the soup pots off the burners
17. Get the two kettles that go out front on the line
18. Pour the soups into these kettles
19. Take the kettles out front to the line
20. Bring the dirty soup pots to the sink

B. Prepping the Vegetables (Cucumbers)
1. Wash your hands
2. Put on plastic gloves
3. Get out a sanitized board
4. Wipe down board with a clean cloth
5. Put board down on counter
6. Get a colander
7. Put vegetables that are going to be prepped in colander
8. Wash vegetables in sink
9. Cut ends of cukes off
10. Slice three peels off cukes
11. Cut cukes into three sections (slice the long way)
12. Take out vegetable slicer
13. Place one section of cucumber on slicer
14. Slice cucumber through until all pieces are separate
15. Place separated pieces into a container
16. Continue Steps 13–15 until you have sliced all cucumbers that are needed
17. Put a layer of plastic wrap over top of container
18. Put the day dot on the container for 3 days
19. Place container in the walk-in cooler

C. Prepping the Vegetables (Onions)
1. Wash your hands
2. Put on plastic gloves
3. Take out a sanitized board
4. Wipe down board with sanitized cloth
5. Put board on counter
6. Take out a colander
7. Put vegetables that are going to be prepped in the colander
8. Wash the vegetables in the sink
9. Peel skins off onions
10. Throw skins into garbage
11. Take out vegetable slicer
12. Place one onion on slicer
13. Slice onion through until all pieces are separate
14. Place separated pieces into a container

15. Continue with Steps 12–14 until you have sliced all onions that are needed
16. Put layer of plastic wrap over top of container
17. Put the day dot on the container for 3 days
18. Place containers in walk-in cooler

D. Making Croutons
   1. Wash your hands
   2. Put on plastic gloves
   3. Get 10 bagels: onion, poppy seed, sun-dried tomato, plain
   4. Put on protective gloves
   5. Cut bagels into halves
   6. Cut bagels into cubes
   7. Get stainless steel bowl
   8. Put bagel cubes into bowl
   9. Go into walk-in cooler
   10. Get garlic butter
   11. Get measuring cup
   12. Portion 8 oz. of garlic butter
   13. Melt garlic butter in microwave
   14. Dump melted garlic butter on bagels that are in bowl
   15. Use your hands to mix the bagel cubes
   16. Take out a baking sheet
   17. Put bagels on the baking sheet
   18. Take dirty dishes to sink

E. Slicing Cheeses
   1. Wash your hands
   2. Put on plastic gloves
   3. Take out a sanitized board
   4. Wipe it down with a clean cloth
   5. Place it on the counter
   6. Pick out the type of cheese you need to slice
   7. Put on protective glove
   8. Take wrapper off cheese
   9. Set slicer to ¾ of an ounce
   10. Set cheese on slicer to slice on automatic
   11. Clear the cheese from the slicer to prep for weighing (continue with this process until all of the cheese is sliced)

F. Dividing the Cheeses
   1. Wash your hands
   2. Put on a pair of plastic gloves
   3. Take out the sanitized board
   4. Wipe down board with a clean cloth
   5. Put the board on the counter
   6. Get some divider papers out
   7. Get a container to store cheese in from rack
   8. Place a paper down
   9. Place a slice of cheese that weighs ¾ ounce on the paper
   10. Place the cheese in the container
   11. Continue with Steps 10–12 until you have separated all of the cheeses
   12. Place a layer of plastic wrap over the containers that have cheese in them

13. Place a day dot on the containers for 7 days
14. Place the containers of cheese in the walk-in cooler

G. Slicing the Meats
   1. Wash your hands
   2. Put on plastic gloves
   3. Get out a sanitized board
   4. Wipe down board with a clean cloth
   5. Put board down on counter
   6. Go into walk-in cooler
   7. Pick out type of meat you need to slice
   8. Put on protective glove
   9. Cut wrapper off meat
   10. Place meat on machine
   11. Set the setting for cutting (it is very important that the slicer is set correctly; ask for assistance if you are not sure)
   12. Set the machine for automatic
   13. Clear the sliced meat from under the slicer
   14. Continue Steps 10–13 until all meat is sliced

H. Weighing the Meats
   1. Wash your hands
   2. Put on plastic gloves
   3. Take out a sanitized board
   4. Wipe down board with sanitized cloth
   5. Put board on counter
   6. Take out scale
   7. Turn on scale
   8. Get some divider papers
   9. Get a container to store meat in
   10. Place a paper on scale
   11. Weigh out meat to correct weight
   12. Take weighed meat off scale and put in container
   13. Continue with Steps 10–12 until you have weighed all of the meat
   14. Place layer of plastic wrap over top of container
   15. Place a day dot on the container for 5 days
   16. Put container of meat in walk-in cooler

I. Cleaning the Slicer
   1. Unplug the machine
   2. Put on protective glove
   3. Get a small red bucket
   4. Fill it with sanitation from the sink
   5. Put a clean rag in the bucket
   6. Take protective guards and pieces off machine
   7. Put protective guards in sink of sanitation
   8. Wipe down machine with sanitized cloth
   9. Clean machine pieces that are in sanitized sink
   10. Put pieces back on machine
   11. Wipe underneath machine

2. Dietary Aide

Time	Sequence Of Activities
12:30 p.m.	Sign in
12:30–4:30	• Help on lunch line, if requested • Portion desserts and salads, if requested • Set up cards if Dietary Assistant is not present • Pick up trays in dining room • Set up dishroom • Wash dishes • Clean dishroom • Set up for dinner • Wrap bread • Wrap silverware
4:30–5:15	Break
5:15–6:00	Serve dinner line
6:00–6:30	Clean dinner line
6:30–8:30	• Wash dishes • Clean dishroom • Wrap silverware • Put cards in order
8:30	Punch out

Key Related Tasks

A. Serving on Line (Dessert, Salad, Bread, Butter)
   1. Listen to caller for type of diet and restrictions
   2. Place appropriate item(s) on tray according to caller's instructions and colored diet cards
      • Blue—Regular Diet
      • Red—Diabetic Diet
      • Green- Soft/Edentulous Diet
      • Pink—Soft/Bland Diet
      • Gold—Restricted Sodium Diet
      • Yellow—Calculated Diet
      • White—Puree Diet
   3. Send tray to next person on line
   4. Repeat Steps 1–3

B. Putting Correct Beverage on Tray
   1. Listen to caller for beverage preference
      • Milk
      • Tea
      • Water
      • Soda

2. Place appropriate items on tray accordingly
   - Milk
   - Tea
   - Water
   - Soda
3. Send tray to next person on line
4. Repeat Steps 1–3
5. If spill occurs, wipe down beverage station with rag

C. Wrapping Silverware
   1. Get clean knife, fork, and spoon
   2. Lay one napkin on table
   3. Place knife on top of the napkin (catercorner, 2 inches from top)
   4. Place fork on top of knife (face up)
   5. Place spoon on top of fork (face up)
   6. Fold top corner over silverware
   7. Fold right side of napkin in
   8. Roll silverware up to left
   9. Pick up finished product and place in pan
   10. Repeat above

E. Positioning Desserts into Bowls
   1. Line up dessert bowls
   2. Choose appropriate scoop to measure dessert
   3. Use utensil to put dessert into bowls
   4. Repeat above

3. Dishwasher

Time	Sequence of Activities
11:00 a.m.	Sign in
11:00–11:30	Refresh restrooms
11:30–11:45	Clean glass doors and case
11:45–12:00	Sweep storefront
12:00–1:45	Wash dishes
1:45–2:15	Lunch
2:15–2:30	Empty trash
2:30–2:45	Sweep and dust mop
2:45–3:00	Mop
3:00–3:15	Vacuum
3:15–4:00	Wash dishes
4:00	Sign out

Key Related Tasks

A. Refresh the Restrooms
   1. Get caddy
   2. Get glass cleaner
   3. Get sponge or paper towels
   4. Go to men's room
   5. Knock on door
   6. Open door
   7. Turn on light
   8. Spray sink with cleaner
   9. Wipe off from left to right with damp sponge
   10. Spray mirror with glass spray
   11. Wipe off mirror from left to right
   12. Check toilet for dirt
   13. Clean if needed with sponge
   14. Check handsoap
   15. Replace if needed
   16. Check toilet paper supply
   17. Restock if needed
   18. Get key from under the sink
   19. Check paper towels
   20. Restock if needed
   21. Open door
   22. Turn off lights
   23. Go to women's room
   24. Repeat Steps 5–22

B. Cleaning Glass Doors and Glass Case
   1. Get caddy
   2. Get 10 paper towels
   3. Go to front door
   4. Spray inside of door
   5. Wipe off thoroughly
   6. Wipe again with clean towel
   7. Spray the other door
   8. Wipe off thoroughly
   9. Wipe again with clean towel
   10. Go outside
   11. Spray outside door
   12. Wipe off thoroughly
   13. Wipe again with clean towel
   14. Spray other door
   15. Wipe off thoroughly
   16. Wipe again with clean towel
   17. Throw away dirty towels
   18. Go to glass case
   19. Spray glass case
   20. Wipe off glass thoroughly
   21. Wipe again with clean towel
   22. Throw away dirty towels
   23. Return glass cleaner to caddy

24. Every 2–3 days, check glass door
25. Refill glass cleaner as needed

C. Filling the Sinks
   1. Put away clean, dry dishes
   2. Clean out 3 sinks
       a. Remove food scraps
       b. Wipe off with a rag
   3. Rinse out sinks
   4. Locate 3 plugs
   5. Plug sinks
   6. Run hot water in sink #1
   7. Squirt 5 pumps of pink detergent in the sink
   8. Fill sink ¾ full with water
   9. Run warm water in sink #2
   10. Fill sink ¾ full with water
   11. Run hot water in sink #3
   12. Add 4 tablets of Steramin to water in sink #3
   13. Fill sink ¾ full with water
   14. Turn off water

D. Washing the Glass Plates
   1. Get a plate
   2. Pick up a sponge
   3. Wash front of plate
   4. Wash back of plate
   5. Dip in clear water
   6. Remove the plate
   7. Look at plate for food
   8. Repeat Steps 3–7 until all food is gone
   9. Put plate in clear water
   10. Continue washing plates
   11. When all the plates are washed, stack plates in the dish drainer
   12. Continue washing the dishes
   13. Never put glass plates in sanitizer

E. Washing the Glass Bowls
   1. Get a glass bowl
   2. Pick up sponge
   3. Wash inside of bowl
   4. Wash outside of bowl
   5. Dip in clear water
   6. Remove the bowl
   7. Look at the bowl for food
   8. Repeat Steps 3–7 until all food is gone from bowl
   9. Put bowl in clear water
   10. Continue washing bowls until all are washed
   11. Remove one bowl from clear water
   12. Dry with towel
   13. Continue to dry all the bowls
   14. Stack bowls on Coke box
   15. When all bowls are dried, take to cabinet behind counter
   16. Put bowls in cabinet

17. Continue washing the dishes
18. Never put bowls in the sanitizer

F. Washing the Pots.
   1. Pick up steel wool
   2. Get a pot
   3. Wash the inside, bottom of the pot
   4. Wash the inside, sides of the pot
   5. Wash the outside, sides of the pot
   6. Wash the outside, bottom of the pot
   7. Dip pot in clear water
   8. Remove the pot
   9. Look inside pot for food
   10. Look on outside of pot for food
   11. Repeat Steps 3–10 until all food is gone
   12. Put pot in sanitizer
   13. Let sit at least 1 minute
   14. Continue washing the pots
   15. Stack pots on the drain rack
   16. Continue washing the pots and pans

G. Washing the Pans
   1. Get a pan
   2. Pick up steel wool
   3. Wash the inside of the pan
   4. Wash the corners
   5. Wash the backside
   6. Dip in clear water
   7. Remove pan
   8. Look on all sides for remaining food
   9. Repeat Steps 3–8 until all food is gone
   10. Put pan in sanitizer
   11. Repeat Steps 1–10 until all pans are washed

H. Emptying the Sinks
   1. Empty dish pan into sink
   2. Remove all 3 sink stoppers
   3. Put stoppers on the soap dish
   4. Wring out sponges
   5. Wring out rags
   6. Put up steel wool
   7. Wait for water to drain
   8. When drained, clean out sink
   9. Remove food scraps

I. Emptying the Trash
   1. Get 1 large trash bag
   2. Get 2 medium bags
   3. Get 2 small bags
   4. Take bags to front
   5. Remove front green trash can
   6. Store bags on green trash can's handle
   7. Empty trash behind counter into green trash can
   8. Reline empty trash can with medium bag

9. Empty trash at sink into green trash can
10. Reline empty trash can with medium bag
11. Go into restrooms
12. Empty trash can by door into green trash can
13. Reline empty trash can with medium bag
14. Empty trash can under sink into green trash can
15. Remove trash bag from green trash can
16. Tie off trash bag
17. Remove trash bag from green trash can
18. If heavy, ask co-worker to help
19. Replace liner in green trash can with large bag
20. Return green trash can to front
21. Unlock back door
22. Open back door
23. Carry trash bags to dumpster
24. Open sliding door on dumpster
25. Throw trash bag into dumpster
26. Close sliding door on dumpster
27. Reenter building
28. Lock back door

J. Dust Mopping
   1. Get dust mop
   2. Get dust treatment spray
   3. Spray the mop
   4. Take mop to front door
   5. Dust mop in "S" figure on the front floor
   6. Dust mop in front of counter
   7. Dust mop between carpet areas
   8. Take dust mop to kitchen
   9. Sweep up dirt into dustpan
   10. Empty dustpan
   11. Unlock back door
   12. Shake dust mop
   13. Close back door
   14. Hang up dust mop

K. Mopping the Floors
   1. Get bucket and mop from outside back door
   2. Push to dish sink
   3. Put detergent in the bucket
   4. Run water until hot
   5. Fill white pail with water
   6. Dump into bucket
   7. Continue Steps 5–6 until bucket is ¾ full
   8. Put wringer on
   9. Put mop in bucket
   10. Push to front
   11. Wring out mop
   12. Mop floor behind counter
   13. Mop in "S" pattern
   14. Mop floor in front
   15. Mop in "S" pattern

16. Mop floor in front of counter
17. Mop in "S" pattern
18. Mop floor between carpets
19. Mop in "S" pattern
20. Rinse mop in bucket

L. Vacuuming the Floor
1. Get vacuum cleaner
2. Take to front
3. Make sure no customers remain
4. Plug in vacuum in the smoking section
5. Vacuum carpet
6. Unplug when done
7. Plug in vacuum in the nonsmoking section
8. Unroll 2 rugs on the carpeted area
9. Vacuum 2 rugs
10. Return 2 rugs to right areas
11. Vacuum nonsmoking section
12. Unplug vacuum
13. Wrap cord on vacuum
14. Return vacuum to back

4. Silverware Roller

Time	Sequence of Activities
9:00 a.m.	Punch in
9:00–9:15	Set up work station
9:15–10:30	Clean chairs
10:30–10:45	Break
10:45–Noon	Roll silverware
Noon–12:30	Break
12:30–1:55	Roll silverware
1:55–2:00	Punch out

Key Related Tasks

A. Punching In
1. Wash hands
2. Go to clock-in station
3. Touch "Clock-in" key
4. Touch "9" key
5. Touch "Enter"
6. Touch "Enter"
7. Touch "Enter"

B. Setting Up Work Area
1. Clean off table
2. Wipe tables (as needed)
3. Ask manager or co-worker for napkins
4. Ask manager or co-worker for bin
5. Organize napkins
6. Organize silverware
7. Move chairs

C. Rolling Silverware
1. Pick up knife
2. Put knife on napkin, horizontally
3. Pick up forks
4. Put forks on napkin, horizontally
5. Fold napkin over silverware
6. Hold silverware in napkin
7. Tightly roll silverware
8. Fold in side
9. Fold in other side
10. Finish rolling silverware and napkin
11. Put napkins with silverware in the bin

D. Cleaning the Chairs
1. Ask co-worker for bucket of sanitizer
2. Clean sides of chair with Windex and a toothbrush
3. Wipe down the chair using a rag and sanitizer
4. Wipe top of back first
5. Wipe arms of chair
6. Wipe seat of chair
7. Wipe legs and crossbar of chair
8. Go to next chair; repeat Steps 2–7 until done

5. Fast Food Order Taker

Time	Sequence of Activities
11:00 a.m.	Punch in
11:00–11:05	Set up work station
11:05–3:00	Take lunch orders
3:00–3:05	Close work station
3:05–3:10	Punch out

Key Related Tasks

A. Entering Normal Lunch Order (not a combo)
1. Greet customer

    2. Ask customer for order
    3. Answer questions regarding menu items
    4. Press food item
    5. Press correct size if nuggets or wings
    6. Ask for sauce if nuggets
    7. Press number corresponding to sauce of choice
    8. Press correct size key
    9. Press fries key
   10. Press correct drink size key
   11. Press correct drink
   12. If special preparation, follow Steps 13–15;
       Press grill
   13. Press food item to be specially prepared
   14. Press appropriate combination of words
   15. Press grill
   16. Press bonus items
   17. Follow Steps 4–16 until entire order is entered
   18. Review order for errors
   19. Correct errors
   20. Press total
   21. Tell customer the total
   22. Tell customer to pay at next window

B. Entering Lunch Combos
    1. Answer questions about combos
    2. Press correct combo button
    3. Press super combo if supersized
    4. Ask for drink of choice
    5. Press medium if regular combo
    6. Press large if supersized
    7. Press drink choice
    8. If special preparation, follow Steps 9–11
    9. Press grill
   10. Press correct combo item
   11. Press appropriate combination of words
   12. Press grill

C. Entering Child's Meal
    1. Press correct child's meal
    2. Ask for sauce choice if nuggets
    3. Enter # corresponding to choice of sauce
    4. Ask for choice of drink
    5. Press child
    6. Press correct drink
       If apple juice, follow Steps 7–14
    7. Press grill
    8. Press child
    9. Press drink
   10. Press plain
   11. Press grill
   12. Press A.J.
   13. Press promo
   14. Press A.J.

Special preparation

15. Press grill
16. Press child's meal
17. Press appropriate words
18. Press grill

D. Entering Senior Citizen Drink with a Food Item
    1. Enter food item
    2. Press small
    3. Press coffee, soft drink, or iced tea
    4. Ask for #'s of cream, sugar, or Equal, if coffee
    5. Enter correct #'s of cream, sugar, Equal
    6. Press 00 to exit
    7. Press promo
    8. Press small
    9. Press drink that was ordered

E. Entering Senior Citizen Drink Without a Food Item
    1. Press senior coffee
    2. Press #1 if senior drink
    3. Press #2 if senior coffee

Case Study

Latonia is an 18-year-old with a primary disability of severe emotional/psychiatric disorder paired with a secondary disability of mental retardation. She has good communication skills and works well with adults. She is prone to angry outbursts at perceived slights in social situations. Latonia's mother has moderate mental retardation and poor communication skills. A community mental health case manager assists Latonia and her mother with educational and daily living decisions.

Latonia is currently enrolled in a supported employment program through her school. She is a cafeteria assistant in an elementary school in her neighborhood. Her wages are provided through a federally funded vocational special needs program.

A situational assessment yielded interesting data regarding Latonia's almost normative work rate. Latonia was able to initiate and complete routine tasks, such as washing trays and pans, wiping tables, and stocking cookies and snack foods.

She displayed deficits in immediate responses to unexpected spills or to food requests that deviated from the posted menu. Latonia also seemed to enjoy watching children's arguments, to a point of interference with her work rate. She would go into a trancelike state as she watched scuffles escalate.

Latonia has applied for a permanent part-time position with the school system. Her employment specialist, mental health worker, and DRS counselor are developing a support system for Latonia at work and at home. The school system is eager to hire Latonia, as she is usually reliable.

Latonia's employment specialist has instituted a management system for Latonia at work. She works in a corner section of the cafeteria during the busiest periods. She is away from the children while she scrubs pots and trays. Latonia works in the public sections during the quietest lunch periods and is always paired with an adult worker. Latonia follows her assigned schedule well and has made a good adjustment. The cafeteria manager is supporting Latonia's quest for permanent employment.

Individual Transition Plan 4

Student Profile

Latonia is an 18-year-old with a primary disability of severe emotional/psychiatric disorder paired with a secondary disability of mental retardation. She has good communication skills and works well with adults.

Individual Transition Plan

Student's Name Latonia S. Jennins

  First M.I. Last

Birthdate 04/16/79 School Wadford High School

Student's ID No. 61 ITP Conference Date 05/11/97

Participants

Name	Position
Latonia	Student
Nancy	Mom
Ray	MH/MR Caseworker
Susan	Teacher
Kate	Employment Specialist

Individual Transition Plan 4

I. Career and Economic Self-Sufficiency	
1. Employment Goal	Permanent part-time position as cafeteria assistant
Level of present performance	Part-time supported employment
Steps needed to accomplish goal	1. Make application to school system. 2. Bring video of Latonia's on-the-job skills to interview. 3. DRS and MH workers accompany Latonia to interview.
Date of completion	3/98
Person(s) responsible for implementation	Latonia, Kate, DRS, Teacher
2. Vocational Education/Training Goal	Continue training through EFE through 6/98.
Level of present performance	1. Decrease on-campus in-class time from 5 hours to 1 hour 2. Increase time at worksite to 4 hours daily by 6/98.
Steps needed to accomplish goal	1. Apply for job. 2. Increase hours in increments. 3. Provide support/wean support.
Date of completion	6/98
Person(s) responsible for implementation	Employment Specialist
3. Postsecondary Education Goal	N/A
Level of present performance	N/A

Individual Transition Plan 4

Steps needed to accomplish goal	N/A
Date of completion	N/A
Person(s) responsible for implementation	N/A

4. Financial/Income Needs Goal	Latonia will open a bank account in her name.
Level of present performance	Receives SSI; puts money in Mom's account. Case manager is payee.
Steps needed to accomplish goal	1. Obtain savings account application. 2. Work with local bank, Social Security Administration for changes. 3. Teach budgeting in school.
Date of completion	11/98
Person(s) responsible for implementation	Latonia, MH/MR Caseworker, Teacher

II. Community Integration and Participation

5. Independent Living Goal	Latonia will live with her family and explore alternatives.
Level of present performance	Same as above. Latonia lives with her mother, aunt, and uncle in a duplex. Her older cousins live nearby and provide ongoing support.
Steps needed to accomplish goal	1. Latonia and her mother will meet with Ray, the MH/MR case manager, to discuss residential options. 2. Latonia will visit local supported living residences with Ray and Mom by 6/98.
Date of completion	6/30/98
Person(s) responsible for implementation	Latonia, MH/MR Caseworker, Mom

Individual Transition Plan 4

6. Transportation/Mobility Goal	N/A
Level of present performance	N/A
Steps needed to accomplish goal	N/A
Date of completion	N/A
Person(s) responsible for implementation	N/A
7. Social Relationships Goal	Latonia will seek assistance in an appropriate manner.
Level of present performance	Interrupts, curses when anxious, "spaces out"
Steps needed to accomplish goal	1. Role playing with counselor. 2. Practice at work in nonthreatening situations.
Date of completion	Ongoing
Person(s) responsible for implementation	Latonia, Employment Specialist, MH Worker
8. Recreation/Leisure Goal	N/A
Level of present performance	N/A
Steps needed to accomplish goal	N/A

Individual Transition Plan 4

Date of completion	N/A
Person(s) responsible for implementation	N/A

III. Personal Competence

9. Health/Safety Goal	N/A
Level of present performance	N/A
Steps needed to accomplish goal	N/A
Date of completion	N/A
Person(s) responsible for implementation	N/A

10. Self-Advocacy/Future Planning	N/A
Level of present performance	N/A
Steps needed to accomplish goal	N/A
Date of completion	N/A
Person(s) responsible for implementation	N/A

Student Career Preference

Food Service Worker/Assistant

Individual Transition Plan 4

Student's Major Transition Needs

1. Permanent part-time employment
2. Anger management
3.
4.
5.
6.
7.
8.
9.

Additional Notes

Clerical Occupations

◆ ◆ ◆ ◆ ◆ ◆ ◆ ◆ ◆ ◆ ◆ ◆ ◆ ◆ ◆ ◆ ◆ ◆ ◆ ◆

Description of Domain

The *Dictionary of Occupational Titles* defines clerical occupations as those concerned with "making, classifying, and filing primarily verbal records. This domain includes activities such as transmitting and receiving data by machines equipped with a typewriter-like keyboard, cold-type typesetting, word processing, and operating machines to duplicate records, correspondence, and reports; to emboss data on metal or plastic plates for addressing and similar identification purposes; to sort, fold, insert, seal, address, and stamp mail; and to open envelopes" (p. 171).

JOB DESCRIPTIONS

1. General Office Aide

Time	Sequence of Activities
10:00 a.m.	Sign in
10:05–Noon	Make and distribute copies
Noon–12:30	Break
12:30–2:25	Make and distribute copies
2:30	Sign out
	*Note: If no copy work is needed, report to supervisor for directions.

Key Related Tasks

    A. Making Copies Using the Automatic Feeder
        1. Go to copy request box
        2. Remove copy request form and materials for today
        3. Look at document to be copied and determine if original is legal size (long) or letter size (short)

4. Adjust document feed tray to appropriate size
   - Move document guide plate to line marked 8½ for legal-size originals
   - Move document guide plate to line marked 11 for letter-size originals
5. Look at document to be copied and determine if the original is one-sided or two-sided
6. Press button under "original" on left side of control panel to light up one-sided or two-sided accordingly
7. Refer to copy request form to determine whether one- or two-sided copy is wanted
8. Press button under "copy" to light up one-sided or two-sided, accordingly
9. Refer to copy request form to determine the number of copies needed
10. Press number of copies requested using the number panel
11. Place the original(s) on the document feed tray
    - face down
    - in correct page order
    - up to 50 pages
12. Touch edges of the original to the two document guide plates
13. Press round green button to start copying
14. When machine stops running, remove originals from the document feed tray
15. Put a paper clip on the upper left side of originals
16. Remove copies from the right side of the machine
17. Refer to copy request form
18. Staple or clip copies according to instructions
19. Refer to copy request form for name of person who requested the work
20. File the original and copies in that person's mailbox

B. Sorting When Making Several Sets of the Original Document
   1. Follow Steps 1–4 above
   2. Press button under "Sort" until sort lights up
   3. Follow Steps 9–20 (*When sort mode is selected, the number of copies should be 20 or less.)

C. Copying from a Book
   1. Go to copy request box
   2. Remove requests for today
   3. Read the copy request form to identify the number of copies
   4. Enter number of copies to be made using number panel
   5. Lift copier cover
   6. Place book print side facing down
   7. Align book binding with book symbol at top of glass
   8. Lower copier cover
   9. Press round green button to start copying
   10. When machine stops running, remove book
   11. Staple or clip copies according to instructions
   12. Refer to copy request form for name of person who requested the work
   13. File the original and copies in that person's mailbox

2. File Clerk

Time	Sequence of Activities
9:00–11:00 a.m.	• Alphabetize and file • Check for inpatient accounts on computer • Purge files
11:00–11:15	Break
11:15–1:00	• Alphabetize and file • Check for inpatient accounts on computer • Purge files

Key Related Tasks

A. Alphabetizing Outpatient Box
   1. Find the D's
   2. Pull them out of box
   3. Alphabetize the D's
   4. Put them back in box
   5. Repeat Steps 1–4 for E, F, G, H, I, and J

B. Merging Outpatients into Files
   1. Pull D's out of box
   2. Go to file cabinets located in the back
   3. Pull appropriate D files
   4. Go back to desk
   5. Merge appropriate invoices in files
   6. Go back to file cabinets
   7. Put merged files into appropriate positions
   8. Pull your next files
   9. Repeat Steps 4–8 until finished with D's
   10. Pull E's out of box
   11. Repeat Steps 2–9 for E's
   12. Pull F's out of box
   13. Repeat Steps 2–9 for F's
   14. Pull G's out of box
   15. Repeat Steps 2–9 for G's
   16. Pull H's out of box
   17. Repeat Steps 2–9 for H's
   18. Pull I's out of box
   19. Repeat Steps 2–9 for I's
   20. Pull J's out of box
   21. Repeat Steps 2–9 for J's

C. Filing Inpatients
   1. Find appropriate letters and lift out of box
   2. Alphabetize each letter set

3. Go back to files
4. Alphabetically refile inpatients
5. Go back to desk

D. Purging Computer Files
   1. Find the numbers with S, K, T, M
   2. Punch in the number using the correct keys
   3. Push enter
   4. Verify name and number
   5. Key in "x"
   6. Check screen for inpatient
   7. If yes, write a check by the name
   8. If no, skip it
   9. Repeat Steps 2–8 above

3. Mail Clerk

Time	Sequence of Activities
7:45–8:00 a.m.	Perform first mail run
8:00–10:00	Sort and distribute mail
10:00–10:10	Perform second mail run
10:10–10:20	Break
10:20–Noon	Sort and distribute mail
Noon–12:10	Perform third mail run
12:10–12:30	Sort and distribute mail
12:30–1:15	Lunch
1:15–2:00	Sort and distribute mail
2:00–2:15	Perform fourth mail run
2:15–3:30	Sort and distribute mail
3:30–3:45	Perform fifth mail run or sort mail
	*During downtime complete address changes.

Key Related Tasks

A. Sorting the Mail—Unidentified Mail
   1. If a specific individual's name is on the envelope, pull out the employee directory
   2. Look up the name and write the department on the envelope
   3. Date stamp envelope
   4. Mark on legal pad under "within the company" column
   5. Place in "within the company" box on mail table
   6. If the name is not found in directory, address to Mr. Smith
   7. Date stamp outside of envelope
   8. Mark on legal pad as "other mail" column

B. Sorting the Mail—LOM Mail
1. Open envelopes manually
2. Count the number of envelopes
3. Record # of envelopes under regular mail column on legal pad
4. Remove contents from envelope
5. Date stamp envelope and draft form only
6. Deliver LOM mail to wire basket labeled LOM on back table

C. Sorting the Mail—VUL Checks
1. Open mail with P.O. Box 26842
2. Count the number of envelopes
3. Record count on legal pad under regular mail column
4. Remove contents from envelope
5. Date stamp envelope and contents
6. Staple check to contents and envelope
7. Deliver VUL Checks to wire basket labeled VUL on back table

D. Sorting the Mail—Return Mail
1. Open envelopes with Green markings
2. Count the # of envelopes
3. Record count on legal pad under return column
4. Date stamp envelope
5. Give to Mrs. Jones, unless the envelope is addressed to any other service representative

E. Sorting the Mail—Globe, Traditional, or Universal
1. Open envelopes with Black lines on right side
2. Count number of envelopes
3. Record number on legal pad under regular column
4. Check contents and look at policy number
5. Separate into 3 stacks according to policy number
6. Date stamp envelope
7. Staple check to envelope
8. Place stacks into wire baskets marked Globe, Traditional, or Universal

4. Mail Room Clerk

Time	Sequence of Activities
10:00 a.m.	Go to work area
10:00–Noon	• Fold, stuff, and count envelopes • Process certified letters
Noon–12:30	Lunch
12:30–3:00	• Fold, stuff, and count envelopes • Process certified letters • Run mail processor machine
	*When the above is completed. extra tasks: check in Federal Express, UPS, etc.; flap mail; weigh large envelopes; count memos; stamp addresses; match certified letter receipts.

Key Related Tasks

A. Running Mail Processor Machine
1. Determine type of mail to be run
2. Hit stop button
3. Hit "1" and enter
4. Hit "1st postage U.S. mail" key and enter
5. For price, punch in number amount and hit enter
6. For labels, hit blue key on top of machine
7. Double-check sealer; change if needed
8. Put stack of mail to be loaded
9. Press start
10. Keep mail in order (if needed)
11. Put mail in trays

B. Checking in Federal Express, UPS, Etc.
1. Review receipt
2. Count packages
3. Sign forms

C. Flapping Mail
1. Separate sealed and unsealed envelopes
2. Stack unsealed mail with flaps nested in previous envelope
3. Take stacks to mail machine

D. Weighing Large Envelopes
1. Pick up letter from bin
2. Put on scale
3. Note price
4. If over $2.90, write on envelope
5. Put priority stickers on

E. Counting Memos
1. Count memos according to department numbers
2. Put department name and number of memos on yellow Post-it
3. Put Post-it on divided memos
4. Separate memos with paper clips or rubber bands
5. Follow department listing and check off departments as you go

F. Stamping Addresses on Light Green Form
1. Get stack of light green certified letter forms
2. Using address stamp, stamp black ink pad
3. Stamp address on form

G. Matching Certified Letter Receipts
1. Sort green receipts according to date
2. Pick out white and green receipts of same date
3. Match receipts according to article number
4. Staple together
5. Keep together according to date

H. Processing Certified Letters
1. Determine if letter has a mailing tag
2. Fill out green and white form
3. Stamp if necessary
4. Fill out light green form (if necessary)
5. Attach certified sticker
6. Attach light green form (if necessary)
7. Weigh if needed
8. Record price

I. Folding Letters
1. Get POR's out of box
2. Pick up letters
3. Remove rubber band
4. Stamp all sheets
5. Pick up single letter
6. Remove paper clip
7. Fold top of letter
8. Fold bottom of letter
9. Check that address shows through
10. Flip and tape
11. Stack and keep in order
12. Count and record cost
13. Clean area

Case Study

Maggie is a 17-year-old who, at age 12, sustained a head injury as the result of a motor vehicle accident. Maggie had always been a leader in elementary and middle schools, maintaining an A average. She excelled in field hockey, played tenor saxophone in the middle school symphonic band, and was well liked by peers and adults. After the accident, Maggie was comatose for 15 days. Upon her return to school after a year in a specialized rehabilitation facility, Maggie was assigned to a combination of resource special education and inclusive classes. She has a part-time assistant for notetaking and is learning to use a voice-activated laptop computer as well. She currently maintains a C average in her classes.

As a result of the injury, Maggie experiences right-hand ataxia, left-side weakness (hemiplegia), and gait instability. Her cognitive impairments are in the areas of short-term memory, attention and concentration, and social skills. She has, in the past, received short-term counseling for depression and suicidal ideation. The counseling was terminated due to Maggie's short-term memory deficits.

Maggie's parents are divorced, and she lives with her father. Her mother has remarried and lives in another state. Maggie's father is an optician and is very involved with her transition planning. He has accepted Maggie's disability and her desire to work and not attend college, after graduation. During the past 18 months, Maggie has worked part time as a dishwasher, sales associate in a craft store, and receptionist in her father's office. Through these experiences, Maggie has learned that she desires office work.

Maggie was assigned an employment specialist through DRS after a transition planning meeting. She and the specialist determined the most appropriate employment sites within a certain radius of Maggie's home. Her father agreed to provide all transportation. Maggie applied and was hired for a part-time office clerk in a large medical facility. Her hours were from 4:00 to 8:00 p.m. on Mondays and Wednesdays and from 9:00 a.m. to 1:00 p.m. on Saturdays. Maggie planned to apply for full-time status after graduation. Maggie chose this job because of the "prestigious" reputation associated with medicine and because she could dress up for work. Also, there were several career advancement opportunities available within the medical facility.

Maggie's duties included sorting documents by file numbers and filing documents. The file system was a color-coded numerical system, with each number 0 to 9 represented by a different color. Accounts were filed based on the last two numbers of the six-digit account number in sections 00 to 99, then reordered by the first four numbers. Maggie reached skill acquisition by the end of her third week but her production rate was still low. Her ataxia contributed to her slow pace. The employment specialist developed a mobile workspace for Maggie with a spare dietary tray on wheels. Because it was also adjustable, Maggie could sit or stand to alleviate fatigue. Her work rate rose an additional 40% with this simple accommodation.

After 5 weeks on the job, Maggie's supervisor received complaints from co-workers that Maggie was getting "too friendly." The complaints indicated that Maggie was touching male co-workers almost daily. Prior to this job placement, Maggie's IEP case manager had developed a contract addressing this issue. Maggie readily signed the contract, agreeing to keep an arm's distance from male co-workers. A meeting was scheduled with the supervisor, employment specialist, and Maggie. The contract was revisited, and the supervisor warned Maggie that the next incident might result in termination. Maggie was tearful and apologetic. Two months went by without incident, until Maggie received a telephone call at home that she did not need to report to work any longer. It seemed that a male co-worker reported that Maggie followed him to the break room every day or to his car after her shift was completed. He found her waiting there twice. Maggie denied the sexually harassing behavior, insisting that she was "just looking for a prom date." The transition planning team has reconvened to assist Maggie with postsecondary options and to deal with the employment termination.

Individual Transition Plan 5

Student Profile

Maggie is a 17-year-old who at age 12 sustained a head injury as the result of a motor vehicle accident. She currently maintains a C average in her classes with an instructional assistant for note taking. She is learning to use a voice-activated computer. She was recently terminated from a job and has requested assistance to develop appropriate social skills in an employment setting.

Individual Transition Plan

Student's Name ___Maggie Stewart_____
　　　　　　　　　　　First　　　　　　　　　　M.I.　　　　　　　　　Last

Birthdate ___1/2/80_____　School ___Pine View High School_____

Student's ID No. ___72_____　ITP Conference Date ___11/7/99_____

Participants

Name	Position
Maggie	Student
Dr. Stewart	Father
Joe Scott	DRS Counselor
Kate Mullins	Teacher, Supported Employment Services (SES)
Sheila Smith	Employment Specialist
Caroline Hawkins	Mental Health Counselor, Community Services Board (CSB)

Individual Transition Plan 5

I. Career and Economic Self-Sufficiency

1. Employment Goal	Maggie will obtain full-time competitive employment with supported employment.
Level of present performance	Part-time employee; recently terminated
Steps needed to accomplish goal	1. Seek job applications independently. 2. Obtain employment. 3. Abide by company rules and regulations.
Date of completion	6/98
Person(s) responsible for implementation	Maggie, DRS Counselor, Employment Specialist

2. Vocational Education/Training Goal	Maggie will develop and maintain appropriate worker interactions.
Level of present performance	Maggie sometimes engages in inappropriate flirting/touching behaviors with male co-workers.
Steps needed to accomplish goal	1. Enroll in support/behavioral group at local CSB (8-week session). 2. Participate fully; practice new skills with SES teacher. 3. Attain 100% compliance.
Date of completion	Ongoing
Person(s) responsible for implementation	Maggie, MH Counselor, SES Teacher

3. Postsecondary Education Goal	N/A
Level of present performance	N/A

Individual Transition Plan 5

Steps needed to accomplish goal	N/A
Date of completion	N/A
Person(s) responsible for implementation	N/A

4. Financial/Income Needs Goal	N/A
Level of present performance	N/A
Steps needed to accomplish goal	N/A
Date of completion	N/A
Person(s) responsible for implementation	N/A

II. Community Integration and Participation

5. Independent Living Goal	Maggie will live with family/partner.
Level of present performance	Maggie lives with her dad. There are no plans to secure independent housing. Her older sister has offered support for the future as well.
Steps needed to accomplish goal	N/A
Date of completion	N/A
Person(s) responsible for implementation	N/A

Individual Transition Plan 5

6. Transportation/Mobility Goal	Maggie will utilize public transportation for persons with disabilities. The local transit system sponsors CARE: Community transportation for Adults in REhabilitation.
Level of present performance	Maggie requires a great deal of support; Dad drives her to and from work.
Steps needed to accomplish goal	1. Obtain CARE card. 2. Practice utilizing CARE to and from school with support until March. 3. Ride CARE from school to home independently by 6/98.
Date of completion	6/98
Person(s) responsible for implementation	Maggie, Dad
7. Social Relationships Goal	Maggie will develop and maintain socially appropriate relationships with males.
Level of present performance	Maggie sometimes engages in flirtatious interactions with unfamiliar/familiar males.
Steps needed to accomplish goal	1. Enroll in support/behavioral group with a mental health counselor. 2. Attend every session, complete assigned tasks in community, with MH counselor support.
Date of completion	Ongoing
Person(s) responsible for implementation	Maggie, MH counselor
8. Recreation/Leisure Goal	Maggie will maintain YWCA membership with 2 visits weekly.
Level of present performance	Maggie infrequently attends adaptive aerobics at the YWCA; wants to rejoin.
Steps needed to accomplish goal	1. Call for schedule. 2. Pay fee. 3. Attend at least 2 visits per seek by June.

Individual Transition Plan 5

Date of completion	6/98
Person(s) responsible for implementation	Maggie, Dad

III. Personal Competence

9. Health/Safety Goal	N/A
Level of present performance	N/A
Steps needed to accomplish goal	N/A
Date of completion	N/A
Person(s) responsible for implementation	N/A

10. Self-Advocacy/Future Planning	Maggie will develop a plan for her future.
Level of present performance	Maggie lives for the moment. She is very impulsive and does not realize the repercussions of her personal behavior.
Steps needed to accomplish goal	1. Maggie will attend counseling for personal growth 1 hour per week. 2. Maggie will develop a personal journal of cause–effect behaviors for 6 months.
Date of completion	Ongoing
Person(s) responsible for implementation	Maggie, MH Counselor

Student Career Preference

Clerical Assistant

Individual Transition Plan 5

Student's Major Transition Needs

1. Maggie must develop appropriate social behaviors with males.

2. Maggie must abide by rules and regulations of any employment site.

3. Maggie will achieve transportation independence.

4. _____

5. _____

6. _____

7. _____

8. _____

9. _____

Additional Notes

Lodging and Related Services Occupations

◆ ◆

Description of Domain

The *Dictionary of Occupational Titles* defines Lodging and Related Services occupations as those concerned with the "cleaning and upkeep of building interiors and the conveying of passengers and freight by elevator" (p. 247).

JOB DESCRIPTIONS

1. Houseman

Time	Sequence of Activities
8:00 a.m.	Punch in, go to laundry room
8:05–10:00	• Strip rooms • Load washers
10:00–10:15	Break
10:15–Noon	• Strip rooms • Deliver/pick up linen
Noon–12:30	Lunch
12:30–3:45	• Fold linens • Deliver clean linen • Collect dirty linen • Process dirty linen
3:45–4:00	Clean carts
4:00	Punch out

Key Related Tasks

    A. Checking Laundry in Dryer
        1. Go to first dryer located to right of door
        2. Check laundry in dryer
        3. Open dryer door
        4. Touch clothes for dryness

5. If damp, close door
6. If dry, unload laundry into cart

B. Folding and Stacking Towels
   1. Fold bath towels and hand towels in thirds
   2. Fold towel in half
   3. Turn bath mat and fold bath mat in thirds widthwise
   4. Smooth out washcloths and stack
   5. Count items when folded
   6. Write down the quantity or tell co-worker

C. Folding Pillowcases
   1. Straighten one pillowcase
   2. Put another pillowcase on top of it and straighten
   3. Fold both pillowcases in half; straighten
   4. Fold in half
   5. Count stack of pillowcases and multiply by 2
   6. Write down quantity or tell co-worker

D. Loading or Unloading the Washer
   1. Go to washer
   2. If washer is stopped, open door
   3. If empty, load with dirty laundry from basket behind you
   4. Firmly close washer door
   5. Set dial on blanket setting and push button
   6. If full, open door
   7. Pull spring bottom cart to washer
   8. Put laundry into basket
   9. Take basket to dryer(s)

E. Loading or Unloading the Dryer
   1. Go to dryer
   2. If dryer is stopped, open door
   3. If dryer is empty, load laundry
   4. Close door to start
   5. If dryer is full, check laundry in dryer and fold items

2. Runner

Time	Sequence of Activities
10:30 a.m.	Punch in
10:30–10:50	Vacuum big dining room
10:50–11:00	Vacuum little dining room
11:00–11:05	Wipe down bus station
11:05–11:10	Straighten bus station
11:10–11:30	Clean windows
11:30 until done	Collect room service trays
After tray collection	Break down bus cart
End of shift/Punch out	Check with supervisor before leaving

Key Related Tasks

A. Collecting Room Service Trays, Floors 8–10
    1. Locate cart in dishroom
    2. If unable to locate, ask co-worker for assistance
    3. Locate three dishpans near dishwasher
    4. If unable to locate, ask co-worker for assistance
    5. Place three dishpans on cart
    6. Wheel cart to elevator using back hallway
    7. Get on elevator; push 8
    8. Get off elevator at 8th floor
    9. Turn right and place cart by railing
    10. Remove dishpan from cart
    11. Go to Room 29
    12. Collect trays, glasses, etc., from floor; load into dishpan
    13. Repeat Step 12 for rooms 30–32 and 01–28, until you arrive back at your cart
    14. When you return to the cart, place dishpan onto cart
    15. Get on elevator
    16. Push 9
    17. Get off elevator at Floor 9
    18. Repeat Steps 9–14
    19. Get on elevator
    20. Push 10
    21. Get off elevator at Floor 10
    22. Repeat Steps 9–14
    23. Get on elevator
    24. Push L (Lobby)
    25. Get off elevator at lobby
    26. Turn right and go to end of wall
    27. Turn left at end of wall to enter back hallway
    28. Push cart through hallway to kitchen

B. Breaking Down the Cart
1. Wheel cart to dishroom
2. Pick up dishpan on top and place it next to dishwasher
3. Return to cart
4. Pick up dishpan in middle of cart and place it next to dishwasher
5. Return to cart
6. Pick up dishpan on bottom of cart and place it next to dishwasher
7. Wheel cart to storage area

3. Silver Polisher

Time	Sequence of Activities
8:00 a.m.	Sign in
8:00–8:30	Straighten work area and set up work station
8:30–10:30	Polish silver
10:30–10:40	Break
10:40–Noon	Polish silver
Noon–12:45	Break
12:45–2:30	Polish silver
2:30–4:00	Remove polish/store items

Key Related Tasks

A. Going to Work Station
1. Enter through employee door
2. Go to 1st doorway on right
3. Push open stairwell door to right
4. Go up stairs to top
5. Pull open door at top
6. Make a right turn
7. Go through hallway
8. Make a right turn in front of steps to cafeteria
9. Go down hallway
10. Go past room service room
11. Go past fire exit hallway
12. Turn right at 1st doorway
13. Enter manager's office
14. Sign in (See Sign-in Instructions)
15. Exit manager's office
16. Turn left
17. Walk down hallway
18. Make immediate right turn past steps to cafeteria on right
19. Walk toward wall

20. Turn right when close to wall
21. Enter work area

B. Going to Lunch Room
   1. Exit work area
   2. Make immediate left
   3. Make a left at hallway
   4. Walk through hallway
   5. Go past room service room
   6. Go past fire exit hallway
   7. Turn right at first door
   8. Enter manager's office
   9. Sign out (See Sign-out Instructions)
  10. Exit manager's office
  11. Turn left outside the door
  12. Go down the hallway
  13. Turn right at steps to cafeteria
  14. Walk up stairs
  15. Pull open door at top
  16. Enter cafeteria

C. Going Back to Work Station
   1. Go to the middle door
   2. Slowly push open the door
   3. Descend stairs
   4. Make immediate left
   5. Make another immediate left
   6. Deposit tray/trash
   7. Turn around ½ circle
   8. Turn left
   9. Walk down hallway
  10. Go past room service room
  11. Go past fire exit hallway
  12. Turn right at first door
  13. Enter manager's office
  14. Sign in (See Sign-in After Lunch Instructions)
  15. Repeat Steps 15–21 of Task A

D. Signing In
   1. Go to manager's office
   2. Locate sign-in sheet
   3. Find name on sheet (last name is first); if you cannot find your name, write in your name
   4. In second block write date of hire
   5. Look at watch/clock for time and write in time in third block
   6. Write initials next to time in fourth block
   7. Go to work station (repeat Steps 15–21 of Task A)

E. Signing Out
   1. Go to manager's office
   2. Locate sign-in sheet
   3. Find name on sheet
   4. Look at watch/clock for time, and write in time in the 9th block
   5. *Sign name* next to the time in the 10th block

F. Setting Up Work Station
   1. Turn on light
   2. Turn on fan
   3. Look at checklist
   4. Locate bucket
   5. Take bucket to sink
   6. Fill bucket ½ full
   7. Return to work area
   8. Put bucket on the floor beside chair
   9. Locate sponges
   10. Put 2 sponges in bucket
   11. Locate toothbrushes
   12. Put 1 toothbrush in bucket
   13. If toothbrushes are not available, see manager
   14. Locate dry rags
   15. Put 2 rags in bucket
   16. Put dry rag on table
   17. If rags not available, go downstairs to uniform department and request rags
   18. Locate silver polish
   19. If polish not available, see manager
   20. Open silver polish container
   21. Put container on work table
   22. Get a piece of silver to be polished and put on table
   23. Put on rubber gloves
   24. Sit down at work table

4. Linen Sorter

Time	Sequence of Activities
8:30 a.m.	Sign in
8:30–10:30	Sort linen
10:30–10:45	Break
10:45–11:30	Sort linen
11:30–12:00	Unload truck
12:00–12:45	Lunch
12:45–2:30	Sort linen
2:30–3:00	Unload truck
3:00–3:30	Sort linen
3:30	Sign out

Key Related Tasks

A. Sorting Linens
   1. Go directly across hallway to Linen Room
   2. Arrange 4 bins, side by side

3. Place black nets into bottom of each bin (if available)
4. Put side panels on bins
5. Drape markers over each bin to distinguish linens
6. Check laundry shoot for stuck linens
7. Sort linens into separate bins
   a. brown terry
   b. white terry
   c. blue terry
   d. sheets
   e. pillow cases
8. Compress linens when filled to the rim (get in and stomp)
   a. brown terry
   b. white terry
   c. blue terry
   d. sheets
   e. pillow cases

B. Load Truck
   1. Help truck driver push filled bins to loading dock
   2. Push filled bins up incline to back of truck
   3. Help driver load bins onto truck

C. Unload Truck
   1. Go to loading dock
   2. Walk up incline to back of truck
   3. Enter truck
   4. Locate clean bin
   5. Assist driver with removing bin from back of truck
   6. Roll bins down incline
   7. Line bins up against wall in hallway

5. Housekeeper

Time	Sequence of Activities
9:00–11:00 a.m.	Clean rooms
11:00–11:30	Lunch
11:30–1:30	Clean rooms
1:30–1:40	Break
1:40 Until Done	Clean rooms

Key Related Tasks

A. Getting Bed Linens
   1. Identify bed size
      a. 1 king bed
      b. 2 double beds

    2. Go to housekeeping cart
    3. Get bed linens
       a. 1 king bed—2 beige sheets and 3 beige pillow cases
       b. 2 double beds—4 white sheets and 4 white pillow cases
    4. Take linens into room
    5. Place linens on table

  B. Applying Bottom Sheet
     1. Straighten mattress pad
     2. Pick up one sheet
     3. Go to side of bed
     4. Unfold sheet top to bottom
     5. Lay sheet on side edge of bed
     6. Take one side edge of sheet
     7. Toss sheet across bed
     8. Pull top of sheet toward headboard
     9. Tuck top edge of sheet under head of mattress
    10. Go to other side of bed
    11. Tuck top edge of sheet under head of mattress
    12. Go to foot of bed
    13. Gently pull sheet to foot to remove wrinkles
    14. Tuck edge of sheet under foot to remove wrinkles
    15. Go to side of bed
    16. Gently pull sheet toward you to remove wrinkles
    17. Tuck sheet along side of mattress under the mattress
    18. Go to other side of bed
    19. Gently pull sheet toward you to remove wrinkles
    20. Tuck sheet along side of mattress under the mattress
    21. Smooth sheet with palm of hands to remove all wrinkles
    22. Tuck any excess sheet to make it tight

  C. Applying Top Sheet
     1. Pick up one sheet
     2. Go to side of bed
     3. Unfold sheet top to bottom
     4. Lay sheet on side edge of bed
     5. Lay raw edge of seam facing up
     6. Take one side edge of sheet
     7. Toss sheet across bed
     8. Pull top of sheet toward headboard
     9. Lay top edge of sheet even with mattress edge at head of bed
    10. Go to other side of bed
    11. Lay top edge of sheet even with mattress edge at head of bed
    12. Go to foot of bed
    13. Gently pull sheet to foot to remove wrinkles
    14. Go to side of bed
    15. Gently pull sheet toward you to remove wrinkles
    16. Go to other side of bed
    17. Gently pull sheet toward you to remove wrinkles
    18. Smooth sheet with palm of hands to remove all wrinkles

  D. Applying Blanket
     1. Pick up blanket
     2. Go to side of bed

3. Lay blanket on side edge of bed
4. Lay shiny edge of blanket toward headboard
5. Take one side edge of blanket
6. Toss blanket across bed
7. Pull top of blanket toward headboard
8. Lay top edge of blanket about 6 inches from mattress edge at head of bed
9. Go to other side of bed
10. Lay top edge of blanket about 6 inches from mattress edge at head of bed
11. Go to foot of bed
12. Gently pull blanket to foot to remove wrinkles
13. Gently pull blanket to foot to remove wrinkles
14. Go to side of bed
15. Gently pull blanket toward you to remove wrinkles
16. Go to other side of bed
17. Gently pull blanket toward you to remove wrinkles
18. Smooth blanket with palm of hands to remove all wrinkles

E. Tucking Blanket and Sheet
1. Go to right-side head of bed
2. Fold top edge of sheet over top edge of blanket
3. Tuck side edge of folded sheet and blanket under mattress
4. Go to left-side head of bed
5. Fold top edge of sheet over top edge of blanket
6. Tuck side edge of folded sheet and blanket under mattress
7. Tuck remaining side of sheet and blanket under mattress working toward foot of bed
8. Go to right-side head of bed
9. Tuck remaining side of sheet and blanket under mattress, working toward foot of bed
10. Go to foot of bed
11. Tuck sheet and blanket under mattress

F. Applying Bedspread
1. Pick up bedspread
2. Go to side of bed
3. Lay bedspread on side edge of bed
4. Locate rounded edge of bedspread
5. Lay rounded edge toward foot of bed
6. Lay squared edge toward headboard
7. Take one side edge of bedspread
8. Toss bedspread across bed
9. Pull bottom of bedspread toward floor at foot of bed
10. Go to side of bed
11. Fold top edge of bedspread back about halfway down the bed
12. Go to other side of bed
13. Fold top edge of bedspread back about half way down the bed
14. Line the seams of the bedspread along the edge of the side of the bed, pulling the bedspread into place
15. Put pillow cases on pillows (See task analysis G for task)
16. Place pillows at head of bed
17. Fold bedspread over pillows

18. Tuck bedspread under pillows
19. Push pillows against headboard
20. Smooth bedspread with palm of hands to remove wrinkles
21. Tuck foot/side corners of bedspread

G. Applying Pillow Cases
   1. Pick up one pillow
   2. Pick up one pillow case
   3. Hold pillow, short side, under chin
   4. Insert thumbs inside of pillow case along folded edge
   5. Grasp outer edge of pillow case with other fingers
   6. Place open edge of pillow case over end of pillow
   7. Pull pillow case on pillow, pulling toward your chin
   8. When pillow case is about halfway on, take pillow from chin
   9. Pull pillow case onto pillow by shaking the pillow case up and down until the pillow slides into the case
  10. Lay pillow on bed and flatten out
  11. Tuck excess edges of pillow case into pillow case opening
  12. Lay pillow to the side
  13. Repeat Steps 1–12

H. Vacuuming the Room
   1. Get vacuum
   2. Take vacuum into room
   3. Unwrap cord
   4. Plug vacuum into bathroom outlet
   5. Push vacuum toward windows
   6. Release vacuum handle
   7. Turn vacuum on
   8. Begin vacuuming
   9. Vacuum while backing out of room until vacuuming completed
  10. Turn vacuum off
  11. Unplug vacuum
  12. Wrap cord
  13. Close curtains
  14. Turn lights off
  15. Push vacuum into hallway
  16. Close the door

I. Dusting the Room
   1. Get terry cloth from cart
   2. Spray dusting solution on cloth
      Dust, by wiping left to right using large strokes
     a. Chest of drawers
     b. Television
     c. Table
     d. Headboard(s) of bed(s)
     e. Nightstands
   3. Return cloth to cart

Case Study

Harold is a 16-year-old student with a recent history of damage due to heavy drug involvement. He was using LSD, marijuana, crack, and heroin on a weekly basis. He was also sniffing aerosols and Butane, and ingesting alcohol. He suffers chronic hallucinations, all tactile. Harold frequently complains of feelings of fire on his face or bugs crawling on his back. He has recently returned to a special education/work program from a residential drug rehabilitation facility.

Harold's medications include Wellbutrin for depression and Risperdal for psychotic symptoms. He demonstrates disorganized thinking, and has a Full Scale IQ of 68 on the *Wechsler Adult Intelligence Scale.* The psychologist has noted that Harold's IQ score may be lower due to drug use and depression.

A recent vocational evaluation indicated that Harold has strengths in basic janitorial and service skills. Harold has expressed a strong desire to work and to "make a lot of money." His work coordinator worked with a large hotel near Harold's home to provide a mentor placement. Harold and the work coordinator attended orientation and initial training sessions together in the housekeeping department. Harold was then weaned from the work coordinator to the head housekeeper, a retired Navy person.

Harold has now been working for 4 months. His mentor has indicated that Harold follows his daily schedule on pretyped index cards provided by the work coordinator. Other staff persons redirect Harold when confusion is noted. DRS has offered to provide support during the upcoming summer months. Harold has requested that his final school year placement be at a hotel.

Individual Transition Plan 6

Student Profile

Harold has traumatic brain injury due to excessive illicit drug use.

Individual Transition Plan

Student's Name Harold K. Reardon
                    First   M.I.   Last

Birthdate 06-11-82   School Kingsroad High School

Student's ID No. 4   ITP Conference Date 01-12-97

. . . .

Participants

Name	Position
Harold	Student
Tom/Anna	Parents
Kathy	EFE Coordinator
Alex	Hotel Mentor
Jon	DRS Counselor
Jim	MH Counselor

Individual Transition Plan 6

I. Career and Economic Self-Sufficiency

1. Employment Goal	Part-time supported employment/individual placement
Level of present performance	Harold works part time (through a grant program) at a local hotel. He requires frequent supervision.
Steps needed to accomplish goal	1. Develop/maintain mentorship at hotel. 2. Develop accommodations for Harold through cue cards/staff assistance.
Date of completion	Ongoing until 6/99
Person(s) responsible for implementation	Harold, EFE Coordinator, Mentor

2. Vocational Education/Training Goal	Harold will complete his vocational certificate program.
Level of present performance	Harold has 2 credits toward his vocational certificate. He has expressed enthusiasm for the program.
Steps needed to accomplish goal	1. Develop ongoing cooperation among school/hotel/DRS staff on Harold's behalf. 2. Maintain school/DRS support.
Date of completion	6/99?
Person(s) responsible for implementation	Harold, EFE Coordinator, DRS Counselor

3. Postsecondary Education Goal	N/A
Level of present performance	Harold has expressed no interest in continued education services beyond his certificate program.

Individual Transition Plan 6

Steps needed to accomplish goal	N/A
Date of completion	N/A
Person(s) responsible for implementation	N/A

4. Financial/Income Needs Goal	Harold will be financially independent to maintain services from agencies.
Level of present performance	Harold's parents do not allow him access to his SSI or weekly paychecks. They claim him on income tax.
Steps needed to accomplish goal	1. Remove Harold as deduction on parents' taxes. 2. Assist Harold in opening/maintaining bank account. 3. Assist Harold in budgeting for clothes, CD's, etc.
Date of completion	9/98
Person(s) responsible for implementation	Harold, Parents, MH Counselor

II. Community Integration and Participation

5. Independent Living Goal	Harold will live in a supervised apartment with two room-mates.
Level of present performance	Harold has basic self-care skills. He can launder clothes and microwave foods.
Steps needed to accomplish goal	1. Increase activities of daily living skills at home. 2. Make application for residential services. 3. Meet with Center for Independent Living staff one time per month.
Date of completion	9/98
Person(s) responsible for implementation	Harold, Parents, MH Counselor

Individual Transition Plan 6

6. Transportation/Mobility Goal	Harold will travel a 1-mile radius from his home without getting lost.
Level of present performance	Harold travels to and from school and work with assistance (school bus). He lives ½ mile from hotel.
Steps needed to accomplish goal	1. Develop map system of laminated photo cards with Harold. (Harold will take and laminate pictures, walk through route.) 2. Walk route with Harold until independence occurs.
Date of completion	After 21 trials or 1 month
Person(s) responsible for implementation	EFE Coordinator, Harold, Mother
7. Social Relationships Goal	Harold will develop and maintain friendships with peers and co-workers.
Level of present performance	Harold is sometimes loud and invades others' personal spaces. He recognizes this and is working on "toning it down."
Steps needed to accomplish goal	1. Explore support groups for teens in recovery and/or with TBI. 2. Role-play with counselor.
Date of completion	Ongoing
Person(s) responsible for implementation	Harold, MH Counselor
8. Recreation/Leisure Goal	Harold will join the YMCA.
Level of present performance	Harold has gained weight from psychotropic medication. He wishes to lose weight by June.
Steps needed to accomplish goal	1. Join YMCA swim club (noncompetitive). 2. Go to YMCA at least 3 times per week.

Individual Transition Plan 6

Date of completion	6/98
Person(s) responsible for implementation	Harold, Parents

III. Personal Competence

9. Health/Safety Goal	Harold will take his medication independently.
Level of present performance	Harold currently relies on his mother to dole out daily medication.
Steps needed to accomplish goal	1. Purchase a 7-day plastic pill container. 2. Set up schedule for refills (Saturday night). 3. Mom will monitor.
Date of completion	5/98
Person(s) responsible for implementation	Harold, Parents
10. Self-Advocacy/Future Planning	Harold will seek support for drug addiction.
Level of present performance	Harold currently becomes very agitated by certain drug-related triggers: songs, settings, former friends.
Steps needed to accomplish goal	1. Research Teen Narcotics Anonymous groups in his area. 2. Attend at least 2 meetings weekly.
Date of completion	12/97
Person(s) responsible for implementation	Harold, Parents, MH Counselor

Student Career Preference

Undecided, but leaning toward custodial position.

Individual Transition Plan 6

Student's Major Transition Needs

1. Maintain mental health needs with medication/support.

2. Increase work hours as appropriate.

3.

4.

5.

6.

7.

8.

9.

Additional Notes

Form © 1995 by PRO-ED, Inc.

Plant Farming Occupations

◆ ◆ ◆ ◆ ◆ ◆ ◆ ◆ ◆ ◆ ◆ ◆ ◆ ◆ ◆ ◆ ◆ ◆ ◆ ◆

Description of Domain

The *Dictionary of Occupational Titles* defines Plant Farming occupations as those concerned with "tilling soil; propagating, cultivating, and harvesting plant life; gathering products of plant life; and caring for parks, gardens, and grounds. Service occupations performed in support of these activities are also included" (p. 285).

JOB DESCRIPTIONS

1. Plant Installation Preparer

Time	Sequence of Activities
8:30 a.m.	Punch in
8:30–11:00	Clean plants (other duties as assigned by supervisor)
11:00–11:10	Break
11:10–1:00	Clean plants
1:00–1:30	Lunch
1:30–4:00	Clean plants (other duties as assigned by supervisor)
4:00–4:10	Break
4:10–5:00	Clean plants (other duties as assigned by supervisor)
5:00	Punch out

Key Related Tasks

    A. Installing the Wick System
        1. Gather materials
           a. Bucket of new top soil
           b. Handful of wicks

2. Read the installment sheet for the Wick System
3. Identify plants needed
4. Take one plant listed from holding area
5. Put plant in cement cleaning area
6. Remove plant from original pot
   a. Grab from stem base
   b. Pull from stem
   c. Push the top of the pot
7. Brush off fertilizer with hand
8. Dump out the extra fertilizer in the pot
9. Place new layer of top soil in the base of original pot
10. Take wicks and crisscross through water drainage holes
11. Place original plant in pot with new top soil
12. Take the wicked plant back to holding area

B. Watering Plants
   1. Gather materials
      a. Hose
      b. Appropriate nozzle
      c. Watering can
   2. Lift each plant
   3. Stick finger in soil to check moisture
   4. Water if needed
   5. Water until it comes out drainage holes (if very dry)
   6. Water only surface (if dry)
   7. Go to next plant

C. Installing Plants
   1. Load truck with plants going to the installation
   2. Ride in the truck
   3. Bring in containers
   4. Remove stickers from container
   5. Replace plants in new containers
   6. Unload new plants from truck
   7. Assemble hanging baskets
      a. Hook in chains with "S" hook
      b. Place plant in hanging basket
   8. Place plants in display area
   9. Clean up with dust buster or hand vacuum

D. Hanging up the Compressor
   1. Locate a wash bucket
   2. Fill bucket with water
   3. Squirt in soap
   4. Put end of hose in soapy water
   5. Stir soapy water
   6. Plug in compressor
   7. Prime
   8. Turn switch on
   9. Grab nozzle
   10. Point nozzle away from you
   11. Unscrew red spray cap
   12. Spray both sides of plant
   13. Stir and go to the next plant

E. Maintaining Plants at Account 1
    1. Gather materials
        a. 2 large trash bags
        b. Gold key for bank's hoses
        c. Extra long garden hose
        d. Pruners and scissors
    2. Place materials in vehicle
    3. Go to job site
    4. Drive to back of building
    5. Turn on left back soaker hose
    6. Turn on right back soaker hose
    7. Maintain right back flower bed
        a. Weed entire bed
        b. Prune and pick dead materials from plants
        c. Water all 4 raised beds
    8. Maintain left back flower bed
        a. Weed entire bed
        b. Prune and pick dead materials from plants
        c. Water all 4 raised beds
    9. Turn off left soaker hose
    10. Turn off right soaker hose
    11. Gather materials/put in vehicle
    12. Drive to front of building
    13. Maintain front flower bed
        a. Weed entire bed
        b. Prune and pick dead material from plants
    14. Water front bed if needed
        a. Take long hose from vehicle
        b. Locate spigot
        c. Use gold key to turn on water
    15. Put materials back in van
    16. Drive back to greenhouse

F. Cleaning Installation
    1. Go to bulletin board in hold area
    2. Write down on list all account names
    3. Go to interior office
    4. Look at calendar inside of door
    5. Place date next to account name on list
    6. Prioritize dates when installations need to be done
    7. Go back to bulletin board in hold area
    8. Identify account sheet that is #1 priority
    9. Locate plants
    10. Look up "Cleaning Instructions" in book
    11. Follow instructions to clean plant
    12. Check off when completed by initialing
    13. If only partially completed, place one initial
    14. Repeat Steps 10–12 until all plants are clean
    15. Go to bulletin board in old hold area
    16. Identify account sheet that is #2 priority
    17. Repeat Steps 9–14 for other plants

G. Cleaning Replacements
   1. Walk to replace envelope in hold area
   2. Pull 1 invoice from "in" envelope
   3. Locate plant by account, plant name, pot size
   4. Clip replacement sheet to "in" envelope
   5. Write initials on replacement sheet
   6. Look up plant and follow directions in book
   7. Carry plant by pot to cleaning area
   8. Check for bugs
   9. Check for soil level
   10. Cover soil
   11. Spray rag, not plants; don't spray any other plants
   12. Handle plants delicately
   13. Rinse plant if needed
   14. Let dry and recheck
   15. Place 1 hand beneath leaf; use smooth gentle strokes
   16. Place check mark next to initials when complete
   17. Repeat Steps 6–15 until all plants are cleaned

H. Cleaning Plants
   1. Gather materials from cleaning shelf
      a. Rags for cleaning
      b. Leaf shine
   2. Dilute leaf shine (1 oz. leaf shine and 8 oz. water)
   3. Sit in chair in holding area
   4. Place plant in front of you
   5. Handle 1 leaf at a time
   6. Stabilize leaf with 1 hand
   7. Wipe off leaf with leaf shine with other hand
   8. Wipe in the direction of leaf skeleton

2. Greenhouse Assistant

Time	Sequence of Activities
2:00 p.m.	Sign in
2:00–3:30	Fill pots or repot cuttings
3:30–3:45	Break
3:45–5:00	Fill pots or repot cuttings
5:00	Sign out

Key Related Tasks

A. Filling Plant Pots with Soil
   1. Line up three rows of five pots

2. Pick up shovel with dominant hand
3. Scoop soil and dump into pot 1
4. Repeat until pot 1 is full
5. Repeat Steps 2–4 for pots 2–15

B. Repotting Cuttings
1. Get pot 1 with soil
2. Pick up cutting with preferred hand
3. Position cutting over center of pot
4. Remove handful of soil with other hand
5. Place cutting down and place soil around the cutting
6. Add soil, if needed
7. Pat down soil around plant to hold in place
8. Repeat Steps 1–7 for pots 2–15

3. Horticultural Worker

Time	Sequence of Activities
12:30 p.m.	Notify supervisor of arrival
12:30–1:30	Remove buds or water plants
1:30–2:00	Break
2:00–4:30	Remove buds or water plants
4:30	Notify supervisor of leaving

Key Related Tasks

A. Removing Dead Buds from Plant
1. Get empty flower pot
2. Go to plants station
3. Start at the top of the table
4. Look at plant and inspect buds
5. Determine if bud is green (alive) or brown and hard (dead)
6. If dead, place fingers of dominant hand in pincer grip at point where bud joins the stem
7. Pinch off dead bud
8. Place dead bud in flower pot
9. Continue above until all plant stems are debudded
10. Move to next plant and repeat Steps 4–9 above

B. Watering Plants
1. Get hose
2. Go to left side head of bed
3. Turn nozzle on
4. Water plant(s)

  5. Step to right
  6. Water plant(s)
  7. Step to right
  8. Water plant(s)
  9. Continue Steps 7 and 8 to end of bed
 10. Go to next bed

 Case Study

Aaron is a 16-year-old with a primary disability of mild neurological disorder, which manifests itself as a learning disability and a secondary emotional disability. Aaron has, for the past 3 years, dressed in clothing mildly reminiscent of Raggedy Andy. He has worn stockings with black and white wide stripes, sailor blouses, and jaunty hats to school. Although he is an object of ridicule among his peers, Aaron seems not to care. He has recently begun to dye his pixie haircut with varying hues of pink, green, and orange. He also carries a Barbie lunchbox.

Aaron was referred to the work coordinator at an alternative high school. As he approached his 17th birthday, Aaron had accumulated only 6 Carnegie units toward graduation. His attendance was poor; he frequently left his campus to go home. He had expressed a mild interest in the education for employment program as an alternative to a traditional diploma track.

The work coordinator met with Aaron for four 30-minute sessions. An interest inventory was completed, as well as conversational probes. As a result, Aaron was taken on a tour of the alternative school's horticulture program. He expressed a desire to work with plants, and a temporary placement was made in the school's greenhouse. The horticulture teacher and work coordinator have emphasized basic employment skills with Aaron, and he has responded well. Aaron has now completed two quarters with the horticulture work program. He was a member of a team of students that successfully developed an exhibit for a local garden show in which a second-place ribbon was awarded.

Aaron has now been hired by a local plant wholesaler to assist with plugs, or tiny plants, for market preparation. Aaron works in the greenhouse and has little to no contact with the public, which is his preference. He plans to complete the 2-year vocational certificate program and maintain his job at the greenhouse.

Individual Transition Plan 7

Student Profile

Aaron is a 16-year-old with a primary disability of mild neurological disorder, which manifests itself as a learning disability and a secondary emotional disability.

Individual Transition Plan

Student's Name <u>Aaron S. Pullen</u>
                          First   M.I.   Last

Birthdate <u>11/12/81</u>   School <u>Beaucraft Technical Center</u>

Student's ID No. <u>3</u>   ITP Conference Date <u>04/30/97</u>

. . . .

Participants

Name	Position
Aaron	Student
Ron/Mary	Parents
Joe	Work Coordinator
Meg	Horticulture Teacher
Eric	Plant Wholesaler Manager
Joan	DRS Counselor

Individual Transition Plan 7

I. Career and Economic Self-Sufficiency

1. Employment Goal	Full-time competitive employment
Level of present performance	Aaron is working part time in a competitive placement in a local business.
Steps needed to accomplish goal	Aaron and the Work Coordinator will meet with the Plant Wholesaler to set up a schedule for increasing hours at work.
Date of completion	6/98
Person(s) responsible for implementation	Aaron, Work Coordinator, Plant Wholesaler
2. Vocational Education/Training Goal	Complete vocational certificate
Level of present performance	Aaron has completed three fourths of his first year in a 2-year vocational certification program.
Steps needed to accomplish goal	Stay in program until 6/99; meet with Work Coordinator at job site one time per month.
Date of completion	6/99
Person(s) responsible for implementation	Work Coordinator, Aaron
3. Postsecondary Education Goal	Aaron does not wish to pursue further educational services.
Level of present performance	N/A

Individual Transition Plan 7

Steps needed to accomplish goal	N/A
Date of completion	N/A
Person(s) responsible for implementation	N/A

4. Financial/Income Needs Goal	Aaron and his family do not wish to pursue assistance in this area.
Level of present performance	N/A
Steps needed to accomplish goal	N/A
Date of completion	N/A
Person(s) responsible for implementation	N/A

II. Community Integration and Participation

5. Independent Living Goal	Aaron will live with friend/partner.
Level of present performance	Aaron has basic activity of daily living skills appropriate to his age and ability. He has weaknesses in budgeting.
Steps needed to accomplish goal	Aaron will use a computer program to budget paychecks. His parents will charge room and board.
Date of completion	Ongoing
Person(s) responsible for implementation	Aaron/Parents

Individual Transition Plan 7

6. Transportation/Mobility Goal	Aaron will maintain driving skills.
Level of present performance	Aaron has a driver's license.
Steps needed to accomplish goal	Aaron will borrow his parents' car when appropriate.
Date of completion	Ongoing
Person(s) responsible for implementation	Aaron/Parents
7. Social Relationships Goal	Aaron will develop and maintain friendships.
Level of present performance	Aaron has a small circle of like-minded friends who attend various schools. He socializes one time per month.
Steps needed to accomplish goal	Aaron will attend an acting class located at a community college with two friends.
Date of completion	6/98
Person(s) responsible for implementation	Aaron
8. Recreation/Leisure Goal	N/A
Level of present performance	Aaron does not need assistance in this area. He plays the guitar with his friends.
Steps needed to accomplish goal	N/A

Individual Transition Plan 7

Date of completion	N/A
Person(s) responsible for implementation	N/A

III. Personal Competence

9. Health/Safety Goal	N/A
Level of present performance	N/A
Steps needed to accomplish goal	N/A
Date of completion	N/A
Person(s) responsible for implementation	N/A

10. Self-Advocacy/Future Planning	Aaron will attend the 1998 Transition Forum with his teacher to increase his knowledge about personal empowerment.
Level of present performance	Aaron has some basic knowledge about his rights in this transition process.
Steps needed to accomplish goal	1. Teacher will notify Aaron of conference dates. 2. Aaron will arrange work schedule.
Date of completion	3/98
Person(s) responsible for implementation	Aaron, Work Coordinator, DRS Counselor

Student Career Preference

Horticulture Assistant

Individual Transition Plan 7

Student's Major Transition Needs

1. Complete vocational certificate program

2. Maintain employment

3. Develop personal advocacy skills

4.

5.

6.

7.

8.

9.

Additional Notes

Information and Message Distribution Occupations

♦ ♦

Description of Domain

The *Dictionary of Occupational Titles* defines Information and Message Distribution occupations as those concerned with the "distribution of information and messages by direct personal or telephone contact, involving such activities as delivering mail, relaying messages by telephone or telegraph equipment, arranging travel accommodations, and directing visitors at reception points" (p. 205).

JOB DESCRIPTIONS

1. Telephone Secretary

Time	Sequence of Activities
10:00 a.m.	Sign in
10:00–Noon	• Give messages to clients • Answer calls and record messages
Noon–12:30	Lunch
12:30–2:30	Answer calls and record messages
2:30–2:45	Break
2:45–4:00	Give messages to clients

Key Related Tasks

A. Signing On
   1. Screen will be black
      a. Type in your name
      b. Press [Return]
   2. Your name will show at top of screen
   3. You are now signed on

B. Answering Phone and Taking Messages
   1. When screen beeps, push line # that shows on screen (line 1, 2, or 3)
   2. Say call phrase
   3. Say person is unavailable (this is their message center, etc.)
   4. Ask if you may take a message
   5. Press Take Message button
   6. Press [1] (or whatever # used that day)
   7. Press [Park] to store message

C. Answering Phone/Message Using Alpha Page
   1. When screen beeps, push line # that shows on screen (line 1, 2, or 3)
   2. Say call phrase
   3. Say person is unavailable (this is their message center, etc.)
   4. Ask if you may take a message
   5. Press [Page] button
   6. Press [1] (or whatever # used that day)
   7. Press [Park] to store message

D. Taking Temporary Information
   1. When screen beeps, press line # that shows on screen (line 1, 2, or 3)
   2. Say call phrase
      (client will state their temporary message)
   3. Press [Take Info] button
   4. Type in message
   5. Press [Stamp]
   6. Press [Special]
   7. Press [Message Taken] to clear screen

E. Clearing Screen if Caller Does Not Wish To Leave Message
   1. Press [Take Info]
   2. Press [Message Taken] button

F. Responding to Hang-Ups
   1. When screen beeps, push line # that shows on screen
      (line 1, 2, or 3)
   2. Say call phrase and person hangs up
   3. Screen will display "Disc"
   4. Press [Take Info]
   5. Press [Message Taken] button

G. Giving Messages to Clients
   1. When screen beeps, press line # that shows on screen (line 1, 2, or 3)
   2. Say call phrase
      Caller will say he or she wants messages
   3. Punch [Take Info] button
   4. Read messages on [R] hand of screen
   5. Press [Message Given] after each message is read off until it shows "no messages"
   6. Press [Message Taken] to clear call after all messages are given

H. Giving Messages to Staff on Business Line
   1. When screen beeps, press line # that shows on screen (line 1, 2, or 3)
   2. Say "Name of Business, may I help you?"
   3. Press in account # (they must know this)

4. Press [Take Info] button
5. Read message on [R] hand of screen
6. Press [Message Given] after each message is read off until it shows "no messages"

2. Librarian's Assistant

Time (Varies daily)	Sequence of Activities (Varies)
1:00–4:00 p.m.	• Unpack hardback books
(Varies daily)	• Unpack talking books and copy invoice
	• Make invoices
	• Unpack paperback books; pull card file box
	• Process books
	• Type labels

Key Related Tasks

A. Unpacking Hardback Books
   1. Get scissors
   2. Open first box
   3. Pull invoice
   4. Place invoice on shelf
   5. Stack books onto cart
   6. Get invoice
   7. Match books to invoice
   8. Check off items on invoice
   9. Put date on top sheet of invoice
   10. Initial top sheet

B. Making an Invoice
   1. Open box of books
   2. Pull invoice; if none, get scrap paper
   3. Attach or write # of company
   4. Write # of books
   5. Put date on top of sheet
   6. Initial top sheet
   7. Put # on plastic covers on sheet
   8. Put invoice on shelf
   9. Shelve books

C. Typing Spine Labels—Talking Books, Young Adults
   1. Turn typewriter on

2. Insert spine label
3. Push index button to insert
4. Get books from shelf
5. Put on cart
6. Pull pink slip
7. Turn roller to blank spine label
8. Look at index #
9. Look at guide sheet
10. Type letter(s)
11. Press index key 2 times
12. Type numbers
13. Press index key
14. Type letters
15. Get scissors
16. Cut spine label
17. Put inside book
18. Put books on shelf

D. Typing Spine Labels—Juvenile Print
1. Turn typewriter on
2. Insert spine label
3. Turn roller to spine label
4. Pull pink slip from box
5. Look at index letters
6. Look at guide sheet
7. Type letter(s)
8. Push index key 2 times
9. Backspace; type numbers
10. Push index key
11. Backspace; type letters
12. Take sheet out
13. Get scissors
14. Cut spine label
15. Put inside book
16. Put books on shelf

E. Processing—All Books Except Reference
1. Attach spine label
2. If YA (Young Adult), put YA sticker above spine label; go to Step 3.
   If L (Large Print), put yellow sticker above spine label; go to Step 3.
   If holiday (pink slip), put appropriate sticker on.
   All other books, no sticker; go to Step 3.
3. Tape spine label
4. Stamp top of book with branch only (not address)
5. Place bar code on upper right side of back cover
6. Place label in the middle of page, inside back cover

F. Processing—Reference Books
1. Attach spine label
2. Write index number inside front cover (upper left-hand corner)
3. Place bar code beneath index number
4. Stamp the branch with address beneath the bar code
5. Stamp date beneath branch address
6. Stamp address on top of book

G. Processing VCR Tapes
    1. Attach spine label to tape
    2. Attach spine label to cover
    3. Stamp address labels with branch
    4. Date address label
    5. Attach branch label to tape
    6. Attach branch label to cover
    7. Put bar code on cover
    8. Attach label "Library is not responsible" on cover

H. Processing Audio Tapes
    1. Attach spine label
    2. Tape spine label
    3. Attach bar code
    4. Insert library's name label on tape
    5. Stamp and date address label
    6. Put label on plastic cover (large part)
    7. Put tape over label
    *   Check work

I. Processing Talking Books
    1. Check spine label
    2. Stamp library's name on tape or place library's name label on tape
    3. Stamp address label—branch, date
    4. Place label on back cover
    5. Tape labels on spine and address
    6. Attach bar code

3. Library Clerk

Time	Sequence of Activities
1:00 p.m.	Sign in
1:00–3:00	Sort books
3:00–3:15	Break
3:15–5:00	Cover or repair books
5:00	Sign out

Key Related Tasks

A. Sorting Books
    1. Obtain cart labeled "To Be Shelved" from Circulation.
    2. Push cart to sorting area
    3. Working from left to right, identify 2 books whose call numbers fall between A and M
    4. Place these books on the shelves labeled A to M according to the first two letters of the call number

5. Repeat Step 4 until you have no more books whose call numbers fall between A and M
6. Place the remaining books on the shelves labeled N to Z according to the first two letters of the call number
7. When all books have been removed from cart, identify a section of A to M shelves that is full
8. Working from left to right, pull 2 books off shelf at a time and arrange them by call number on the cart
9. Continue Step 8 until no books remain in section
10. Push cart to Circulation
11. Record entry in log
12. Assign tag to cart

B. Covering Books
   1. Obtain book from Kap-Co shelf
   2. Choose 2 sheets of Easy Cover to fit front and back covers of book
   3. Measure and cut 2 strips of Easy Bind tape to fit length of book but not overlapping
   4. Place 1 piece of Easy Bind tape around bone folder
   5. Remove narrow white strip from Easy Bind tape
   6. Place adhesive strip into the inside crease of the back cover
   7. Remove paper strip from side of Easy Bind tape facing page
   8. Working from the center and out, smooth the tape onto the page using the bone folder
   9. Remove paper strip from side of Easy Bind tape facing back cover
   10. Working from center and out, smooth the tape onto the inside of the cover using the bone folder
   11. Repeat Steps 4–10 for front cover
   12. Place one sheet of Easy Cover on flat surface, paper side up
   13. Place book on the paper with the front of the book facing you
   14. Align the top and right edges of the book's spine edge ¼ inch past the edge of the Easy Cover spine
   15. Slide book to left so that book's spine edge is ¼ inch past the edge of the Easy Cover spine
   16. Using pencil, mark book's bottom and right edge on Easy Cover
   17. Repeat Steps 12–16 for the front cover of the book
   18. Referring to penciled-in lines, cut each piece of Easy Cover to fit book
   19. Align Easy Cover on back cover of book
   20. Remove paper from spine of Easy Cover
   21. Starting from center, smooth Easy Cover onto book's spine
   22. Remove remaining paper from sheet of Easy Cover
   23. Gently curl Easy Cover back and smooth onto cover of book using bone folder
   24. Repeat Steps 19–23 for front cover of book
   25. Pop any air bubbles in Easy Cover with pin
   26. Place book between two pieces of computer paper on shelf
   27. Place weight on top of book

C. Repairing Books—Tip-In
   1. Choose books from "Tip-In" shelf according to this priority:
      a. Medical journals
      b. Reference materials
      c. Other monographs

2. Remove work order and replacement copies from book
3. Check work order for specific instructions
4. If book is to be sent out for repair
   a. Remove small pieces of damaged pages with tweezers
   b. Placing ruler against next page, remove large pieces of damaged pages with Exacto Knife
   c. Replace work order in book
   d. Place book on "Already Reviewed" shelf
   e. Throw away scrap paper
5. If book is to be tipped-in here:
   a. Remove small pieces of damaged pages with tweezers
   b. Placing ruler against next page, remove large pieces of damaged pages with Exacto knife
   c. Fit replacement copy in book so that pages are aligned with the rest of book (If there are multiple replacement copies, make certain that the margins on the copies are uniform so that all trimming and fitting can be done with the pages held together; if the margins are not uniform, each copy will need to be trimmed and fit individually)
   d. Starting with left edge of replacement copy, pencil in lines on top and bottom margins of copy to indicate where it needs to be trimmed to fit
   e. Place replacement copy at 90-degree angle on plastic graph on desk
   f. Place ruler along left side of replacement copy so that edge is aligned with penciled lines
   g. Trim excess paper from left side of replacement copy using Exacto knife
   h. Repeat Steps 4–8 above as necessary for top, bottom, and right margins of replacement copy
   i. Throw away scrap paper
   j. Place piece of computer paper horizontally on plastic graph
   k. Place replacement copy horizontally on plastic graph so that left edge of copy is at top
   l. Place second piece of computer paper horizontally on replacement copy, leaving ⅛-inch strip
   m. Starting from middle of page, brush glue to left and then to right of the ⅛-inch strip
   n. Remove top piece of computer paper
   o. If more than one replacement copy needs to be tipped-in, repeat Steps G–N for each page; starting with the bottom page, glue the pages together by lining up the corners and smoothing down the glued pages as you add them
   p. Turn replacement copy to other side so that glued edge is at bottom facing away
   q. Holding replacement copy at the top with one hand, run a long strip of blue with nozzle of glue bottle along bottom of copy
   r. Fit glued edges of replacement copy into book
   s. Place wax paper between glued replacement copy and other pages
   t. Using fingers, smooth both sides of replacement copy so that it fits neatly into book
   u. Close book
   v. Place book on stacks on work table with heaviest books on bottom of pile

      w. Insert wooden palettes between books and place brick on top of stack

      x. Clean work area

4. Receptionist

Time	Sequence of Activities
8:00 a.m.	Clock in
8:00–10:30	Answer telephone
10:30–10:45	Break
10:45–1:00	Answer telephone
1:00–1:30	Break
1:30–3:30	Answer telephone
3:30–3:45	Break
3:45–5:00	Answer telephone
5:00	Clock out

Key Related Tasks

A. Answering a Call
   1. Pick up receiver
   2. Press RLS key
   3. Say business' name

B. Transferring a Call to an Extension
   1. Press TRANS key
   2. Then press the 3-digit extension as shown on monitor
   3. Press RLS key

C. Transferring a Call to Voice Mail
   1. Press 2nd TRANS key
   2. Press 5
   3. Then enter the 3-digit extension as shown on monitor

D. Putting a Call on Hold
   1. Say business' name
   2. Listen to request
   3. Type in 3-digit extension of person requested
   4. Press hold
   5. Press RLS

E. Retrieving a Call Back
   1. Press the HOLD button
   2. Calls will come back in the order you put them on hold

F. Calling for Help
1. Pick up receiver
2. Press RLS key
3. Press ICM key
4. Press either extension 007 or extension 009
5. When you hear the tone, begin to talk

G. Leaving a Message on Someone's Voice Mail
1. Press RLS key
2. Type in 436
3. Type in extension starting with 3, then three digits on the monitor
4. Person's recording will begin; press # to bypass the recording
5. You will hear a beep; then leave your message

H. Resetting Extensions
1. Control P (at the same time)
2. Type LEVEL 8
3. Press return
4. Press F
5. Use arrow keys to tab over to desired extension
6. Press R (the extension will appear dimmed)
7. Exit the screen by hitting ESC twice and E once
8. The extension will appear dimmed on the screen
9. To put the extension back on the monitor, follow Steps 1, 2, 3, 4, and 8
10. It should be fine after that

Case Study

Anna is an 18-year-old senior in a large suburban school district. She has a primary disability of spinal cord injury and a secondary disability of mild head trauma due to a snow skiing accident. She has excellent communication skills and maintains a B average in all Carnegie unit subjects. She uses a puff-power wheelchair for mobility and has no functional use of her arms or legs. Anna has a peer assistant for basic aid.

Anna and her parents recently participated in a PATH for transition planning. Anna indicated a desire to defer postsecondary educational options for 2 years; instead, she would like to work using her communication skills.

An assessment revealed that Anna would benefit from assistive technology with computer systems for employment. A mouthstick to push telephone buttons and a voice-activated computer system would allow Anna to work in an office, depending on the job duties. A rehabilitation engineer teamed with the high school exceptional education employment specialist to assist Anna in a work study internship during her second semester. During various interviews, employers were provided information regarding Anna's skills and accommodation needs.

The rehab engineer installed a mount for the phone and a mouthstick so that Anna could access the phone independently. He also built a box for the phone that allowed the employment specialist to hear the phone for training purposes. This was used for the first month of training until she became more comfortable with handling customers. A headset replaced the telephone, which is now standard in most offices. To record personal messages for employees instead of allowing the client to use the voice-mail system, another system was devised. A tape recorder was mounted next to the phone. The machine was left on to record and was set to pause. Anna turned off the pause button to record the message and turned it back on after the message was recorded, all with her mouthstick. Anna can play back information as she needs to when retrieval is necessary. She can then send E-mail messages with the voice-activated dictation system.

The headset systems presented an immediate problem. A headset was used to talk on the phone. The voice-activated computer system (Dragon dictate) also used a headset for input. Because of the obvious issue with two headsets, the rehab engineer built a gooseneck mounted on her desk to allow her to access Dragon dictate when the phone was not busy. Also, two document holders were purchased to display information about frequently asked questions. This reduced the need for co-worker support.

Anna has been at her position for 4 months now. She can handle the majority of incoming calls without any assistance, and when people call for specific assistance, Anna successfully reroutes the calls. She gets along with co-workers and has been offered full-time employment after graduation.

Individual Transition Plan 8

Student Profile

Anna is an 18-year-old senior in a large suburban school district. She has a primary disability of spinal cord injury and a secondary disability of mild head trauma due to a snow skiing accident. She maintains a B average in all college preparatory subjects. She has excellent verbal communication skills.

Individual Transition Plan

Student's Name ___Anna Walsh___
 First M.I. Last

Birthdate ___1/31/80___   School ___River Bend High School___

Student's ID No. ___15___   ITP Conference Date ___2/01/00___

Participants

Name	Position
Anna Walsh	Student
Tom, Grace Walsh	Parents
Sam Gardner	Rehab Engineer, Department of Rehabilitative Services
Tina Nguyen	Counselor, DRS
Maureen Blackwell	Guidance Counselor
Peter Callahan	Exceptional Education Employment Specialist

Individual Transition Plan 8

I. Career and Economic Self-Sufficiency

1. Employment Goal	Full-time competitive employment
Level of present performance	1. Anna works part time in an office. 2. She needs several technical assistance accommodations (ongoing).
Steps needed to accomplish goal	1. Job analysis specific to Anna's needs 2. Make accommodations 3. Provide ongoing support until Anna is 98% independent
Date of completion	6/98
Person(s) responsible for implementation	Rehab Engineer (DRS), Employment Specialist, Anna

2. Vocational Education/Training Goal	N/A
Level of present performance	N/A
Steps needed to accomplish goal	N/A
Date of completion	N/A
Person(s) responsible for implementation	N/A

3. Postsecondary Education Goal	Anna has chosen to defer postsecondary education for 2 years.
Level of present performance	N/A

Individual Transition Plan 8

Steps needed to accomplish goal	N/A
Date of completion	N/A
Person(s) responsible for implementation	N/A
4. Financial/Income Needs Goal	N/A
Level of present performance	N/A
Steps needed to accomplish goal	N/A
Date of completion	N/A
Person(s) responsible for implementation	N/A

II. Community Integration and Participation

5. Independent Living Goal	N/A
Level of present performance	N/A
Steps needed to accomplish goal	N/A
Date of completion	N/A
Person(s) responsible for implementation	N/A

Individual Transition Plan 8

6. Transportation/Mobility Goal	Anna will use local adaptive transportation (CARE).
Level of present performance	Anna is dependent upon her parents for all transportation needs.
Steps needed to accomplish goal	1. Make appointment with doctor for CARE medical form; attend appointment 2. Send completed application to CARE 3. Obtain CARE card 4. Practice one time with DRS counselor 5. Independent by 3/20/00
Date of completion	3/20/00
Person(s) responsible for implementation	Anna, Parents, DRS Counselor
7. Social Relationships Goal	N/A
Level of present performance	N/A
Steps needed to accomplish goal	N/A
Date of completion	N/A
Person(s) responsible for implementation	N/A
8. Recreation/Leisure Goal	N/A
Level of present performance	N/A
Steps needed to accomplish goal	N/A

Individual Transition Plan 8

Date of completion	N/A
Person(s) responsible for implementation	N/A

III. Personal Competence

9. Health/Safety Goal	N/A
Level of present performance	N/A
Steps needed to accomplish goal	N/A
Date of completion	N/A
Person(s) responsible for implementation	N/A

10. Self-Advocacy/Future Planning	N/A
Level of present performance	N/A
Steps needed to accomplish goal	N/A
Date of completion	N/A
Person(s) responsible for implementation	N/A

Student Career Preference

Undecided

Individual Transition Plan 8

Student's Major Transition Needs

1. Independence on worksite
2. _____
3. _____
4. _____
5. _____
6. _____
7. _____
8. _____
9. _____

Additional Notes

Anna will work for the next 2 years. She will apply to local colleges in her state in 2 years.

Computing and
Account-Recording Occupations

◆ ◆ ◆ ◆ ◆ ◆ ◆ ◆ ◆ ◆ ◆ ◆ ◆ ◆ ◆ ◆ ◆ ◆ ◆

Description of Domain

The *Dictionary of Occupational Titles* defines Computing and
Account-Recording occupations as those concerned with "systematiz-
ing information about transactions and activities into accounts and
quantitative records, and paying and receiving money. It includes
such activities as keeping and verifying records of business and
financial transactions; receiving and disbursing money in banks and
other establishments; operating data processing and peripheral
equipment; computing and verifying amounts due for goods and services; preparing payrolls, timekeeping records, and duty rosters; com-
bining data and performing computations to create statistical
records; and computing costs of production in relation to other factors
to determine profit and loss" (p. 181).

JOB DESCRIPTIONS

1. Toll Collector

Time*	Sequence of Activities
7:00 a.m.	Punch in
7:00–7:20	Get bank; set up work station
7:20–10:00	Collect tolls
10:00–10:15	Break
10:15–12:00	Collect tolls
12:00–12:45	Lunch
12:45–3:10	Collect tolls
3:10–3:15	Close lane
3:15–3:30	Close up work station; deposit cash
3:30	Punch out

*Shifts vary from day to day: Morning
7:00–3:30; Evening 3:30–11:30; Late Night
11:30–7:00.

Key Related Tasks

A. Setting Up Work Station
   1. Put money in drawer
   2. Open coins to get started
   3. Put bills in selected bins
   4. Make enough setups to get started
   5. Make 3 setup piles of change
      a. 65 cents
      b. 35 cents
      c. 15 cents
      * It does not matter what coins are used as long as they equal the appropriate amount.
   6. Fold receipts for easy access
   7. Make 4 folded piles of 1 dollar bills
   8. Take cones from in front of your lane and put in front of lane to be closed
   9. Go back to booth
   10. Turn 3 switches on front panel to "on" position
   11. Turn vault switch in back of booth to "on" position
   12. Finish making setups (approximately 12 each)
   13. Fold receipts

B. Collecting 35-Cent Tolls
   1. Observe vehicle
   2. Determine classification for vehicle payment amount
   3. Greet patron
   4. Accept payment
   5. Deposit correct toll
   6. Give directions if necessary
   7. Give receipt if necessary
   8. Return correct change
   9. Thank patron

C. Collecting Free Passage Cards
   1. Observe vehicle
   2. Determine classification for vehicle payment amount
   3. Greet patron
   4. Accept manilla card
   5. Check card for completeness
   6. Give blank card back
   7. Press #5 classification button
   8. Thank patron
   9. Write # on back of card
   10. Place card in slot

D. Collecting from Prepaid Vehicles
   1. Observe vehicle
   2. Determine classification for vehicle payment amount
   3. Greet patron
   4. Receive prepaid card
      or, if bus, stamp blue card
   5. Press #6 classification button

6. Thank patron
7. Write # on back of card and fill out card
8. Place card in slot

E. Collecting 45-Cent, 55-Cent, and 65-Cent Tolls
1. Observe vehicle
2. Classify correctly
3. Greet patron
4. Accept payment
5. Press corresponding classification button
6. Deposit correct toll
7. Give correct change
8. Give directions if necessary
9. Give appropriate receipt
10. Thank patron

2. Bookstore Cashier

Time	Sequence of Activities
1:00 p.m.	Punch in
1:05–3:30	Assist customers or perform inventory*
3:30–3:40	Break
3:40–5:00	Assist customers or perform inventory
5:00	Punch out
	*When customers are not in the store, perform inventory.

Key Related Tasks

A. Ringing up Items and Taking Payments
1. Enter price of item
2. Press category button
   SCHS—school supplies; white price label
   SG-G—"soft goods"; green label
   GEN 20%—books and magazines (label says G-20)
   GEN 40%—some books (label says G-40)
3. Repeat Steps 1–2 for each item
4. Press subtotal
5. Tell customer amount owed
6. Determine how customer wishes to pay
   a. Cash payment
      1) Enter amount of cash
      2) Press AMT TEND/CASH button
      3) Read display for change
      4) Count out change from drawer

      5) Close drawer
      6) Hand change to customer
   b. Check payment
      1) Underline phone # & SS # on check
      2) Check ID
      3) Initial top left corner of check
      4) Enter amount of check into register
      5) Press CHECK button
      6) Insert check into validator, blank side up and lines toward back
      7) Press VALIDATE
      8) Remove check from validator
      9) Place check under change compartment
      10) Close drawer
      11) Rip receipt from register
      12) Give receipt to customer
   c. Credit card payment
      1) Run card through machine, strip down and facing right
      2) Enter subtotal on card machine
      3) Press enter
      4) Reenter subtotal
      5) Press enter
      6) Press CRED CARD button on register
      7) Remove receipt from credit card printer
      8) Give receipt to customer to sign and write phone #
      9) Separate white and yellow pages
      10) Put white copy into card validator (in front of receipt), blank side facing you
      11) Press VALIDATE button
      12) Remove white copy
      13) Put white copy in box on top shelf of cabinet
      14) Rip receipt from register
      15) Staple register receipt to yellow copy and give to customer

B. Generating Refunds
  1. Greet customers
  2. Ask for receipt
  3. Read receipt to determine method payment used
   a. If by cash or check
      1) Press refund item (2nd row of keys, last one on right)
      2) Press price of item
      3) Press category button
      4) Repeat Steps 1–3 for each item
      5) Get refund slip pad from top drawer
      6) Slide top refund slip, blank side up, on to validator on top of register
      7) Press VALIDATE button
      8) Remove refund slip
      9) Ask customer to complete top portion of refund slip and sign the bottom at "received by"
      10) Complete middle portion of refund slip
      11) Draw lines through rows not used
      12) Press subtotal button

      13) Read display for refund amount

      14) Give money to customer

      15) Close drawer

      16) Rip receipt from register

      17) Give receipt to customer

      18) Put refund slip in cabinet, top shelf, in box

    b. If credit card purchase

      1) Follow Steps 1–12 of "cash or check" list

      2) Go to credit card machine

      3) Press #2

      4) Press blue enter button

      5) Slide credit card through machine

      6) Enter refund amount

      7) Reenter refund amount

      8) Go back to register

      9) Press CRED CARD button

      10) Tear transaction off credit card printer

      11) Ask customer to sign white slip and write phone #

      12) Separate white and yellow copies

      13) Insert white copy blank side facing you in card validator

      14) Press VALIDATE

      15) Circle amount on front and put your name

      16) Put white copy in box, on top shelf of cabinet

C. Completing Clothing Inventory

    1. Identify inventory book titled "Clothing"

    2. Pick up book

    3. Take book to T-shirt section located in front of store near door

    4. Identify specific item of clothing on rack

    5. Turn to specific page that each item is located on, matching number code on item with code on page

    6. Verify price of item; if item does not have price on it, let manager know

    7. Count that specific item of clothing and record number counted on row that reads "Floor Stock"

    8. Continue Steps 3–7, working from front of store down each row until all items of clothing in each category have been accounted for

3. Accounting Clerk

Time	Sequence of Activities
8:25 a.m.	Go to work station
8:30–10:30	Check writing
10:30–10:45	Break
10:45–11:30	Sort mail
11:30–Noon	Deliver mail
Noon–1:00	Lunch
1:00–3:30	Credit processing
3:30–4:00	File cover sheets
4:00	Go home

Key Related Tasks

A. Writing Checks
   1. Rip check from bottom
   2. Match up to correct line by matching with "check # box" in book
   3. Take refund request form
   4. Write in the invoice # on the check (order # on request form)
   5. Write in today's date on check
   6. Look at refund request form
   7. Write in the name of the person on the check
   8. Look at refund request form for amount of refund
   9. Write in the number amount on the check
   10. Write in the written amount on check
   11. Write check # from upper left-hand side into the book on the same line
   12. Write order # into box right next to check # "Accounts Receivable Refunds"
   13. Look at the "Office Use Only" box
   14. Write in the check #
   15. Write in the date
   16. Paper clip check to refund request form
   17. When finished, give to Amy
   18. Take checks out of book
   19. Place inside book
   20. Put away book
   21. Double check work
   22. Give to Mr. X

B. Processing Credits
   1. Take MC/VISA summary sheet
   2. Write in store # (82)
   3. Write in date

    4. Tell machine that it will be "credit" by pushing #3
    5. Put in card number
    6. Press blue enter button
    7. Put in expiration date (must be a 4-digit #)
       Example: 3/99 would be 03/99
    8. Hit enter button
    9. Put in today's day number
  10. Hit enter button
  11. Copy "REC" credit slip on red line
  12. Copy "REC = #" on refund request form under "Office Use Box"
  13. Look at the MC/VISA summary sheet
  14. Write in the name
  15. Write in order number
  16. Write in the amount in <brackets>
  17. Press clear button (will say 001 clear)
  18. Press 3 again
  19. Start on next credit slip
  20. When finished, clip slips and leave with sheet
  21. Staple refund request forms
  22. Double-check work
  23. Give to supervisor

C. Processing Credits for Void Transactions
    1. Press clear
    2. Press 4
      (Terminal response: VOID . . . enter sale amount)
    3. Key in dollar amount of transaction to be voided
    4. Press enter
      (Terminal response: Acct number)
    5. Key in account number
    6. Press enter
      (Terminal response: Exp date)
    7. Key in expiration date
    8. Press enter
      (Terminal response: Verify amount)
    9. Key in dollar amount of transaction to be voided
  10. Press enter
      (Terminal response: Record number)
  11. Key in record number of transaction to be voided
  12. Press enter
      (Terminal response: VOID COMPLETE)
  13. Now you can start over and key in the correct amount of the slip you
      just voided

D. Processing Credits for Detail Transactions
    1. Press clear
      (Terminal should say: "### CITINET")
    2. Press enter
      (Terminal should say: "FUNCTION")
    3. Press 4
      (Terminal should say: "ENTER CODE")
    4. Press 2
    5. Press enter

(Terminal should say: "RECORD NUMBER")

6. Key in the *record number* (the number you write on the slip) of the slip that you are trying to look at
7. Press enter
   (Terminal should say the credit card number of the card you are trying to find)
8. Press number button
   (Terminal should say the authorization number and type of card)
9. Press number button again
   (Terminal should say the amount that you put in)
   If the amount that you put in does not match what is on the slip, then *VOID* this

E. Sorting Mail
   1. Go to second floor to get mail
   2. Go to wicker basket
   3. Take envelopes
   4. Bring back down to desk
   5. Open first envelope
   6. Take everything out of envelope
   7. Put envelope in a pile (to save)
   8. Look at 1st item on cover sheet and put in place to make a pile
   9. Look at 2nd item on cover sheet and put in place to make a pile
   10. Look at 3rd item and make pile
   11. Look at 4th item and make pile
   12. Look at 5th item and make pile
   13. Look at 6th item and make pile
   14. Look at 7th item and make pile
   15. Put cover sheet in a pile
   16. After finished, get "received" stamp and pad
   17. Change stamp to today's date
   18. Stamp financing paperwork on back of slip and on application
   19. Stamp: refund request forms
   20. Stamp: tax exempt forms
   21. Stamp: backs of cash receipt pages
   22. Stamp: customer credit forms
   23. Stamp: other

F. Closing
   1. Add amounts on summary sheet
   2. Write total on summary sheet in brackets <   >
   3. Press <u>clear</u> on transaction machine
   4. Press <u>enter</u>
   5. Press <u>4</u>
   6. Press <u>3</u>
   7. Press <u>enter</u>
   8. This will give the <u>number of transactions</u>
      *Match it with summary sheet
   9. Press <u>enter</u>
   10. This will give the dollar amount
      *Match it with summary sheet; if match, go to next step. If amounts do not match, re-add the summary sheet; when amounts match, continue.

11. Press <u>clear</u> on the transaction machine
12. Press <u>9</u>
    Terminal will display "Trans Count"
13. Key in the <u>number of transactions</u> (how many credits or names) from the summary sheet
14. Press enter
    Terminal will display "total amount"
15. Key in <u>total</u> (summary) from the summary sheet
16. Press enter
17. When terminal is finished completing transmission, it will display "OK 038604_ _"
18. Record the number on the <u>batch header ticket</u>
19. Write in (on batch header ticket) the <u>net total</u>
20. Write the number of transactions on the bottom right of the batch header ticket
21. Attach <u>header ticket</u> to credit vouchers and place in box, above desk
22. Give refund request forms to Susan
23. Give summary sheet to Scott or put in his box (box: to be coded)

4. Microfilm Clerk

Time	Sequence of Activities
8:30–9:00 a.m.	Set up work station
9:00 until complete	Copy check register
After copying check register, until break	Processing or microfilming checks
10:30–10:45	Break
After break until done or lunch	Processing or microfilming checks
Noon–12:45	Lunch
12:45–4:50	Processing or microfilming checks
4:50	Close down

Key Related Tasks

A. Setting Up Work Area
   1. Set up calculator
   2. Set up date machine
   3. Put paper clips, sticky fingers, and staple remover on desk top
   4. Pull check register copies and checks to be processed
   5. Pull aprons (backup work)

B. Making Copy of the Check Register
   1. Memorize date of box to be processed or write it on piece of paper
   2. Take piece of paper to original check register in the log (blue) book

3. Locate appropriate pages by date
4. Take check register apart to get pages out
5. Remove pages
6. Take pages to copy machine area
7. Tear pages and place in order
8. Set copy machine on 8½ × 11 and set to reduce at 64
9. Straighten pages so they are all straight
10. Place straightened pile face down in feeder and lightly push forward
11. Push green start button. *DO NOT* touch papers!
12. Collate new copies
13. Ensure that you can read them and that they are reduced properly
14. Retrieve originals (top machine)
15. Move away from copy machine
16. Put originals in order
17. Return originals to check register and replace them
18. Rebind the book and place in cabinet
19. Take new copies to microfilm room
20. Put new copies in order
21. Check to see that all pages are there
22. Place merchandise (#5) checks in front of expense (#3) checks

C. Processing Checks
1. Tear top check off pile
2. Read vendor number (top left-hand corner of check)
3. Match vendor number on check with vendor number on apron (top left corner on green and white computer sheet)
4. Pull off all aprons with corresponding vendor number
5. If check has *NO* backup aprons (work receipts), write MB (missing backup) beside check number on check register
6. Put check on top of apron(s)
7. Remove all staples and stack papers matching top left-hand corner; papers must be facing forward as if you were reading them
8. Pull out any cash register, credit card, etc., receipts; staples *do not* need to be removed from receipts
9. Paper clip check to backup work (aprons and all other documents) in top left corner
10. Place receipts in envelope
11. Tape envelope closed
12. Write "check number" on envelope
13. Paper clip envelope to back of check and backups
14. Place paper clipped stack on center of work table; checks *must* be in order, so if stacking work, place at bottom of pile facing up
15. CHECK OFF (RED PENCIL) THE CHECK NUMBER COMPLETED ON CHECK REGISTER
16. Keeping checks in order numerically, pull top check and attached backup from pile
17. Look at amount on check and amount on apron(s); if same, go to Step 33
18. If not the same, add up all apron totals, check this total with the check total; if same, go to Step 33
19. If not same, pull adding machine tape and check all numbers with apron numbers to ensure that calculator was punched properly
If a mistake, correct

If same total, go to step 33

If not the same, subtract check amount from apron amounts (total); this is the difference to look for

20. Ensure that all aprons have been accounted for; IF BACKUP IS LESS THAN CHECK, YOU HAVE A BACKUP MISSING
21. Check box you are working on: it might be out of place
22. Check missing backup folder
23. Check OPEN file to see if backup is in there (vendor number and voucher number)
24. Check with employee who does cash requirements
25. If no backup, write MB (missing backup) on each register
    IF BACKUP IS MORE THAN CHECK, SOMETHING WAS NOT SELECTED
26. Check the voucher numbers on the aprons with the voucher numbers on the check; if all aprons belong with the check, then one item on an apron must not have been selected
27. Add the voucher numbers up on the check and ensure each voucher total matches that of the apron that goes with it—one or more of them will NOT!
28. Look at the invoice number to see which one was not selected
29. Make a copy of the apron and backup that goes with it (small copy machine)
30. Highlight the total that was not selected (on duplicate copy) and file to be selected (OPEN FILE)
31. Put original backup with the check and process it normally
32. Slide or take off paper clip; insert papers (10) into date paid punch machine and pull lever; too many papers will be difficult to stamp and require extra "wasted" time
33. Ensure that stamp goes cleanly through all work
34. Replace paper clip (top left corner)
35. Stack upside down with the work facing same direction (paper clips should stack on top of each other). When this pile becomes large enough that it begins to fall (not stack easily), place it in rear of box with work facing toward front of box—paper clips should be on left side of papers (lying sideways)

D. Microfilming Checks
    1. Blow (clean) compressed air into microfilm machine
    2. Reset item counter to 0
    3. Check film supply
    4. Locate appropriate check register
    5. Locate next check to be filmed; verify it with the check register
    6. Turn on machine
    7. Pull check to be filmed from stack
    8. Make sure it has no MB (check register)
       If MB:
       a. Locate MB and film
       b. If not located, film note
       c. Make note on film box
    9. For each check, press BLIP LEVER and space (5 counts)
    10. Film check (face up)
    11. Film backup
    12. Make sure each item is filmed without overlapping another document

13. Ensure that items "fall" in same order as filmed
14. Finish entire check or more (repeat Steps 7–13)
15. Gather documents belonging to each check and straighten
16. Staple documents
17. Refile in box in order
18. Continue Steps 7–17
   Note: If machine "flutters," begin unloading film process—Checklist on the wall

E. Loading Film
   1. Get a new tape
   2. Record on box label:
      a. Store name
      b. New tape number
      c. First check number to be filmed
   3. Turn off lights
   4. Load film
   5. Turn on lights
   6. Replace film cartridge in film machine
   7. Reset film cartridge (push button next to numbers)
   8. Turn on film machine
   9. Press Leader Trailer switch
   10. Begin filming

F. Researching Checks on Computer
   1. Ask if computer is not being used
   2. If open, have a seat
   3. No matter what's on the screen, press <u>Cmd</u> and <u>1</u> at the same time; Expense Payables Clerical Menu should appear
   4. Enter in 20
   5. Press <u>ENTER</u>; should have A/P Voucher Inquiry
   6. Enter vendor name
   7. Enter invoice number or name
   8. Make sure it is entered exactly the same as listed on apron (may have to use space bar to delete extra numbers or letters)
   9. Press <u>ENTER</u>; list with checks should be displayed
   10. Locate correct amount in question
   11. If no check number appears beside amount, it has not been selected to be paid
   12. File in OPEN FILE
   13. If check number listed write date and check number (these are on computer screen) on apron
   14. Do all missing backups to be researched and either file them or stack them to be filed
   15. File all OPEN FILE work in OPEN FILE
   16. For backup with date and check number, locate check run (appropriate)
   17. Find check
   18. Find check register and check number on register
   19. Rebalance check
   20. Erase MB on check register if check balances
   21. If check does not balance, make sure MB or appropriate mark is on check register
   22. Place backup with check and refile check in box

23. Finish refiling all researched MB
24. Continue whatever next appropriate task

G. Closing Down
   1. Cross off last check # on check register sheet
   2. Replace process checks into back of box
   3. Complete processing on any checks that were started
   4. Stack on already processed pile
   5. Place processed pile in very back of box; checks should be facing forward, numerically in order, and on their side (paper clip on left side)
   6. Figure number of checks processed (subtract first number from last number)
   7. Mark last check number so you know where to begin next day

Case Study

Lynnlee is a 17-year-old student enrolled in a large urban high school. She has been diagnosed with a mild learning disability and an emotional disorder related to early childhood abuse. Her teachers feel that Lynnlee has very poor self-esteem due to failures in various endeavors: clubs, boyfriends, and maternal relationship. She also has difficulty learning new tasks and displays impatience with classmates' immature behaviors.

A formal vocational evaluation stated that Lynnlee would benefit from a supportive environment. She displayed strengths in basic keyboarding and data entry skills. Lynnlee also expressed a desire to work in the fashion industry. The work coordinator met with Lynnlee, her marketing teacher, mother, and the DRS counselor to strategize employment options prior to an IEP meeting. The team agreed on having Lynnlee start out with 20 hours per week at a location on the bus line. Lynnlee agreed to attempt an associate's position in a local factory outlet store. The work coordinator had developed a good rapport with the store manager with a prior successful placement.

Lynnlee began her training the following week with a set schedule of three afternoons and all day Saturday. The schedule's consistency was reassuring to Lynnlee. The job required Lynnlee to hang new stock on special hangers for the first 2 hours of each shift; to assist at the cash register for up to 2 hours per shift; and then to report to the stock room to review the daily computerized stock lists.

A system of least prompts using verbal and modeling cues was used. Lynnlee and the work coordinator developed compensatory strategies using diagrams for assistance with the cashier skills. For example, a diagram was developed listing various steps to take when processing different payment types (check, credit card, cash, etc.). Other employees noticed the cue cards and requested that they be laminated to use as refreshers for all employees. This request was Lynnlee's first step toward acceptance and independence at work. The work coordinator was able to fade assistance by the third week.

Lynnlee has made friends at work and plans to attend the holiday party in a few weeks. She plans to slowly increase her hours by graduation and to take some adult education classes in advanced computer skills in the fall.

Individual Transition Plan 9

Student Profile

Lynnlee has mild a learning disability and an emotional disorder related to early childhood abuse.

Individual Transition Plan

Student's Name ___Lynnlee R. Jones_____
                    First   M.I.   Last

Birthdate ___01/12/80_____ School ___Fairfax High School_____

Student's ID No. ___6_____ ITP Conference Date ___04/12/97_____

Participants

Name	Position
Lynnlee	Student
Lee	Mom
Betsy	Work Coordinator
Steve	DRS Counselor
Blinda	Marketing Teacher

Individual Transition Plan 9

I. Career and Economic Self-Sufficiency

1. Employment Goal	Lynnlee will gain competitive employment as a stock clerk.
Level of present performance	Lynnlee works part time, with support, at a factory outlet store.
Steps needed to accomplish goal	1. Increase hours by 4/98 2. Maintain, increase good work skills
Date of completion	6/98
Person(s) responsible for implementation	Lynnlee, Work Coordinator, DRS Counselor

2. Vocational Education/Training Goal	N/A
Level of present performance	Lynnlee is completing this program.
Steps needed to accomplish goal	N/A
Date of completion	N/A
Person(s) responsible for implementation	N/A

3. Postsecondary Education Goal	To increase advanced computer skills
Level of present performance	Lynnlee has completed keyboarding spreadsheet skills utilizing Microsoft Office/Excel. She received a B+.

Individual Transition Plan 9

Steps needed to accomplish goal	1. *Complete senior year credits* 2. *Obtain summer/fall continuing adult education brochures* 3. *Enroll in one class Fall '98*
Date of completion	1/99
Person(s) responsible for implementation	*Lynnlee, Mother, Case Manager*

4. Financial/Income Needs Goal	N/A
Level of present performance	*Lynnlee has independent skills in this area. No assistance requested.*
Steps needed to accomplish goal	N/A
Date of completion	N/A
Person(s) responsible for implementation	N/A

II. Community Integration and Participation

5. Independent Living Goal	*Lynnlee will obtain an apartment with partner/friend.*
Level of present performance	*Lynnlee lives at home with her mother and cousin. She has basic activities of daily living skills.*
Steps needed to accomplish goal	1. *Develop a savings account for independent residential goal.* 2. *Save a minimum of $150 per month until ready to move out.*
Date of completion	1/99
Person(s) responsible for implementation	*Lynnlee*

Individual Transition Plan 9

6. Transportation/Mobility Goal	N/A
Level of present performance	Lynnlee has a driver's license.
Steps needed to accomplish goal	N/A
Date of completion	N/A
Person(s) responsible for implementation	N/A

7. Social Relationships Goal	Lynnlee will increase social activities.
Level of present performance	Lynnlee responds to adults as peers. She has recently begun to develop friendships with co-workers.
Steps needed to accomplish goal	1. Attend at least one activity with a co-worker per month. 2. Initiate at least one activity with a friend per month.
Date of completion	12/99
Person(s) responsible for implementation	Lynnlee, Work Coordinator

8. Recreation/Leisure Goal	Lynnlee will join her church choir.
Level of present performance	Lynnlee has a beautiful voice but was afraid to join the choir. A new co-worker has urged her to join.
Steps needed to accomplish goal	1. Call choir director. 2. Attend one practice within 14 days. 3. Join choir.

Individual Transition Plan 9

Date of completion	1/98
Person(s) responsible for implementation	Lynnlee, Mom

III. Personal Competence

9. Health/Safety Goal	N/A
Level of present performance	Lynnlee jogs 4 times weekly.
Steps needed to accomplish goal	N/A
Date of completion	N/A
Person(s) responsible for implementation	N/A

10. Self-Advocacy/Future Planning	Lynnlee will recognize her personal strengths.
Level of present performance	Lynnlee has low self-esteem but is improving since her employment began.
Steps needed to accomplish goal	1. Develop a daily journal to measure growth/goals. 2. Review, as appropriate with DRS Counselor.
Date of completion	6/98
Person(s) responsible for implementation	Lynnlee

Student Career Preference

Short term: Warehouse stock clerk
Long term: Inventory control specialist

Individual Transition Plan 9

Student's Major Transition Needs

1. Maintain work ethic, excellent skills at work.

2. Raise self-esteem through personal activities.

3. Increase social contacts.

4.

5.

6.

7.

8.

9.

Additional Notes

About the Contributors

◆ ◆

Paula K. Davis, Ph.D., is an associate professor in the Rehabilitation Institute at Southern Illinois University at Carbondale. Prior to obtaining her doctorate, she worked in a variety of community-based programs for people with developmental disabilities. Her interests are in assisting people with developmental disabilities to play an active role in their own habilitation, including expressing their preferences and making choices about their programs.

David Michael Mank, Ph.D., is director of Indiana University's Institute for the Study of Developmental Disabilities (ISDD), the University Affiliated Program (UAP) of Indiana. In addition, he is a full professor in the School of Education's Program in Special Education, Department of Curriculum and Instruction. He is a prolific writer and researcher with an extensive background in education and employment for persons with disabilities. His interests also include a focus on the transition of persons with disabilities from school to work. Mank is a member of the editorial boards of the *Journal of the Association for People with Severe Handicaps* (JASH), the *Journal of Vocational Rehabilitation,* and the *Journal of Disability Policy Studies,* and a consulting editor for the journal of *Mental Retardation.* His work has been recognized at the national level with an appointment to the executive board of the Foundation of the Association for Persons in Supported Employment and at an international level as an appointee to the World Association for Supported Employment.

Ernest L. Pancsofar, Ph.D., is currently an assistant professor at Central Connecticut State University in New Britain. Working closely with Communitas, Inc., in Manchester, Connecticut, Pancsofar translates current research and best practices into staff development modules for family members, teachers, and students in training to be the primary agents of support for individuals of all abilities. He is currently the book review editor for *The Journal of Vocational Rehabilitation* and is on the editorial board of *The Journal of Staff Development.*

Pamela Sherron Targett, M.Ed., is program manager of the Employment Services Division at Virginia Commonwealth University Rehabilitation Research and Training Center on Supported Employment, Richmond. She has been involved with supported employment direct services since 1986. Her background also includes teaching adult basic education classes and personnel management. She also has co-authored a number of journal articles and book chapters on supported employment and other disability-related issues.

George P. Tilson, Ed.D., is senior vice president of TransCen, Inc., and is on the faculty at George Washington University, Washington, D.C. Since 1975, his career has centered on vocational preparation, employment, and independent living of people with disabilities. He has worked as a special educator, job placement specialist, program manager, and human resources consultant and trainer. His current specialization is translating theory into practice in the area of job development and placement.

Paul Wehman, Ph.D., is Professor at the Department of Physical Medicine and Rehabilitation, Medical College of Virginia, and Director of the Rehabilitation Research and Training Center, Virginia Commonwealth University, Richmond. Internationally recognized for his service and scholarly contributions in the fields of special education, psychology, and vocational rehabilitation, Wehman is the recipient of the 1990 Joseph P. Kennedy, Jr., Foundation Award in Mental Retardation and of the Distinguished Service Award from the President's Committee on Employment for Persons with Disabilities in 1992. He is the author or editor of over 100 books, research monographs, journal articles, and chapters in the areas of traumatic brain injury, mental retardation, supported employment, and special education. He also is editor of the *Journal of Vocational Rehabilitation,* an international journal published by Elsevier. Specific research interests include transition from school to work, supported employment, developmental disabilities, and brain injury.

Michael D. West, Ph.D., has direct service experiences in special education, residential programs, vocational services, and general community functioning. He currently is a research associate with the Rehabilitation Research and Training Center on Supported Employment at Virginia Commonwealth University. He has authored or co-authored numerous journal articles and book chapters on supported employment, special education, and other disability-related issues.

Katherine M. Wittig, M.Ed., has worked in the fields of rehabilitation, education, and community support services for persons with disabilities for the past 20 years. Wittig served as the director of project transition in Bangor, Maine, for 6 years. She has co-authored several chapters in textbooks edited by Paul Wehman. She is currently the work coordinator for vocational special needs students in Henrico County, Virginia.

Index

◆ ◆ ◆ ◆ ◆ ◆ ◆ ◆ ◆ ◆ ◆ ◆ ◆ ◆ ◆ ◆ ◆ ◆ ◆ ◆

ADA. *See* Americans with Disabilities Act
AFDC. *See* Aid to Families with Dependent Children
Aid to Families with Dependent Children (AFDC)
  and supported employment, 91–92
Americans with Disabilities Act (ADA) of 1990, 63, 64, 72, 73, 77
Assessment. *See* Vocational assessment, functional

Behavior analysis, 80
Brain injuries. *See* Traumatic brain injury
Business
  partnerships, 63–76
    business culture understanding, 65–66
    customer service principles for job placement and supported employment professionals, 72–74
    expansion of relationships, 66
    human resource practice enhancement, 68
    job coach as consultant, 67
    materials for training programs, 67
    obstacles, 70–71
    productivity, 68
    skills utilized, 66
    supported employment and workforce diversity, 65
    training, and sponsorship opportunities, 67
  relationships, maintaining, 12–13
  representatives
    identification, 10
    initial visit, 10–11
    making contact, 10, 33–39
  trends in supported employment and business, 63
  and vocational curriculum development, 4–5, 52–54

Career planning, 119
Case studies
  building and related services occupations, 173–179
  clerical occupations, 246–253
  community living, 128–129
  computing and account-recording occupations, 314–320
  food and beverage preparation occupations, 231–237
  information and message distribution occupations, 294–300
  lodging and related services occupations, 265–271
  plant farming occupations, 278–284
  production and stock clerk occupations, 210–216
  sales occupations, 193–199
Center for Psychiatric Research, 87–88
Chaining, in vocational training
  backward, 104
  forward, 104
Chamber of Commerce
  and labor market, 29
Checklist
  as assessment tool, 41
Children
  and supported employment, 91–92
"Choose–Get–Keep" approach, 87–88
Circles of Support, 119
Client screening, 132–133
Cognitive strategies
  and job-site training, 80
Community
  assessment schedule, 42–43
  job resources, 10
  living, 111–130
    case studies, 128–129
    decisions, 121–123
    lifestyle evaluation, 124–127
    overview, 111–112
    person-centered planning, 119–127
    plans compared, 120
    quality of life, 121
    residential options, 112–119
      continuum approach, 112–115
      supported living, 115–119
  trainers, 27
  vocational planning and analysis, 7–13
  vocational training, 27
Community Services Board (CSB), 159
Consumers
  assessment, and supported employment, 79–80
  and follow-along strategies, 152–155

and job retention
    satisfaction surveys, 152–155
    self-evaluation, 152
    update form, 152, 154
Corporations
    involvement in supported employment, 88
Counseling
    and job-site training, 80
Cross-training, 5
CSB. *See* Community Services Board
Cueing
    self-administered, 144
    in vocational training, 102–104
Culture
    and business understanding, 65–66
Curriculum guides, 19–21
Customer consultation strategy, 81

Deinstitutionalization, 111
Department of Rehabilitative Services (DRS), 159
Dictionary of Occupational Titles (DOT), 159
Disabled persons
    and U.S. Department of Labor regulations, 27
    wages paid, 84
DOL. *See* U.S. Department of Labor
DOT. *See Dictionary of Occupational Titles*
DRS. *See* Department of Rehabilitative Services

Economic Development Office
    and labor market, 29
Economics
    and job loss, 138–139
ED. *See* Emotional disturbance
Education for Employment Program (EFE), 159
Educators
    as providers of consistent job descriptions and
        task segments, 6
EFE. *See* Education for Employment Program
Elderly
    and supported employment, 91–92
Emotional disturbance (ED), 159
Employee integration strategy, 81
Employers
    as customers of supported employment profes-
        sionals, 68–70
    what they are looking for in supported employ-
        ment professionals, 71
Employment
    client screening, 132–133
    economic disincentives, 92
    opportunities, 11–12, 63
    outcomes and typicality, 64–65
    postemployment support services, 131–133

supported
    implementation
        basic placement, 82
        cluster placement, 83
        multiple placement, 82–83
    individual placement
        assessment and follow-along, 80–81
        consumer assessment, 79–80
        corporate involvement, 88
        job development, 78–79
        job placement, 80
        job-site training, 80
        outcomes, 83–86
            benefit–cost, 86
            inclusion, 84–85
            ongoing support, 85
        population applications, 87–88
        support strategies, 81
        support systems, 81
        trends and issues, 86–89
    for persons with severe disabilities, 77–78
    regulations, 132
    segregated to competitive employment,
        90–93
    success rate, 89–90
    technologies, 79
    and workforce diversity, 65
    vocational objectives
        selection, 14
        writing instructions, 14–15
            specifying criteria of adequate perfor-
                mance, 15
            specifying desired performance, 15
            specifying performance conditions, 15
Employment specialist, role, 142–145

Fair Labor Standards Act (FLSA), 98
Family involvement
    and job retention, 140–141
FLSA. *See* Fair Labor Standards Act
Follow-along strategies, 148–155
    consumer
        satisfaction surveys, 152–155
        self-evaluation, 152
        update form, 152, 154
    job update form, 152, 153
    off-site intervention, 149
    on-site intervention, 148–149
    scheduling contacts, 149–150
    supervisor's evaluations, 150–152
    support group, 150
Foster homes, 113
Funding, 133–137

coordination of sources, 133–134
  follow-along services, 134–137
Futures planning, 119

Gestures
  and vocational training, 101–102
Group facilities, large, 113
Group homes, 113

HCB. *See* Home and Community-Based Waiver
  programs
Health
  and job retention, 138
Home and Community-Based (HCB) Waiver programs, 134
Home of Your Own project, 118, 119
Housing. *See also* Residential living
  cooperatives, 119
  foster homes, 113
  group homes, 113
  independent living, 113, 119
Human resources, 68

IEP. *See* Individual Employment Plan; Individual-
  ized Education Plan
Illinois Planning Council on Developmental Dis-
  abilities, 129
Independent living
  as residential option, 113
  skills, 25–26
Individualized Education Plan (IEP), 13, 25, 37, 97
Individual Employment Plan (IEP), 159
Individual Transition Plan (ITP), 42, 97, 159
Individuals with Disabilities Education Act
  Amendments of 1997, 25
Institute for Community Inclusion, 91
Institute on Disability/University Affiliated Pro-
  gram at the University of New Hampshire, 118
Intervention
  off-site, 149
  on-site, 148–149
Interview process, 68
ITP. *See* Individual Transition Plan

Jargon
  and job skills, 11–12
Job Accommodation Network, 46
Jobs
  assessment tools, 39–42, 57–60
  and evaluation of student, 8
  resources in community, 10
  tasks for assessment, 39, 55–56
Job carving, 30

Job coach
  as consultant, 67
  as facilitator, 81
Job descriptions
  consistency, 6
  occupations. *See* Occupations, job descriptions
Job development, 78–79
Job evaluation
  with students with motor impairment, 8
Job market. *See* Labor market
Job performance level, determination, 99
Job placement, 80
  basic, 82
  cluster, 83
  individual, 78–89
  multiple, 82–83
  professionals, 71
Job retention, 131–158
  extended services
    funding, 133–137
      coordination of sources, 133–134
      follow-along services, 134–137
    planning and implementing, 148–155
  family involvement, 140–141
  follow-along strategies, 148–155
    consumer
      satisfaction surveys, 152–155
      self-evaluation, 152
      update form, 152, 154
    job update form, 152, 153
    off-site intervention, 149
    on-site intervention, 148–149
    scheduling contacts, 149–150
    supervisor's evaluations, 150–152
    support group, 150
  job choice, 141–142
  job loss factors, 137–140
    economics, 138–139
    physical and mental health, 138
    productivity, 138
    responsibility, 139
  natural supports, 145–147
  overview, 131
  postemployment support services, 131–133
  role of employment specialist, 142–145
  self-administered consequences, 145
  self-management strategies, 143–145
  and supported employment programs, regula-
    tions, 132
Job-site vocational training, 80
  modifications, 107–109
    instructional program change, 108
    task analysis change, 107

work environment adaptations, 108
worker's responsibilities, 108–109
reinforcement procedures, 105–106
delivery reinforcement, 106
paycheck as reinforcer, 106
timing, 105

Labor market, analysis, 28–30
Labor trends
identification in community, 9
LD. *See* Learning disability
Learning disability (LD), 159
Least restrictive alternative (LRA), 112
Least restrictive environment (LRE), 112
Lifestyle
community living, evaluation, 124–127
Lifestyle Assessment, 124–125
Likert scale, 84–85, 124
LRA. *See* Least restrictive alternative
LRE. *See* Least restrictive environment

Meals on Wheels, 117
Medicaid
and supported employment, 91–92, 134
Mental health (MH), 159
Mental illness, and supported employment, 87–88
Mental retardation (MR), 160
MH. *See* Mental health
MHA. *See* MHA Cooperative; Mutual Housing Association
MHA Cooperative, 119
Modeling
and vocational training, 101–102
Motor impairment
assessment, 7–8
student evaluation and job evaluation, 8
MR. *See* Mental retardation
Mutual Housing Association (MHA), 119

Natural supports, 65
and job retention, 145–147
Neighborhood Living Project, 127
Networking the environment, 81
Normalization, 111

Occupations, job descriptions, 161–320
building and related services, 161–179
case study, 173–179
general utility, 169–173
groundskeeper, 167–168
janitor, 163–165
pool cleaner, 161–163
porter, 165–167
clerical, 239–253

case study, 246–253
file clerk, 241–242
general office aide, 239–240
mail clerk, 242–243
mail room clerk, 244–245
computing and account-recording, 301–320
accounting clerk, 306–309
bookstore cashier, 303–305
case study, 314–320
microfilm clerk, 309–313
toll collector, 301–303
food and beverage preparation, 217–237
case study, 231–237
dietary aide, 221–222
dishwasher, 222–227
fast food order taker, 228–230
linebacker, 217–220
silverware roller, 227–228
information and message distribution, 285–300
case study, 294–300
librarian's assistant, 287–289
library clerk, 289–292
receptionist, 292–293
telephone secretary, 285–287
lodging and related services, 255–271
case study, 265–271
housekeeper, 261–264
houseman, 255–256
linen sorter, 260–261
runner, 257–258
silver polisher, 258–260
plant farming, 273–284
case study, 278–284
greenhouse assistant, 276–277
horticultural worker, 277–278
plant installation preparer, 273–276
production and stock clerk, 201–216
box packer, 201–203
case study, 210–216
engraver, 208–210
order picker, 203–206
warehouse assistant, 206–207
sales, 181–199
case study, 193–199
courtesy clerk, 185
customer assistant, 181–184
customer service representative, 189–192
movie video clerk, 187–189
telemarketer, 186
Outsourcing
and cross-training, 5

Parents
and goal planning process for students, 13
and students' abilities and desires, 30–33
and teacher assistance, 31
Partnerships, 63–76
business culture understanding, 65–66
expansion of relationships, 66
human resource practice enhancement, 68
job coach as consultant, 67
materials for training programs, 67
productivity, 68
skills utilized, 66
supported employment and workforce diversity, 65
training opportunities sponsorship, 67
PASS. See Plan for Achieving Self-Support
PATH. See Personal Alternatives for Tomorrow
with Hope; Planning Alternative Tomorrows
with Hope
Paycheck
as reinforcer in vocational training, 106
Personal Alternatives for Tomorrow with Hope
(PATH), 32–33
Physical assists
and vocational training, 101–102
Plan for Achieving Self-Support (PASS)
and job retention, 134
Planning Alternative Tomorrows with Hope
(PATH), 160
Positioning
and students' abilities, 42
Production data
recording, 41–42
reporting, 47
Productivity
in business partnership, 68
and job retention, 138
Prompts, in vocational training, 99–102
guidelines for use, 103
least intrusive, 102
response, 99–102
Public Law 105-17. See Individuals with Disabilities Education Act Amendments of 1997

Quality of life, 121, 125, 126

Rehabilitation Act Amendments of 1992, 63, 64,
91, 133, 135, 145–146, 152, 155
Rehabilitation organizations, 70, 71, 89
Rehabilitation Research and Training Center on
Supported Employment at Virginia Commonwealth University (VCU-RRTC), 90–91, 92,
136

Rehabilitation services
eligibility, 26–27
Rehabilitation Services Administration, 89
Residential living. See also Housing
options, 112–119
continuum approach, 112–115
supported living, 115–119
Residential Outcomes System (ROS), 124, 127
ROS. See Residential Outcomes System

School-to-work transition, 25
SEIS. See Supported Employment Information
System
Self-instruction, 144
Self-management
consequences, 145
strategies, 143–145
Semi-independent living, 113
Sequencing, 14
SGA. See Substantial gainful activity
Situational assessment, 43
Skills. See also Occupations, job descriptions
utilized in business partnership, 66
Social Security Administration (SSA), 77, 90, 160
Social Security Disability Insurance (SSDI)
and supported employment, 91–92
and vocational curriculum for competitive
employment, 160
Special Olympics, 84
SSA. See Social Security Administration
SSDI. See Social Security Disability Insurance
SSI. See Supplemental Security Income
Students
abilities and desires, 30–33, 44–45, 47
assessment of strengths and weaknesses, 6–7,
39–40
and goal planning process with parents, 13
interests and preferences in job selection, 44,
47
with motor impairment, job evaluation, 8
positioning considerations, 42
questions to generate profile data, 32, 49–51
skills, 44–45, 47
skills and learning analysis, 57–60
support needs, 45–46
Substantial gainful activity (SGA)
and supported employment, 92
Supplemental Security Income (SSI)
and supported employment, 91–92, 134
and vocational curriculum for competitive
employment, 160
Supported Employment Information System
(SEIS), 137–138

Support groups, 150
  postemployment, 131–133
Survey
  as assessment tool, 40

Tasks
  analysis, 40–41, 99–100
  analysis change, 107
  analytic assessment, examples, 17–18, 20
  developing for teaching, 19–22
    curriculum guides, 19–21
    developing curricula from skill sequences,
      22
    dividing skills into small steps, 21–22
    field testing, 22
    resources, 19
  job assessment, 39, 55–56
  segments, consistency, 6
  and skill sequencing, 15–18
TBI. *See* Traumatic brain injury
Teachers
  assistance with parents, 31
  awareness of curriculum changes, 3–4
  familiarization with local labor market, 30
  presence in vocational training, 106–107
  role with local business representatives, 33–39
  staffing challenges, 42
  and students' abilities and desires, 30–33
  and support needs of students, 45–46
  and transportation, 42
  and U.S. Department of Labor regulations, 98
Teaching
  task analysis development, 19–22
    curriculum guides, 19–21
    developing curricula from skill sequences,
      22
    dividing skills into small steps, 21–22
    field testing, 22
    resources, 19
Trainers
  community-based, 27
  as providers of consistent job descriptions and
    task segments, 6
TransCen, Inc., 70, 71, 72
Transition planning. *See* Vocational assessment,
  functional
Training programs
  job-site, 80
  materials, 67
  sponsorship opportunities, 67
  and supported employment, 72, 80
Transportation
  role in vocational planning and assessment, 42

Traumatic brain injury (TBI)
  and supported employment, 87, 133, 136
  vocational curriculum for competitive employ-
    ment, 160

Unemployment, 3, 4
U.S. Congress, 77
U.S. Department of Health and Human Services
  Administration on Developmental Disabilities,
  118
U.S. Department of Labor (DOL)
  and persons with severe disabilities, 77–78
  regulations and local businesses, 35
  vocational exploration, 27
  vocational training, 98
  wages paid to persons with disabilities, 84

VCU-RRTC. *See* Rehabilitation Research and
  Training Center on Supported Employment at
  Virginia Commonwealth University
Verbal instructions
  and vocational training, 101–102, 144
Verbal labeling, 144
Vocational assessment, functional, 25–61
  business review, example, 52–55
  community-based programs, 26–46
    assessment implementation, 28–46
    purpose, 27–28, 29
  considerations, 42–43
  department review, example, 55–56
  outline for writing a vocational situational
    assessment report, 46–48
  overview, 25–26
  skills and learning analysis, example, 57–60
  student profile, example, 49–51
Vocational curriculum, 3–23. *See also* Occupations, job descriptions
  community analysis, 7–13
    business relationships, maintaining, 12–13
    business representatives
      identification, 10
      initial visit, 10–11
      making contact, 10, 33–39, 52–54
    labor trends, identification, 9
    review of success, 9
    work opportunities, observation, 11–12
  development, 4–6, 52–54
    business-referenced, 4–5
    cross-training, 5
    detail, 5–6
    flexibility, 5
    job descriptions, consistency, 6
    objective and focus, 6

task segments, consistency, 6
goals, annual, 13–15
  identification, 13–14
  sequencing, 14
  vocational objectives
    selection, 14
    writing instructions, 14–15
      specifying criteria of adequate perfor-
        mance, 15
      specifying desired performance, 15
      specifying performance conditions, 15
guides, 19–21
overview, 3–4
population analysis, 6–7
task analysis
  analytic assessment, examples, 17–18, 20
  developing for teaching, 19–22
    curriculum guides, 19–21
    developing curricula from skill
      sequences, 22
    dividing skills into small steps, 21–22
    field testing, 22
    resources, 19
    and skill sequencing, 15–18
vocational planning, 7–13, 52–54
Vocational Integration Index, 142
Vocational Rehabilitation (VR)
  and job retention, 133, 146
  regulations, 78, 90
Vocational training
  community-based, 27
  job-site

modifications, 107–109
  instructional program change, 108
  task analysis change, 107
  work environment adaptations, 108
  worker's responsibilities, 108–109
reinforcement procedures, 105–106
  delivery reinforcement, 106
  paycheck as reinforcer, 106
  timing, 105
overview, 97–98
teacher presence, 106–107
techniques, 98–104
  chaining
    backward, 104
    forward, 104
  cueing, 102–104
  job performance level, determination, 99
  prompts, 99–102
    guidelines for use, 103
    least intrusive, 102
    response, 99–102
  task analysis, 99–100
VR. *See* Vocational Rehabilitation

Work environment
  adaptations for vocational training, 108
Workforce, diversity, 64–65

Young Women's Christian Association
YWCA. *See* Young Women's Christian Association